AF744018

Sales and Service Digital Transformation

Jun Yang

Sales and Service Digital Transformation

The Arrival of CRM3.0 Era

中国科学技术出版社
CHINA SCIENCE AND TECHNOLOGY PRESS

Springer

Jun Yang
Beijing Rongya Botong Information
Technology Co., Ltd.
Beijing, China

ISBN 978-981-96-5960-9 ISBN 978-981-96-5961-6 (eBook)
https://doi.org/10.1007/978-981-96-5961-6

Jointly published with China Science and Technology Press Co., Ltd.
The print edition is not for sale in China (Mainland). Customers from China (Mainland) please order the print book from: China Science and Technology Press Co., Ltd.
ISBN of the Co-Publisher's edition: 9787504696885

Translation from the Chinese Simplified language edition: "营销和服务数字化转型: CRM3.0 时代的来临" by Jun Yang, © China Science and Technology Press Co., Ltd. 2020. Published by China Science and Technology Press Co., Ltd. All Rights Reserved.

© China Science and Technology Press Co., Ltd. 2025

This work is subject to copyright. All rights are solely and exclusively licensed by the Publisher, whether the whole or part of the material is concerned, specifically the rights of reprinting, reuse of illustrations, recitation, broadcasting, reproduction on microfilms or in any other physical way, and transmission or information storage and retrieval, electronic adaptation, computer software, or by similar or dissimilar methodology now known or hereafter developed.
The use of general descriptive names, registered names, trademarks, service marks, etc. in this publication does not imply, even in the absence of a specific statement, that such names are exempt from the relevant protective laws and regulations and therefore free for general use.
The publishers, the authors, and the editors are safe to assume that the advice and information in this book are believed to be true and accurate at the date of publication. Neither the publishers nor the authors or the editors give a warranty, express or implied, with respect to the material contained herein or for any errors or omissions that may have been made. The publishers remain neutral with regard to jurisdictional claims in published maps and institutional affiliations.

This Springer imprint is published by the registered company Springer Nature Singapore Pte Ltd.
The registered company address is: 152 Beach Road, #21-01/04 Gateway East, Singapore 189721, Singapore

If disposing of this product, please recycle the paper.

Preface

The first edition of "Sales and Service Digital Transformation—The Arrival of CRM3.0 Era" was officially published in July 2020. Over the past two years, it has been well received by readers. However, in my communication with many readers, I also deeply felt the inadequacies of the content in the first edition. For example, where is the integration of sales and service with digitalization reflected? How does CRM3.0 in the digital age embody digitalization? What does its innovation include?

Therefore, in this book, I will introduce the CRM3.0 in the digital age more systematically and comprehensively, that is, the innovation of the sales and service theoretical system, the innovation of digital tools and products, the innovation of the value assessment system, and the innovation of the support system. This book also introduces some practical cases of industry innovation and transformation.

Entrepreneurs have been constantly searching for a formula that can enable their businesses to sustainably grow. But what is the right formula? It is to advance with the times! There are enterprises that have lasted for a hundred years, but there are no enterprises that have remained unchanged for a hundred years! How entrepreneurs find their own path of development based on the specific circumstances, trends, and situation determines how high and far an enterprise can go.

As we entered the year 2020, consumer purchasing methods, channels, and word-of-mouth propagation have undergone earth-shaking changes. The emergence of the novel coronavirus pandemic has further intensified this trend. After the pandemic, the modes and methods of doing business will undergo significant changes as well. It's a survival of the fittest world, where companies looking to overtake on curves and ultimately rise from the ashes like a phoenix, need to actively join in the transformation wave rather than being bystanders. In the digital age, the digital innovation and transformation of enterprises is an irreversible trend. Upgrading from a traditional product and service company to a digital-driven high-tech company is the only way for enterprises to maintain their vitality.

This book is primarily written for sales and service personnel in enterprises that are currently engaged in or preparing for digital transformation, as well as related readers in the field of digitization, and practitioners in the field of customer relationship management. This book focuses on four themes: CRM3.0, digital innovation

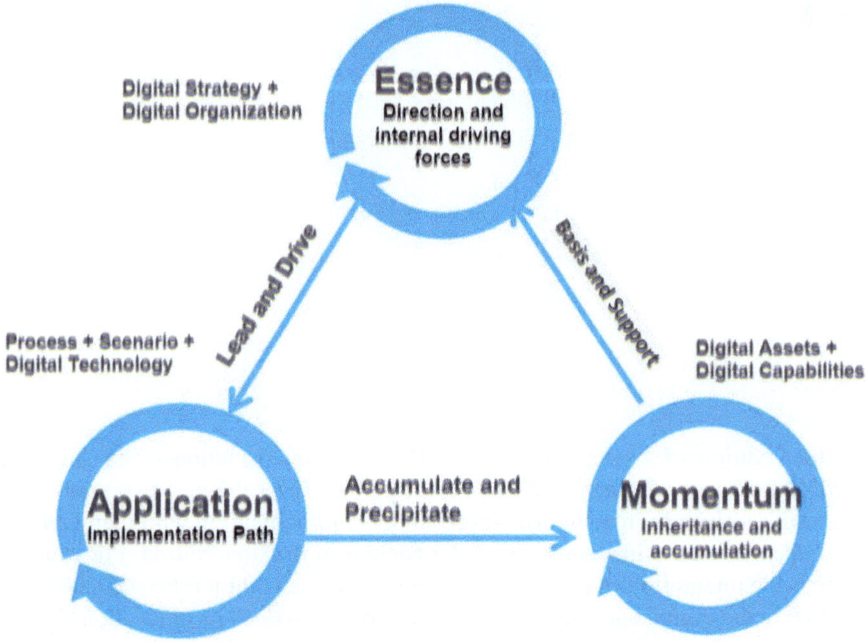

Fig. 1 The Three Pillars of Sales and Service Digitalization

and transformation of sales, digital innovation and transformation of services, and the construction of a digital support system. It explains digital innovation and transformation of sales and services in the digital age from different perspectives such as theoretical systems, business models, value output, and digital tools.

I. The Three Pillars of Sales and Service Digitalization

As shown in Fig. 1, the digitalization of sales and services is composed of essence, application, and momentum. Essence refers to digital strategy and digital organization, which are the direction and internal driving force of digital transformation; Application refers to processes, scenarios, and digital technology, which are the implementation paths of digital transformation; Momentum refers to digital assets and digital capabilities, which are the inheritance and accumulation of digitalization.

The relationship between essence, application, and momentum is as follows: The digital strategy leads the path of digital implementation, and the construction of self-driven digital organizations and position settings within the enterprise generate powerful internal driving forces. This enables organizations and employees to burst with strong enthusiasm and vitality for digital innovation and transformation, and continuously use digital technology to optimize processes and scenarios, promoting digital transformation. The application of digital technology in processes and scenarios will continue to accumulate digital assets and precipitate digital capabilities for enterprises. The accumulated digital assets will provide a basis for decision-making for the digital strategy, and the precipitated digital capabilities will provide support for the construction of digital organizations and position settings.

In summary, the digitalization of sales and service is not just about digital technology and some new technologies, it also includes all aspects of enterprise management and operation, such as strategy, organization, business model, process, scenario, and data assets.

II. Broadly Defined CRM

Customer Relationship Management, in a broader sense, can be considered as the improvement, innovation, or transformation measures taken by enterprises to enhance their core competitiveness in areas such as marketing, sales, service, channels, and customer management. It can be on the strategic level, it can also be on tactical levels such as business models, profit models, and operation modes, it can be on management levels such as organizational structure, assessment, and processes, and it can also be on technological levels such as digital tools and information systems. Therefore, in a broader sense, Customer Relationship Management is the innovation and transformation of customer-related businesses.

III. Narrowly Defined CRM

Narrowly defined, CRM is a digital system and tools for managing aspects like marketing, sales, service, channels, and customers. Therefore, in the narrow sense, CRM is the carrier of digital innovation and transformation for customer-related businesses and the realization of digital tools for business's innovation and transformation.

IV. The Difference Between Digital Innovation and Transformation

I believe that digital transformation refers to helping businesses achieve new business models, profit models, operation models, etc., through digital technology and capabilities, that is, changing lanes to achieve absolute advantages in competition in different ways. This is a qualitative change. Digital innovation refers to optimizing

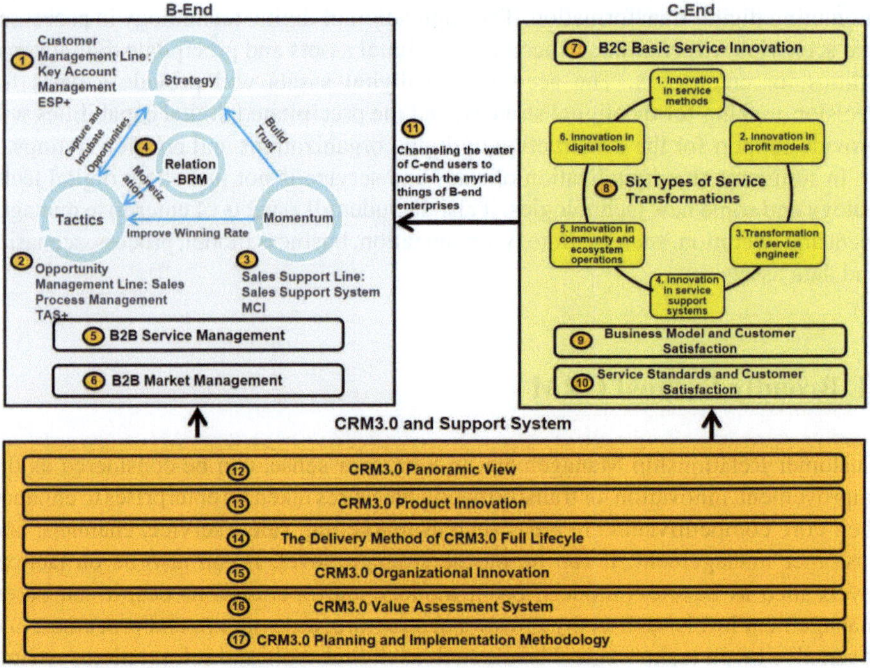

Fig. 2 Content Map of This Book

and improving original models and processes through digital technology and capabilities, that is, running in circles, still on the original track, but more efficient, agile, and intelligent than competitors, thus far ahead of competitors. This is a quantitative change.

V. Content Mind Map

In Fig. 2, I gather all the relevant content together and outline the interconnections between them.

VI. B-end Digital Transformation

The B2B (Business-to-Business) sales in the digital age can be summarized into the three chapters of Upholding the Right Path, Deploying Surprise Forces and Accumulating Momentum. Upholding the Right Path refers to key account management which is more about direction and strategy, not pursuing short-term goals. Deploying

Surprise Forces is sales process management that focuses more on short-term results with whether or not a deal is won as a measure of success. Accumulating Momentum is sales support system management. These three components make up the dynamic, visible part of B2B, often integrated with processes and scenarios. B2B also has a static, invisible part, which is business relationship management composed of enterprise connection resource management and project behavior management.

1. Key Account Management—ESP+ (Enterprise Selling Process Plus)

Regarding the first part of the three-stage digital transformation of B2B sales—key account management, this book has optimized the ESP methodology, making it more practical and is named as ESP+. Key account management is centered around three core tasks: "establishing one's own advantages, isolating competitors, and incubating business opportunities", implemented through ESP+.

2. Sales Process Management—TAS+ (Targeting Account Selling Plus)

Regarding the second part of the B2B sales digital transformation trilogy, Sales Process Management, this book optimizes the methodology of sales process management, making it more grounded, efficient, targeted, and easier to implement, and is named TAS+. Sales process management is divided into two major parts and thirteen elements, with internal and external coordination, and a combination of action and stillness: "action" against competitors, constantly changing to overcome the enemy; "stillness" for sales personnel, to be efficient, fair, transparent, and let them charge into battle with peace of mind.

3. Sales Support System Management—MCI (Match, Coordinate, Integrate)

Regarding the third part of the three-stage digital transformation of B2B sales—sales support system management (MCI), it is about establishing systematic advantages for the company and building a moat around the enterprise. This book focuses on how to solve three major problems, namely resource match, process coordination, and resource integration capability, and proposes the MCI method.

4. Business Relationship Management—BRM

Business Relationship Management (BRM) is an extension of Customer Relationship Management (CRM). It is the relationship among people, enterprise and projects that a company can collect, accumulate, analyze, optimize, and utilize during the sales process. It consists of Enterprise Connection Management (ECM) and Project Behavior Management (PBM), which will form data asset accumulation and realize scenario and process empowerment through data asset driving.

5. B2B Service Management

The innovation and transformation of B2B services in the digital age will involve three main service stages: B2B sales process service, B2B delivery process service, and B2B after-sales process service. The five areas of after-sales service innovation and transformation are: ① cost reduction and efficiency improvement; ② all-employee sales; ③ long-term stability; ④ profit center; ⑤ transformation and change of track.

6. B2B Market Management

The five main components of B2B market management are: ① sales plan management; ② marketing budget management; ③ cost management; ④ marketing activity management; ⑤ marketing activity assessment management.

VII. Digital Transformation of C-end Services

New era, new service. How can we emancipate our minds, break the deadlock through service transformation, reinvent ourselves, and make service the core competitiveness of enterprises and the start of sales?

7. B2C Basic Service Innovation

Innovation in B2C basic services encompasses nine areas: ① User experience; ② Omni-channel; ③ Work order management; ④ Service network management; ⑤ Spare parts management; ⑥ Defective product management; ⑦ Quality management; ⑧ Technical support and training; ⑨ Settlement management.

8. Six Types of Innovation in Service Digital Transformation

Digital transformation of services includes six types of innovation: ① Innovation in service methods; ② Innovation in profit models; ③ Transformation of service engineer positioning and capabilities; ④ Innovation in service support systems; ⑤ Innovation in community and ecosystem operations; ⑥ Innovation in digital tools.

9. Business Model and Customer Satisfaction

There is a contradiction between the traditional service business model and customer service satisfaction, which affects the improvement of service experience. A new service business model is proposed, which ultimately establishes a more reasonable business model through service butlerization, service network platformization, Employee Makerization, and Income Ecologization, in order to improve user satisfaction.

10. Service Standards and Customer Satisfaction

It is a misconception for companies to try to improve service satisfaction by raising service standards. In fact, service satisfaction is the gap between the service customers expect and the service they perceive. Through five steps, we can manage user satisfaction more reasonably and with better returns. These five steps are: ① rationally setting service standards; ② appropriately lowering user expectations; ③ increasing user tolerance threshold and appropriately creating touching moments for users; ④ rationally resolving complaints; ⑤ comprehensively monitoring unexpected incidents.

VIII. C-end Empowers B-end

11. Watering B-end Enterprises with C-end User Water

This book introduces how to use service as a means to water B-end with C-end user water through five steps. These five steps are: ① decentralization, operating individual brands of service personnel; ② integrating touchpoints, building a smart service platform; ③ service endorsement, igniting the community; ④ ecological parallel, co-creation and win-win; ⑤ service tuning, focusing on the community.

IX. CRM3.0 and Digital Transformation Support System

This book introduces the three eras of customer relationship management development in China over the past 20 years: ① the CRM1.0 era centered on products; ② the CRM2.0 era centered on solutions and best practices; ③ the CRM3.0 era centered on business value and digital transformation. The book also introduces the five essential elements in the CRM3.0 era: ① building a theoretical system; ② industry innovation; ③ establishing a value assessment system and operating system; ④ innovative charging model; ⑤ digital tool innovation.

12. CRM3.0 Panoramic View

This book introduces what a complete customer relationship management includes in the digital age, that is, the concept of CRM3.0 in the digital age. It is a panoramic description of customer relationship management, explaining customer relationship management from the demands of the client, CRM software manufacturers, CRM implementers, and CRM consultants. CRM3.0 describes the nine main aspects that complete customer relationship management should include: ① function; ② business; ③ industry; ④ delivery management; ⑤ organizational adaptation; ⑥ operational efficiency and business value monitoring and evaluation; ⑦ operational management; ⑧ digital technology; ⑨ version iteration evolution.

13. CRM3.0 Product Innovation

In the digital age, traditional customer relationship management gradually becomes the customer relationship management application middle platform, CRM3.0 also needs to build four other core components: ① CRM intelligent brain; ② CRM intelligent terminal; ③ CRM win-win platform; ④ CRM data asset platform.

14. CRM3.0 Full Lifecycle Delivery Method

This book introduces how to build a successful delivery system in the digital age through the full lifecycle delivery method. It focuses on how to focus on software selection to digital innovation, from focusing on software functions to focusing on business output, from focusing on project launch to focusing on continuous input and output over a longer period.

15. CRM3.0 Organizational Innovation

CRM3.0 organizational innovation, that is, building a self-evolving organization driven by digital transformation, introduces the digital drive The five steps of business model transformation are introduced, as well as the differences between traditional IT departments, digital empowerment departments, and self-evolving organizations driven by digitalization. It focuses on how to build a self-evolving organization that drives digital transformation at the group level, that is, only when the "power is large enough, the level is high enough, and the return is sufficient", it is possible to truly establish a self-evolving organization that drives digital transformation at the group level.

16. CRM3.0 Value Assessment System

This book introduces the value assessment system of CRM3.0, and takes the value assessment system of B2B sales as an example, introducing five dimensions and the secondary indicators of each dimension. The five dimensions are: ① customer management ability; ② control ability of the order process; ③ resource scheduling and management ability; ④ employee improvement ability; ⑤ enterprise direction matching ability.

17. CRM3.0 Planning and Implementation Methodology

In the three stages of digital planning, digital design, and digital empowerment, digital innovation and transformation are designed and implemented through methods such as RMB-PT and CRM3.0 four-dimensional planning method (MSTT).

Beijing, China　　　　Jun Yang

Competing Interests The author has no competing interests to declare that are relevant to the content of this manuscript.

Contents

Chapter 1
The Arrival of the CRM 3.0 Era

A Twenty-Year Essay on China Customer Relationship Management Market

I started developing Siebel 7.0 in the core R&D team of Siebel Canada in March 1999. After returning to China in October 2002, I founded a customer relationship management company. It's been over twenty years in this field. Over these years, I have experienced the ups and downs of the customer relationship management market, alternating between hope and disappointment. Now, I would like to share my views on the domestic customer relationship management market over the past twenty years from the perspective of a participant.

The history of the rise of the customer relationship management market is not very long. In a sense, the rise of Siebel CRM represents the rise of the customer relationship management market. Siebel was established in 1993, Siebel CRM began to sweep the world in 1995, and by 2000, Siebel's market value reached 50 billion US dollars, and then it began to decline. If calculated this way, the customer relationship management market has a history of about thirty years. The rise of CRM in China should have occurred around 2000, with the emergence of companies like PowerCRM, Turbo CRM and MyCRM, so it has a history of more than 20 years.

As shown in Fig. 1.1, the domestic customer relationship management market has gone through three stages since 2000.

The First Stage: CRM1.0 Era—Product-Centered Market

2000–2005 was the first stage of customer relationship management, when the market size was not large, it was a billion-yuan market. CRM at this stage is mainly sold by product, with standalone versions, enterprise versions, etc. When selling customer

© China Science and Technology Press Co., Ltd. 2025
J. Yang, *Sales and Service Digital Transformation*,
https://doi.org/10.1007/978-981-96-5961-6_1

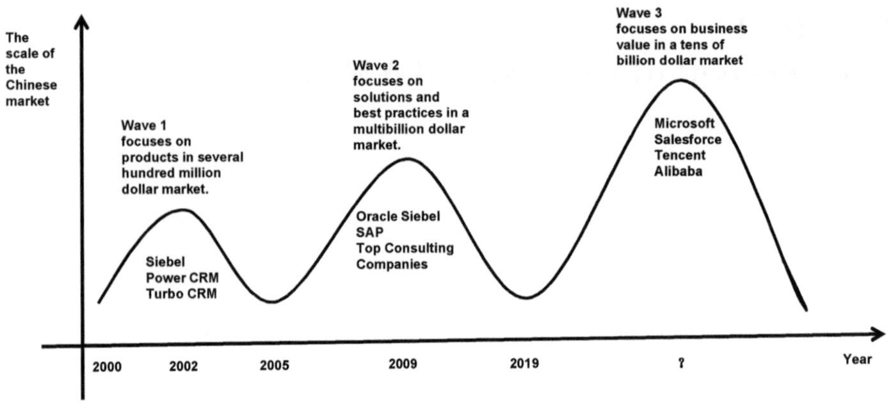

Fig. 1.1 Three waves of CRM market in China

relationship management products, companies mainly demonstrate the product interface to customers and introduce product functions; at the same time, they also We will introduce to customers whether a two-tier structure is better or a multi-tier structure is better, whether a client/server (Client/Server, CS) structure is better or a browser/server (Browser/ Server, BS) structure is better.

At that time, Siebel was not widely used in China. Instead, domestic software vendors such as PowerCRM, Turbo CRM, and MyCRM were more advanced. I don't know if anyone still remembers PowerCRM now, but it was indeed flourishing in the field of CRM in China at that time.

Another CRM company that must be mentioned is Turbo CRM. At the time, Turbo CRM claimed to be the largest CRM vendor in China. In 2001, when I was at Siebel Canada, colleagues showed me information about Turbo CRM. At that time, this company claimed that its annual sales had reached millions of dollars.

At that stage of the market, the Chinese market was too small and basically no vendors could make a profit. At that time, I also founded a customer relationship management company and developed and sold customer relationship management products "Redbook", including standalone version, SME version, and large enterprise version. It even ranked in the top five in the sales ranking of management software from Federal Software, but we really couldn't sell many copies, and it didn't make any money.

Second Stage: CRM2.0 Era—A Market Centered on Solutions and Best Practices

After 2005, influenced by the strong demand in telecommunications, energy, finance, and automobile industries, big customers like Huawei emerged. At the same time, many companies went public with Initial Public Offerings (IPOs), one of the fundraising investments was customer relationship management. Therefore, the Chinese customer relationship management market entered a rapid rise period.

During this period, many projects were promoted by large international consulting companies, such as IBM, Accenture, Capgemini, and the "Big Four" accounting firms (PwC, Deloitte, KPMG, Ernst & Young). Due to the dominance of large consulting companies with international backgrounds, the scale of the projects during this period was also quite large, and CRM consultants charged higher fees. I remember when I was in charge of bank and securities CRM projects in 2007, almost every phase was around 3 million US dollars in scale, and the most common consultant fee was 500 US dollars a day. The senior consultant fee that IBM quoted to me at that time was 2,000 US dollars per day. Moreover, at that time, clients had great respect for CRM vendors and provided good working environments for consultants.

During this period, what vendors were competing for were best practices and industry solutions. Chinese CRM companies basically missed out on large customers because they lacked accumulation in this area and did not have the assistance of international consulting companies to promote. During this period, there was essentially a competition between the CRM of two companies, namely Oracle Siebel and SAP CRM.

During the CRM boom from 2007 to 2011, many companies still reaped dividends. The scale of the CRM market at this stage could be between one billion and several billion US dollars.

Third Stage: CRM3.0 Era—A Market Centered on Business Value and Digital Transformation

In 2012, when I was in charge of the Oracle Siebel solution at IBM GBS, I clearly felt that the CRM market was gradually shrinking. Firstly, the size of the opportunities has become smaller and smaller, the projects which were originally at the level of tens of millions have shrunk to several million. Furthermore, as soon as there is an opportunity, mainstream software vendors and major consulting companies would swarm in, the CRM market has turned into a red ocean battlefield.

2019 was a very difficult year for the CRM market, and the next few years may be even more challenging. Currently, the shrinking trend of the CRM market can be seen from the number of staff in the CRM teams of major consulting firms. However, 2019 also saw a sudden rise in hope for the CRM market. From an international perspective, the proportion of CRM software companies in all software company mergers and acquisitions is the highest. From the Chinese domestic market's perspective, BAT (Baidu, Alibaba, and Tencent) continues to step up its investment in the CRM field, and various kinds of capital are continuously flowing into the B2B market, particularly in the area of digital empowerment and transformation.

I believe that it's not the CRM market that is shrinking, but the traditional CRM field is shrinking, while new CRM fields are emerging and exploding rapidly. I believe that the following reasons have accelerated the shrinkage of the traditional CRM field over the past decade:

1. Lack of business value

Over the past decade or so, CRM consulting has been standardized by PPT deliverables, and CRM products have been standardized by system launch. The project fee has no direct relationship with whether it generates business value for customers. This kind of CRM model is becoming increasingly difficult for customers to accept. Leading enterprises have basically gone through one or even several rounds of CRM products, their honeymoon period with CRM has passed, and they have moved from a period of anticipation to a period of calm. If we can't impress customers from business value and ROI, then customers are unwilling to make blind large investments.

2. Improvement of customer's own capabilities

A large number of CRM experts who used to work at consulting firms have now joined the ranks of clients. You will find that many of the Chief Information Officers (CIOs), Chief Technology Officers (CTOs), and Chief Digital Officers (CDOs) at leading companies come from consulting firms such as IBM, AC, Deloitte, PwC, KPMG, Ernst & Young, etc. Therefore, the CRM consulting ability and self-development ability of these top enterprises are now no less than those of the suppliers. Many projects are solved internally through their own research and development.

3. CRM Cloudification

CRM cloudification is gradually becoming mainstream now. Because it is a rental model, and many companies want to use out-of-the-box native features, the annual software license fees and overall secondary development implementation costs have both decreased. Those CRM projects worth tens of millions or even hundreds of millions are also becoming less and less.

4. Economic growth slows down

Due to the impact of the COVID-19 pandemic, the overall economic growth has slowed down, and the operating conditions of various industries have also declined to varying degrees. Therefore, companies naturally reduce their budgets for consulting and informatization projects.

The new CRM field focuses on the digital age. Traditional CRM achieves a complete transformation through the reconstruction of digital models, digital technologies, and digital assets, thereby helping companies innovate and transform in business models, business scenarios, and business processes, enhancing the output of business value, building the core competitiveness of companies, and realizing the innovation and transformation of companies. This is the new competition track for CRM, which I call the CRM 3.0 era.

From a market perspective, it's not that there are fewer CRM projects, but there are fewer CRM projects without business value, without business innovation, and without digital technology empowerment. In the next ten years, for domestic companies, it will definitely be a decade of surging digital transformation and digital innovation, and a trillion-dollar A market of trillion-scale. Customer Relationship Management (CRM) will be an important part of this market, that is, how to help enterprises in sales, service, customer and channel fields, through digital models, digital technology, and accumulation of digital assets, to form the core competitiveness of enterprises and generate measurable huge business value. This area will definitely be the largest market in the field of CRM in the next decade, and it is also a market of hundreds of billions or even trillions. Whichever CRM company can meet the needs of this wave of market, that company can enjoy this wave of dividends.

As shown in Fig. 1.2, to win this market, I believe that companies must have five key capabilities:

(1) Innovation in theoretical system: The current theoretical system of CRM was formed twenty years ago, which can be considered as a product of the information age. In the digital age, companies must have a new CRM theoretical system to possibly build a market of tens of billions or even trillions.
(2) Industry innovation: CRM companies must have new models for the industry (business models, profit models, and operation models, etc.), new processes, new organizations, new assessments, new functions, etc.

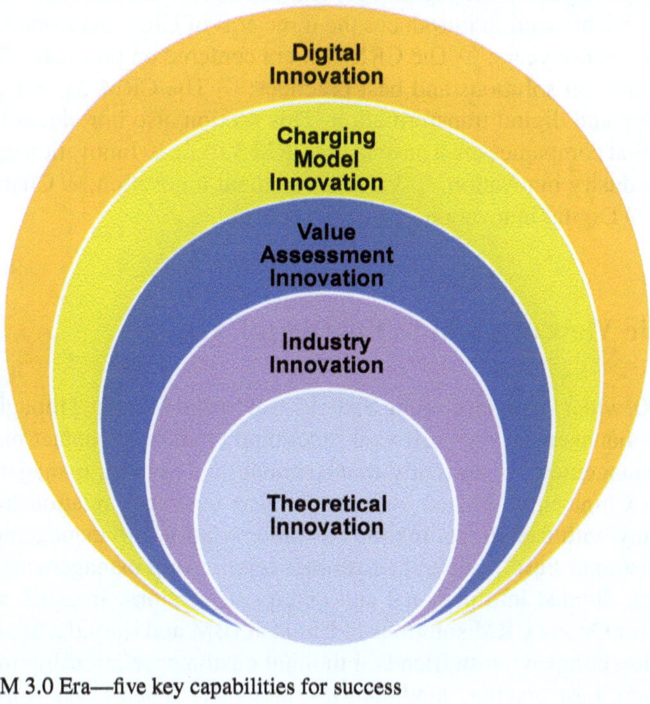

Fig. 1.2 CRM 3.0 Era—five key capabilities for success

(3) Value assessment innovation: CRM companies must have a practical CRM business value assessment system. It is already difficult to convince customers with the previous PPT deliverables and system launch as standards.
(4) Charging model innovation: In addition to the cloud charging model, CRM companies must actively explore new charging models, such as operation by proxy, sharing based on business value output; such as building a CRM field ecosystem platform, helping companies on the platform to dock demand and supply through charging platform fees, etc.
(5) Digital innovation: The new CRM not only needs to use digital technology, but also needs to transform the traditional CRM product architecture, such as building a CRM intelligent brain, CRM intelligent terminal, CRM win–win platform, CRM data asset platform, etc.

In the CRM 3.0 era, so far, I believe that no company has built its own "very wide and deep moat" in the five areas of theoretical system innovation, industry innovation, value assessment system innovation, charging model innovation, and digital innovation. In the digital age, the CRM market is calling for a new king to emerge. The trend makes heroes, and I believe that in the near future, a company will emerge that can become the leader of CRM in the digital age.

As a practitioner of CRM, I also hope that the next ten years will be a decade when CRM rises again in the digital age, and the market is booming.

Summary > This section introduces the three eras of CRM development in China over the past twenty years: ① The CRM 1.0 era centered on products; ② The CRM 2.0 era centered on solutions and best practices; ③ The CRM 3.0 era centered on business value and digital transformation. This section also introduces the five key capabilities that companies must have in the CRM 3.0 era: ① Innovation in theoretical system; ② Industry innovation; ③ Value assessment innovation; ④ Charging model innovation; ⑤ Digital innovation.

Panoramic View of CRM in the Digital Age

Around 2000, when I was developing Siebel 7.0 at Siebel Canada, I thought customer relationship management was software functionality such as contact management, customer management, opportunity management, and activity management. After returning to China in 2002 and starting the first customer relationship management company with friends, selling the customer relationship management product "Rongbo Customer Pass", I thought customer relationship management was a software product, divided into personal and enterprise versions. In 2012, when I was responsible for Oracle CRM solutions in China at IBM and started a financial digitization solution company with friends, I thought customer relationship management was a solution, best practice, methodology, and PPT. When I was responsible for global service digital innovation and informatization construction at Haier Group, I thought customer relationship management was business value, innovation, and transformation. As I was responsible for customer relationship management sales at Microsoft, I believe customer relationship management is a digital empowerment tool. From this, it can be seen that from different perspectives, the understanding and demand for customer relationship management are different, which is also a main reason why customer relationship management always fails to meet customer expectations: customers have different evaluation standards for customer relationship management.

The current basic classification of customer relationship management still uses the outdated method from twenty years ago, divided into operational customer relationship management, analytical customer relationship management, and collaborative customer relationship management, and later added social customer relationship management; in terms of functions, it is divided into market management, sales management, service management, channel management, member management, etc. This definition of customer relationship management is flat, focusing only on software functionality. Its problems are:

(1) It does not reflect the relationship between customer relationship management and important factors such as customer business models, processes, scenarios, organizations, positions, and assessments.
(2) It does not reflect the customer's demand for business value output.
(3) It does not consider the empowerment, innovation, and transformation of digital applications.
(4) It does not consider industry characteristics.

I designed the customer relationship management model for the digital age—CRM3.0 panoramic view (see Fig. 1.3). Before introducing it, I want to share my view on customer relationship management in the digital age: it is not that CRM using digital technology can be called customer relationship management in the digital age. Rather, customer relationship management that can satisfy customers and bring value to customers in the digital age is customer relationship management in the digital age. Digital technology is just a tool, and our purpose of applying customer relationship management is to bring value to customers in the digital age.

The CRM3.0 panoramic view described in Fig. 1.3 is closely related to the five key capabilities required for CRM3.0 success: ① Innovation of the theoretical system corresponding to functions and business; ② Industry innovation corresponding to the industry; ③ Value assessment innovation corresponding to operational efficiency and business value evaluation monitoring; ④ Charging model innovation corresponding to operational management; ⑤ Digital innovation corresponding to digital applications.

The reason it is called a panoramic view is that it is all-encompassing. It explains customer relationship management from the demand perspectives of four groups: the client, the customer relationship management software manufacturer, the customer relationship management consultant, and the customer relationship management implementer. It consists of nine parts: ① Function; ② Business; ③ Industry; ④ Delivery management; ⑤ Organizational adaptation;⑥ Operational efficiency and business value evaluation monitoring; ⑦ Operational management; ⑧

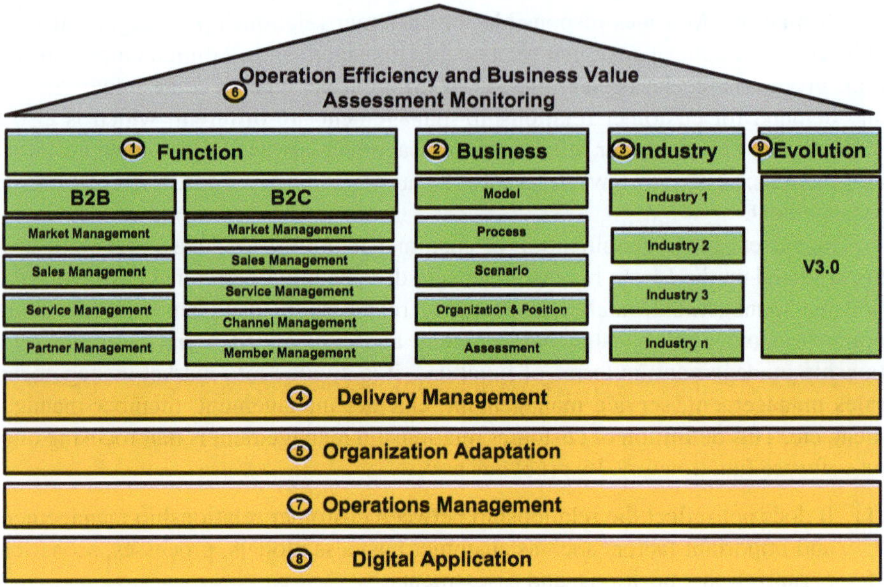

Fig. 1.3 Panorama of CRM 3.0

Digital application; ⑨ Evolution. Next, I will introduce the nine main components of CRM3.0:

Function

In the function, we have designed a new methodology and model for CRM to achieve innovation in the theoretical system of customer relationship management.

1. B2B model

(1) Sales management B2B sales management consists of key account management, sales process management, and sales support. The system is composed of three parts. In addition, it is also related to business relationship management and other content.

(2) Market Management Under the B2B model, whether customer relationship management includes market management has always been a contentious issue. Many people believe that B2B does not have market management. I believe there is, but it is different from traditional sales. For the B2B model, market management should consist of five parts: ① sales plan management; ② market budget management; ③ cost management; ④ market activity management; ⑤ market activity evaluation management.

(3) Service Management B2B services involve three main stages: B2B sales process service, B2B delivery process service, and B2B after-sales process service.

After-sales service innovation and transformation mainly involve five areas:① Service grading support system; ② Sales and service integration; ③ Enterprise network resource management; ④ Service productization;⑤ Customer service value-added platform.

(4) Partner Management B2B companies often use solution-based sales, channels are often called partners, and partners often manage in different ways depending on the solutions, industries, and regions they are responsible for. For example, there are industry-specific partners, solution-specific partners, region-specific partners, and partners for major customers. The key to B2B partner management is to establish the best partner classification and coverage mechanism, establish a partner sharing and training mechanism, and establish a partner business opportunity reporting mechanism, etc.

2. B2C Model

(1) Service Management The digital transformation of services involves the repositioning of services, how to plan and design the transformation, and how to innovate in six aspects: service methods, profit models, service personnel capabilities, service support systems, community ecological operations, and digital tools, as well as how to use C-end users to empower B-end businesses, etc.

(2) Market, Sales, Channel, and Member Management The market, sales, channel, and member management of B2C are often associated with new retail, and there is a lot of deep research on this part, so I won't go into too much detail here.

Business

In business, we design new business models for customer relationship management to achieve innovation in the theoretical system of customer relationship management.

Any customer relationship management project cannot go online with just functionality, it must involve business. Business is determined by the model, process, scenario, organizational position, and assessment.

As shown in Fig. 1.4, I will explain in detail in the later text how to plan business from the five aspects of model, process, scenario, organizational position, and assessment in the MSTT four-dimensional planning method of CRM3.0 and the case analysis of B2B sales.

Industry

In each industry, we will design solutions with industry characteristics, enter the segmented track of customer relationship management, and achieve innovation in the industry of customer relationship management.

Each industry has its own characteristics, and no customer relationship management solution can meet the needs of all industries, so when designing a customer

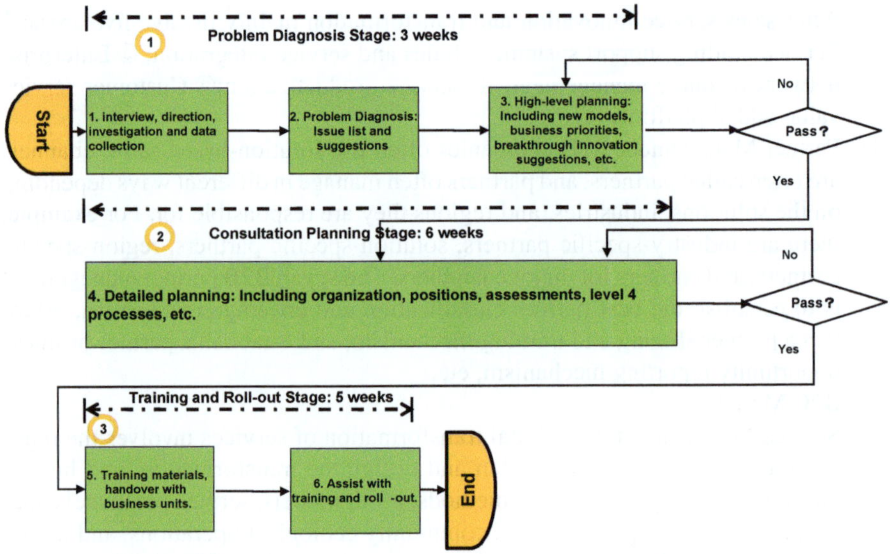

Fig. 1.4 Project planning stages

relationship management solution, it must be targeted at industry characteristics. But on the other hand, we must also consider learning from the experience of other industries. Some pain points have no solutions in this industry because the benchmark companies in this industry cannot solve them; so at this time, we must cross industries to find solutions, because this pain point may be easily solved in other industries.

Delivery Management

Currently, the delivery methods of customer relationship management in various companies are not much different from those I used when I worked at Siebel twenty years ago. Twenty years ago, we could regard customer relationship management as a software, as long as it could share data and have automated processes after the product was launched. But today, twenty years later, enterprises generally link customer relationship management with digital transformation, model changes, and process innovation in various fields such as customer management, marketing, sales, services, channel management, etc., and they generally require the output of business value. Therefore, in the digital age, the delivery method of customer relationship management also needs to keep up with the times. I believe that enterprises should adopt a full lifecycle delivery method, which will cause three changes in the delivery of customer relationship management projects: ① from focusing on software selection to focusing on digital innovation; ② from focusing on software functions to focusing

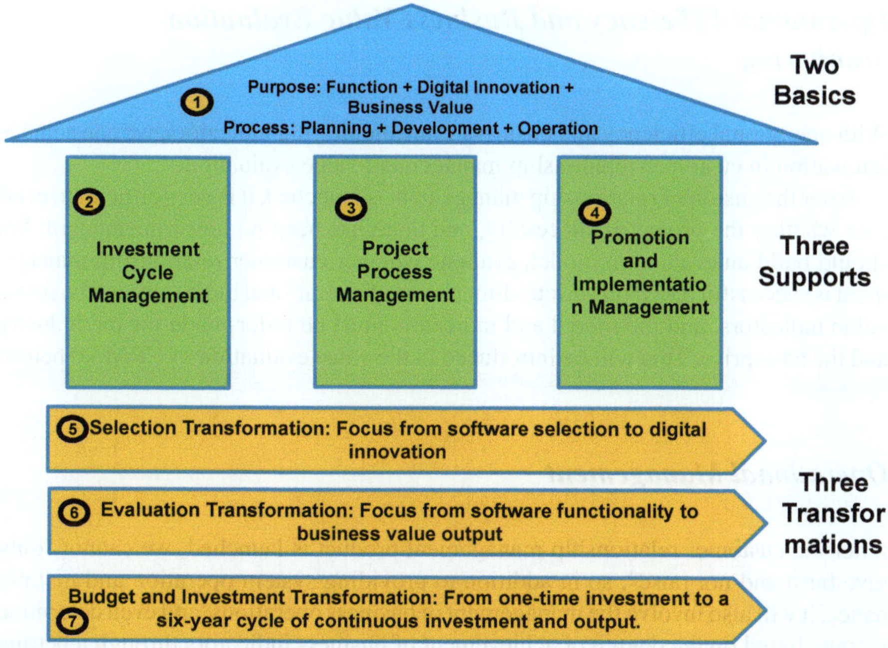

Fig. 1.5 Full lifecycle CRM delivery method

on business value output; ③ from focusing on one-time investment to focusing on continuous investment output every six years. For details, see the relevant sections on the full lifecycle customer relationship management delivery method, which will not be elaborated here.

Figure 1.5 is a panoramic view of the full lifecycle delivery method of customer relationship management. Enterprises must avoid "only giving birth and not raising" in customer relationship management, do not invest all the money in the software launch stage, and are reluctant to spend money in the subsequent operation stage; do not only focus on the Scope of Work (SOW) function, but ignore the business value.

Organizational Adaptation

The traditional IT department is established for the purpose of software project launch and the safe and normal operation of hardware and software. Its integration with the business department is poor. Since the IT department is often a cost center, they do not have a say in the business department. If we want to carry out digital transformation and generate business value from the customer relationship management system, we must build an architecture and mechanism that can drive digital transformation within the enterprise.

Operational Efficiency and Business Value Evaluation Monitoring

With operational efficiency and business value monitoring indicators, we can achieve innovation in customer relationship management value evaluation.

After the customer relationship management is launched, it is very difficult to evaluate whether the project is successful, and there has been no uniform standard. We should build an evaluation model, evaluate whether customer relationship management is successful based on various dimensions of operational indicators and business value indicators, and the model and indicators must be tailor-made for the industry and the enterprise. This will be introduced in the value evaluation of CRM3.0 below.

Operational Management

After the customer relationship management product is launched, we cannot "only give birth and not raise", so in addition to providing system operation and maintenance, it will also involve the management of business operations, and even determine income based on the degree of achievement of business indicators through a betting method. This is also a new profit method for customer relationship management, that is, the innovation of the customer relationship management charging model.

Digital Application

Customer relationship management applies a new product system, technical architecture, and digital technology, which is the innovation of digital customer relationship management.

The various technologies involved in customer relationship management, whether they are based on the cloud or installed locally; what technical architecture is adopted; what digital technologies are adopted, such as mobile, big data, artificial intelligence (AI), Internet of Things, social software, cloud, face recognition, maps, blockchain, etc. These will be introduced in the digital product innovation of CRM3.0 below.

Evolution and Iteration

As mentioned earlier, customer relationship management will keep up with the times, continuously iterate and evolve, and produce new versions. The In the era of digitization, we refer to customer relationship management as CRM3.0, which will certainly evolve into new versions in the future.

Summary > This section introduces what a complete customer relationship management includes in the digital age.

The concept of CRM3.0 is a panoramic description of customer relationship management, which explains customer relationship management from the perspectives of the client, customer relationship management software vendors, customer relationship management consultants, and customer relationship management implementers. It describes the nine main aspects that a complete customer relationship management should include: ① Function; ② Business; ③ Industry; ④ Delivery management; ⑤ Organizational adaptation; ⑥ Operational efficiency and business value monitoring and evaluation; ⑦ Operation management; ⑧ Digital application; ⑨ Evolution and iteration.

CRM Product Innovation in the Digital Age

In the digital age, how should customer relationship management products evolve and innovate? I believe that the three major standards for measuring whether the digital transformation of sales and services is successful are: ①Availability of sales and services; ②Satisfaction of sales and services; ③Dependence on sales and services. Therefore, CRM3.0 products also need to support these three characteristics.

As shown in Fig. 1.6, the standards for measuring whether the digital transformation of sales and services is successful are:

(1) Availability means that sales and services are ubiquitous, and customers and users can access and obtain sales and services at any time and place.

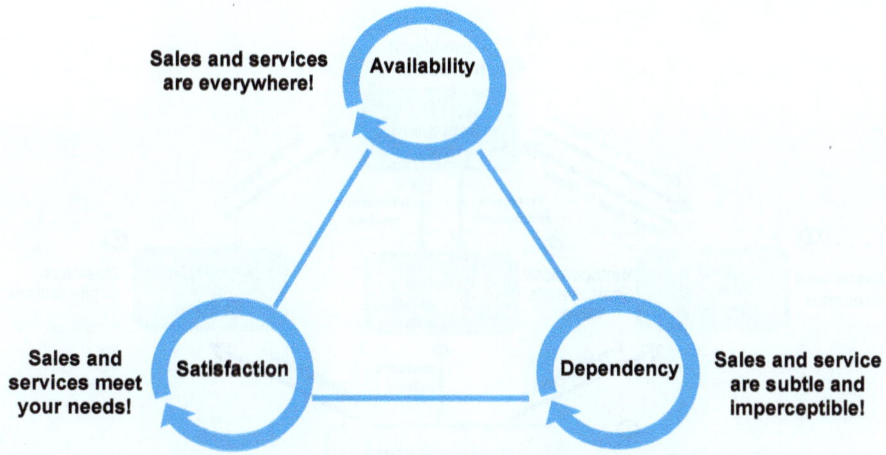

Fig. 1.6 Three standards for measuring sales and service success in the digital age

(2) Satisfaction means that sales and services are provided as needed by customers. We always provide the right sales and services to customers and users at the right time and place.
(3) Dependence means that sales and services are subtly integrated. Marketing and services should be like sunlight, air, and water, making customers and users dependent, using them every day, and forming habits.

In order to achieve the above three standards and successfully innovate and transform sales and services digitally, customer relationship management products also need to keep up with the times and innovate.

As shown in Fig. 1.7, the composition of customer relationship management products in the digital age needs to be restructured. It needs to meet the expectations and requirements of customers for customer relationship management in the digital age, and also needs to fully apply various advanced technologies of the digital age to achieve product and function evolution.

Customer relationship management products in the digital age consist of five core components, namely the traditional customer relationship management application platform, customer relationship management intelligent brain, customer relationship management intelligent terminal, customer relationship management win–win platform, and customer relationship management data asset platform. These five core components also reflect the five major trends of customer relationship management in the digital age: platform support, intelligent management, business scenario, operational ecology, and digital business.

(1) Customer Relationship Management Application Platform (Platform Support) refers to traditional customer relationship management. Entering the digital age, customer relationship management's requirements for intelligence, real-time, customer interaction, and experience accumulation are getting higher and

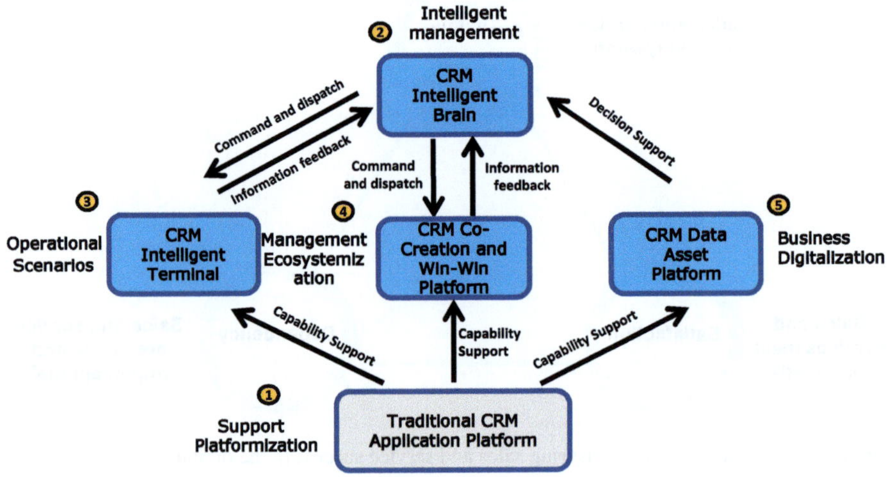

Fig. 1.7 Five core components of CRM3.0 product

higher. Traditional customer relationship management mainly focuses on the implementation of processes and functions, so traditional customer relationship management gradually moves backward, becoming the application platform for sales and services, as well as the ability to output sales and services.

(2) Customer Relationship Management Intelligent Brain (Intelligent Management) is the command center in sales and services, turning the post-correction in the past sales and service process into pre-prevention and mid-course correction.

(3) Customer Relationship Management Intelligent Terminal (Business Scenario) is the business platform for sales and service personnel. The platform is also their maker platform and customer management platform. Through this intelligent terminal, every sales and service personnel is their own CEO, completing a self-driven, self-evolving, and self-profitable process.

(4) The Customer Relationship Management Co-creation and Win–Win Platform (Operational Ecologization) is a platform for all stakeholders in sales and service to interact and add value. Through this platform, we can not only strengthen the stickiness with customers and users, but also perceive the needs of customers and users, and provide one-on-one butler services and personalized product sales.

(5) The Customer Relationship Management Data Asset Platform (Business Digitization) The data assets and experience accumulation in sales and service make customer relationship management a platform that can continuously learn and progress, accumulate experience, and grow on its own.

The following is a detailed introduction to the five core components of customer relationship management in the digital age:

Traditional Customer Relationship Management Application Platform—Supporting Platformization

In the digital age, traditional customer relationship management gradually moves backward to become a platform, that is, to become a capability output center, so customer relationship management supporting platformization is a trend. Because customer relationship management supporting platformization has become a trend, therefore, the platform technology cloudification and microserviceization are also inevitable.

The Seven Command Centers of the Customer Relationship Management Wisdom Brain—Management Wisdom

In the digital age, customer relationship management needs to be equipped with the wings of wisdom, to have its own command center, that is, management wisdom, to build a customer relationship management wisdom brain. This will transform the post-punishment correction in the past sales and service process into pre-prevention and mid-course correction. In order to achieve the customer relationship management wisdom brain, customer relationship management products will also apply a series of new digital technologies, such as artificial intelligence, Internet of Things (IOT), edge computing, and cloud computing, etc.

As shown in Fig. 1.8, the customer relationship management wisdom brain consists of seven command centers:

(1) Work Distribution Center: At the right time, in the right scene, through the right channel, push the right work, and assign it to the right executor.
(2) Skill Center: Guide employees to use the most appropriate methods, tools, and skills in the sales and service process.
(3) Emergency Response Center: In the sales and service process, if an emergency occurs, provide assistance and support at the first time, such as remote expert support, product flash delivery, etc.
(4) Work Guide Center: In the sales and service process, guide employees on how to comply and how to execute according to standardized processes.
(5) Experience and Demand Perception Center: In the sales and service process, collect and feedback customer experience and needs in real-time, recommend touching suggestions. When a negative event is discovered, intervene and correct it in time.

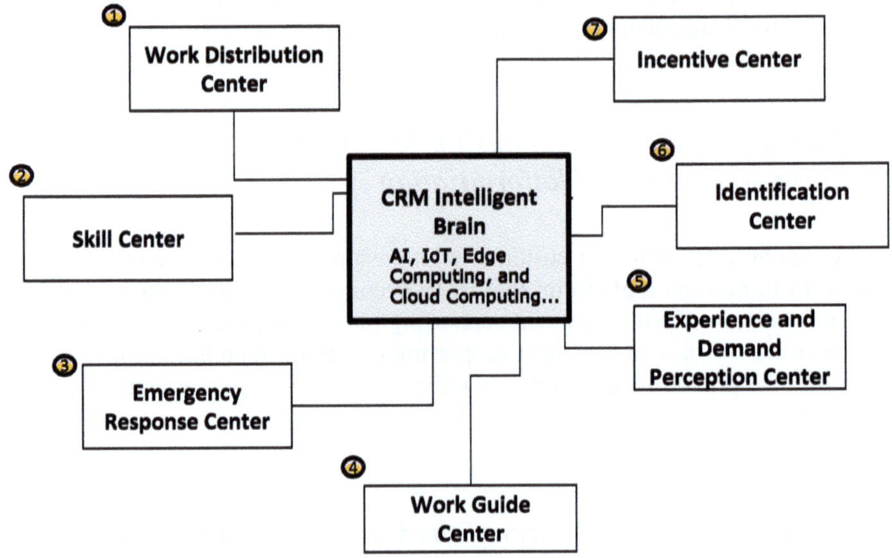

Fig. 1.8 CRM intelligent brain

(6) Identification Center: Identify and correct problems in the sales and service process in real-time, such as non-standard photo uploads and false work orders in service, and false sales leads and contacts in marketing, etc.
(7) Incentive Center: Employee income and incentive calculator, real-time calculation of employee basic income, value-added income, and social income.

The Six Capabilities of the Customer Relationship Management Intelligent Terminal—Operational Scenario

In the digital age, CRM can create different scenarios for sales and service at different times and spaces. To successfully achieve digital transformation of sales and service in these scenarios, to achieve ubiquitous sales and service, as needed and subtly, intelligent mobile terminals are indispensable. (Intelligent mobile terminals are not only the business platform for sales and service personnel, but also their creative platform and customer management platform. Through this intelligent terminal, each sales and service personnel is their own CEO, capable of completing a self-driven, self-evolving, and self-profitable process.) In the process of implementing the intelligent terminal of customer relationship management, it is necessary to apply various digital technologies such as mobile, social, Internet of Things, and artificial intelligence. As shown in Fig. 1.9, the intelligent terminal of customer relationship management needs to achieve the following six capabilities:

(1) Self-planning ability: With the assistance of the intelligent brain of customer relationship management, employees can achieve self-work planning, customer, user operations, etc.

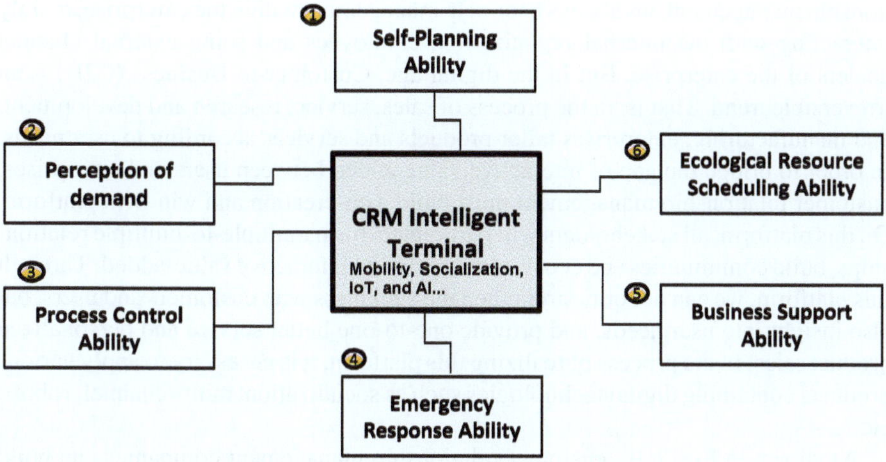

Fig. 1.9 CRM intelligent terminal

(2) Perception of demand: With the assistance of the intelligent brain of customer relationship management, employees can actively perceive the experience and needs of customers and users, and take measures to enhance the experience and promote products.
(3) Process control ability: With the assistance of the intelligent brain of customer relationship management, employees can carry out standardized and standardized sales and service operations.
(4) Emergency response ability: With the assistance of the intelligent brain of customer relationship management, when problems cannot be solved, customer dissatisfaction and other emergencies occur, employees can smoothly and quickly solve problems and improve user satisfaction.
(5) Business support ability: With the assistance of the intelligent brain of customer relationship management, employees can obtain various sales and service support capabilities from the middle and back office, such as expert support, industry support, etc.
(6) Ecological resource scheduling ability: With the assistance of the intelligent brain of customer relationship management, resources from various ecological partners inside and outside the group can be scheduled to coordinate sales and service.

Customer Relationship Management Co-Creation and Win–win Platform—Operation Ecologicalization

Traditional customer relationship management has always been unable to solve the problem of how to let customers and users participate in customer relationship management and form high-stickiness interaction. That is, traditional customer relationship management has always been self-management within the enterprise, mainly interacting with the internal organization, employees and some external channel dealers of the enterprise. But in the digital age, Customer-to-Business (C2B) is an irreversible trend. That is, in the process of sales, service, research and development, and manufacturing, enterprises tailor products and services according to user needs. In order to bridge the gap of interactive value-added between users and enterprises, customer relationship management must build a co-creation and win–win platform. On this platform, all stakeholders will participate, form multiple-to-multiple relationships, build communities and ecosystems, and form interactive value-added. Through this platform, we can not only strengthen the stickiness with customers and users, but also insight into user needs, and provide one-to-one butler service and personalized product sales. In the process of realizing this platform, it is necessary to apply various products containing digital technologies such as socialization, multi-channel, robots, etc.

As shown in Fig. 1.10, customer relationship management companies can build a customer relationship management co-creation and win–win platform for the following four types of institutions and people:

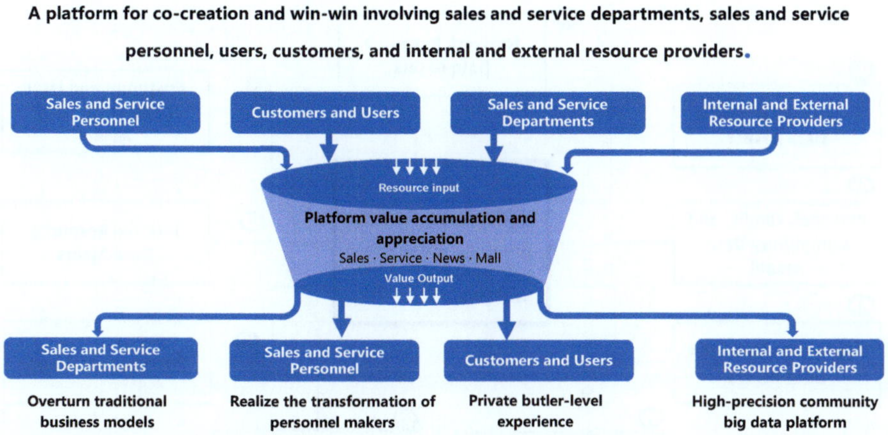

Fig. 1.10 CRM co-creation and win–win platform

(1) Sales and service institutions: Subvert traditional sales and service models, from centralized to decentralized; from sales and service entrances to butler platforms and ecological communities.
(2) Sales and service personnel: Realize the transformation of sales and service personnel into creators, from sales and service personnel. To the customer user steward; from passively arranging tasks to actively starting a business; from selling goods to earn commissions to maintaining customers and users to earn commissions.
(3) Customers and users achieve a private steward-level experience, from basic services and rights services to one-on-one full-time steward-level services.
(4) Internal and external resource parties build a highly accurate community big data platform, from advertising to community big data interaction; from single-item dissemination to demand excavation to force service upgrades.

Nine Major Assets of Customer Relationship Management Data Asset Platform—Business Digitization

Traditional customer relationship management mainly focuses on process optimization and improvement, which we call best practices. However, the accumulation and application of data assets related to sales and services have always been a weak point. In the digital age, the empowerment of technology and the acquisition of massive scene data make the construction of a customer relationship management data asset platform a must. The customer relationship management data asset platform makes customer relationship management a platform that can continuously learn and progress, accumulate experience, and grow on its own. To achieve this

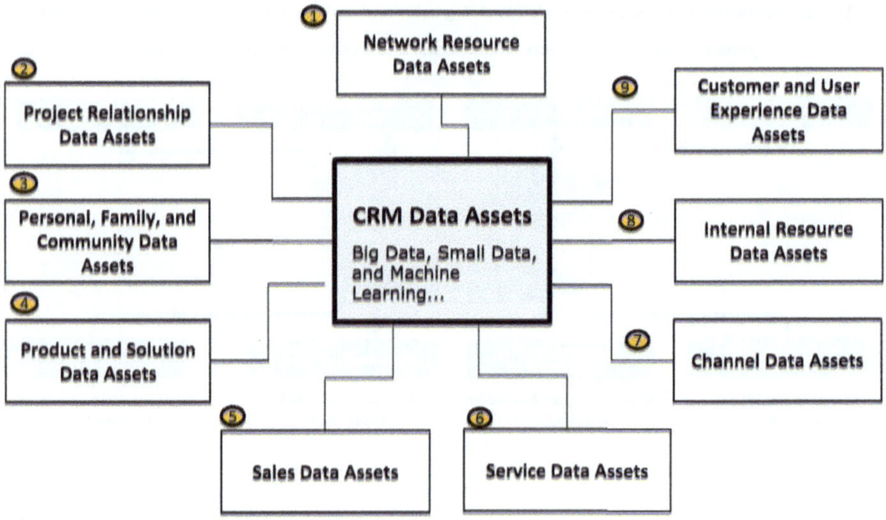

Fig. 1.11 CRM data asset platform

platform, it is necessary to apply various digital technologies and products such as big data, small data, and machine learning.

As shown in Fig. 1.11, the CRM data asset platform consists of nine major categories of data assets:

(1) Network resource data assets are the accumulation and analysis of network resources in B2B business, which are the core resources and digital assets of the enterprise, that is, the enterprise network resource data in business relationship management.
(2) Project relationship data assets are the accumulation and analysis of historical information of projects in B2B business, which are the core digital assets of the enterprise, that is, the historical information data of projects in business relationship management.
(3) Personal, family, and community data assets center on individuals, families, and communities, displaying panoramic information, including the information of products and solutions owned. And establish complex many-to-many relationships for individuals, families, and communities, showing the current status and forecast results of individuals, families, and communities from various dimensions, such as product and service satisfaction, penetration of various products, comparison with competitive products, future procurement needs, etc.
(4) Product and solution data assets are the accumulation of experience and effective data summary with products and solutions as the theme. For example, product and solution trends and customized needs, product quality bank, product self-intelligent model (automatic detection, automatic diagnosis, automatic repair, automatic feedback), etc.

(5) Sales data assets are the accumulation of experience and effective data summary in all market promotion and sales processes. For example, production and sales collaborative forecasting, sales lead conversion forecasting, best order winning step suggestions, etc.
(6) Service data assets are the accumulation of effective data and experience summary in all after-sales processes. For example, spare parts demand forecasting for each service outlet, intelligent dispatch model, intelligent fault diagnosis, etc.
(7) Channel data assets are the accumulation of effective data and experience summary in all channel management processes. Such as channel capacity forecasting, procurement forecasting, production planning, false order diagnosis, etc.
(8) Internal resource data assets are the accumulation of effective data and experience summary in the process of internal resource management of the enterprise. Such as sales and service capability estimation, network layout planning, etc.
(9) Customer and user experience data assets are the accumulation of effective data and experience summary related to all customer and user experiences. Such as customer emotion fluctuation model, creation of touching suggestions, best way of word-of-mouth communication, etc.

Summary > This section introduces the five core components of CRM 3.0 products in the digital age: ① Customer relationship.

Management intelligence brain; ② Customer relationship management intelligent terminal; ③ Customer relationship management win–win platform; ④ Customer relationship management data asset platform; ⑤ Customer relationship management application middleware.

Digital Age Customer Relationship Management Subdivision Track

Domestic customer relationship management will enter the industry and functional subdivision track. It is difficult for general CRM manufacturers to emerge as companies with a market value of tens of billions or even hundreds of billions of dollars like Siebel and Salesforce:

(1) Without the support of the global market, it goes without saying that due to language, culture and other factors, domestic manufacturers' customer relationship management products are difficult to occupy the global market, and there are some opportunities only in some countries that are friendly to us and have similar cultures.
(2) The domestic customer relationship management market has not formed a market scale that matches the national power. The domestic customer relationship management market has experienced ups and downs for more than 20

years. At present, due to inconsistent statistical methods, it is difficult to have a particularly accurate market scale estimate. I think the annual usage license scale is between several billion and tens of billions. This customer relationship management market scale is difficult to match the status of China as the world's second largest economic entity, and there is a big gap with the customer relationship management market scale of many countries in Europe and America. Why is there such a big gap? I think this is caused by the different management genes of domestic and foreign companies. Take coffee as an example, European and American countries may regard coffee as a necessity of life, a part of life; but Chinese people do not have this habit, coffee may only be the choice of a small number of people, most people still choose to drink tea.

According to China's economic scale, the domestic customer relationship management market should be a scale of tens of billions or even hundreds of billions. The reason why the current market scale is so small is actually because our customer relationship management manufacturers have not developed a customer relationship management like tea that can meet the needs of the vast majority of Chinese enterprises.

Chinese enterprises generally pay attention to results, and the customer relationship management they need is the customer relationship management that has visible investment returns. Why do so many companies spend a lot of money on CCTV advertising, and now live on various social media? In fact, these methods can make investment returns visible and can be realized in time. Why should it be visible and timely? Because for building core competitiveness, widening the "moat" and so on, except for a few companies that will think about these issues, most companies will not care about it.

If the return on investment in customer relationship management is not visible and timely, in fact, more than 95% of Chinese enterprise audiences have been excluded. Recently, SCRM has received some attention. In fact, it is the private domain traffic built by enterprises themselves. Chinese enterprises recognize that traffic is money, and the cost of acquiring new customers can be quantified, so the return of SCRM is visible and can be realized in time.

Below are the opportunities I think exist in the domestic customer relationship management market:

The Traditional Customer Relationship Management Track

Traditional customer relationship management includes standard functions of various modules such as market, sales, channels, services, customer management, etc., and covers many industries' customer relationship management. In this market, international manufacturers have micro Foreign manufacturers include Salesforce (a customer relationship management software service provider established in March 1999), SAP, Oracle, etc.; domestic manufacturers include Neocrm, Sharecrm, etc.

This market has entered a mature stage, and the market capacity will not change much.

If customer relationship management manufacturers want to achieve rapid development in the traditional customer relationship management market, they often need to win large orders, that is, to win customer relationship management projects of at least several million yuan. But such projects are often done by two types of companies:

(1) "Carp Leaping Over the Dragon Gate" type companies are often thousands of people in size, with sales of tens of billions, facing a process of breaking out of their cocoon and becoming a butterfly from tens of billions to hundreds of billions or even hundreds of billions in scale. These companies say they want to do customer relationship management, but in fact, it is because the company has reached a certain scale and wants to find a good way to transform in the field of sales and service to help the company grow quickly and become stronger.
(2) "Head" companies These companies often have tens of thousands of people, with a market value of hundreds of billions. They often have a budget for the customer relationship management track every year.

In summary, these two types of companies often have high requirements for the brand, solutions, and cases of customer relationship management manufacturers. For customer relationship management companies that are new to this track, if you do not have enough funds, do not have enough scale and brand support, and do not have top industry experts, it is very difficult to grow.

Segmenting the Customer Relationship Management Track

I believe that the hope for the future market of customer relationship management in China lies in the segmented track, just like the vertical search from Baidu to Meituan, Ctrip, etc. This segmented track can accommodate dozens or even more customer relationship management "unicorns", and the scale of each track may not necessarily be smaller than the traditional customer relationship management track.

The segmented customer relationship management track is divided into industry-segmented customer relationship management track and function-segmented customer relationship management track.

(1) Industry-segmented customer relationship management track: Many domestic industries have a market scale of trillions of yuan, such as automobiles, home appliances 3C, medical health, retail, finance, manufacturing, etc. These industries all need to innovate and transform digitally in the fields of sales and service. As long as the industry-segmented customer relationship management has industry characteristics and meets the principle of visible and timely realization of investment returns, there will be a lot of market opportunities.

(2) Function-segmented customer relationship management track: The traditional customer relationship management theoretical system and methodology are not perfect, and many places can be innovated, refined, and improved. For example, SCRM is a product not found in traditional customer relationship management. In addition, like enterprise relationship resource management, project behavior management, sales support system, etc., there is no related theoretical system and perfect product function in traditional customer relationship management.

We can discover segmented tracks based on the five key success capabilities of CRM 3.0 introduced earlier.

(1) Theoretical system innovation: As mentioned earlier, SCRM is in a sense a customer relationship management theoretical system innovation based on private domain traffic acquisition, and it can meet the principle of visible and timely realization of investment returns. But this is just a very small part of the innovation in customer relationship management theory, and there is still a lot of space for CRM innovation, such as enterprise relationship resource management. In fact, many Chinese companies initially used customer One of the reasons for customer relationship management is the fear of salespeople taking away connections. China is a society where relationships are important, and it's not an exaggeration to say so. In my more than twenty years in the field of customer relationship management, countless companies, especially those whose target customers are large customers, have expressed the need to manage their company's relationship resources, but there is still no such mature product on the market. The construction of a new theoretical system and methodology, if universal, is a functional subdivision of the customer relationship management track, and if it is industry-related, it is an industry subdivision of the customer relationship management track.
(2) Industry Innovation: The industry characteristics of the mainstream customer relationship management products on the market are not obvious. To apply to industry customers, a lot of customization is often required. The understanding of industry business by current customer relationship management vendors, as well as the ability to drive industry transformation and innovation through customer relationship management products, is insufficient, often relying on consulting implementation partners to complete. The industry track is a blue ocean for customer relationship management vendors, and the capacity of each track may not be smaller than the traditional domestic customer relationship management market. For example, the annual sales of the domestic home appliance 3C field are over a trillion yuan, and there are hundreds of thousands of specialty stores and service outlets. If our customer relationship management can solve industry pain points, such as production and sales coordination, integrated sales and service, intelligent dispatch, spare parts prediction, production capacity prediction, intelligent production scheduling, etc., it will definitely create a billion or even tens of billions of customer relationship management market. If we consider the upstream and downstream enterprises of home appliances, the scale will be even larger. If we empower various new technologies,

such as the Internet of Things, AI, big data, mobility, socialization, etc., and apply them to various customer relationship management business scenarios, then this customer relationship management vendor facing the industry track has the opportunity to become a high-valued "unicorn". The construction of innovative products in the industry is considered an industry subdivision of the customer relationship management track.

(3) Value Assessment Innovation: Chinese companies usually pay more attention to return on investment, and a customer relationship management value assessment system must be established to realize the principle of visible and timely realization of return on investment in customer relationship management. Customer relationship management vendors generally charge customers based on system go-live, and whether there is business value is the customer's business. This point is increasingly difficult to be recognized and accepted in Chinese enterprises. If customer relationship management vendors have tools that can evaluate various indicators of the enterprise before the system goes live, monitor key business indicators after the system goes live, and analyze return on investment through quantifying business indicators, it will be easier to win customers and projects. The construction of a new value assessment system, if universal, is a functional subdivision of the customer relationship management track, and if it is industry-related, it is an industry subdivision of the customer relationship management track.

(4) Charging Model Innovation: The innovation of the charging model needs to be based on the establishment of a value assessment system. If business value can be quantified, the charge for customer relationship management can be defined according to the output of business value, rather than charging based on the current number of usage licenses and development workload. We often say that what customers need is a hole in the wall, not a drill. So for customer relationship management, what customers actually need is business value, not software. Charging based on business value is more in line with the true meaning of SAAS service, that is, software is service. Take the home appliance industry as an example, after using the customer relationship management after-sales service module, about 10 million service engineer in-warranty visits can be reduced each year. If each visit costs 50 yuan, it can reduce the company's cost by 500 million yuan each year, and it is reasonable to talk about tens of millions of CRM charges each year. The innovation of the charging model often has strong industry characteristics and individualized characteristics of the enterprise, so it generally belongs to the industry subdivision of the customer relationship management track.

(5) Digital Innovation: Digital innovation refers to transformation and innovation using digital technology. It can Transforming the architecture of traditional customer relationship management (CRM) products, such as creating a CRM intelligent brain, CRM intelligent terminal, CRM win–win platform, CRM data asset platform, etc., can also empower business models, scenarios, and processes. If digital innovation is to innovate the general CRM functions, it is

the CRM track of functional segmentation; if it is to innovate industry-related applications, it is the CRM track of industry segmentation.

Summary > This section introduces the opportunities and challenges faced by CRM vendors in the digital age on traditional tracks and segmented tracks. And it details how to find CRM opportunities on the functional segmentation track and industry segmentation track through the five key capabilities of CRM 3.0.

CRM in the Digital Age Cross-Border Track

When it comes to CRM products, what people generally refer to is the CRM used internally by enterprises, that is, traditional CRM. But entering the digital age, with the integration of digital technology and scenarios, the boundaries of CRM products are becoming wider and even cross-border. For example, SCRM is not only used by internal employees, but also involves a large number of active users. In addition, e-commerce, WeChat, TikTok, etc., in some sense, are also a kind of CRM.

I believe that, broadly speaking, CRM has two key points: one is related to the enterprise, and the other involves the market, sales, service, channels, and customers, etc. As long as these two conditions are met, it can be considered as broad CRM. Therefore, from the perspective of usage, CRM can be divided into three categories:

(1) CRM used internally by enterprises.
(2) C2B CRM.
(3) C2C2B CRM.

C2B CRM and C2C2B CRM are derivatives of the digital age, but they are developing rapidly and are both trillion-yuan scale tracks, growing much faster than CRM used internally by enterprises. The reason for this, I believe, is mainly because these two types of CRM can meet the conditions driven by capital and can quickly occupy the market with the power of capital.

Many cases show that business models that grow rapidly driven by capital often have the following characteristics: ①High frequency of participation by C-end customers; ②Simple transaction model; ③Act as a platform matchmaker or connector; ④The key to competition lies in traffic and supply chain.

Next, we will introduce these three types of CRM, and analyze which type of CRM has the characteristics of quickly occupying the market driven by capital.

CRM Used Internally by Enterprises

The current mainstream CRM products are all CRM used internally by enterprises, which is also the orthodox CRM in everyone's mind. From the earliest Siebel to the current Salesforce, Microsoft Dynamics CRM. Whether it is SAAS service or local installation, it focuses on product functions and shows its value through different product functions. Although this type of CRM manages individual customer information,

However, it is primarily used by internal employees. Let's see if it has the characteristics of being capital-driven:

(1) High frequency of participation by C-end customers: It is mainly used by internal employees, and C-end individual customers do not participate or participate to a limited extent.
(2) Simple transaction model: These products often win with very complex functions and solutions as prerequisites, usually going through bidding processes, making the transaction process very complex.
(3) Acting as a platform for matchmaking or as a connector: These products are exclusively for internal use by companies and do not act as matchmakers or connectors.
(4) The key to competition lies in traffic and supply chain: Competition lies in product functions, solutions, and industry knowledge, unrelated to traffic and supply chain.

As can be seen, customer relationship management for internal use by companies is not suitable for capital-driven. The traditional customer relationship management field has always been a difficult area for capital to invade and conquer. It requires time to continuously refine products, projects to accumulate solutions, gradually establish industry reputation, and build its own partner network. Without ten or even twenty years, it is difficult to succeed. It is rare to hear of any traditional customer relationship management vendors that have quickly captured the market in a few years. Siebel is an exception, it rose when CRM was a blue ocean market, with little competition, and it is now difficult for the customer relationship management market to have such an opportunity again.

C2B CRM

Next, let's see if there is high growth space for capital-driven in the focus on C2B customer relationship management. Let's first look at what C2B customer relationship management is.

C2B customer relationship management refers to the focus on the value-added interaction between individuals and businesses. It is not a CRM that focuses on internal use by companies, but focuses on connecting individuals and businesses, completing value-added customer relationship management through information exchange, demand matching, and transaction matchmaking.

As shown in Fig. 1.12, the most successful area of this type of customer relationship management is the docking of individuals and business sales, such as Tmall, JD.com, Pinduoduo, and other e-commerce platforms.

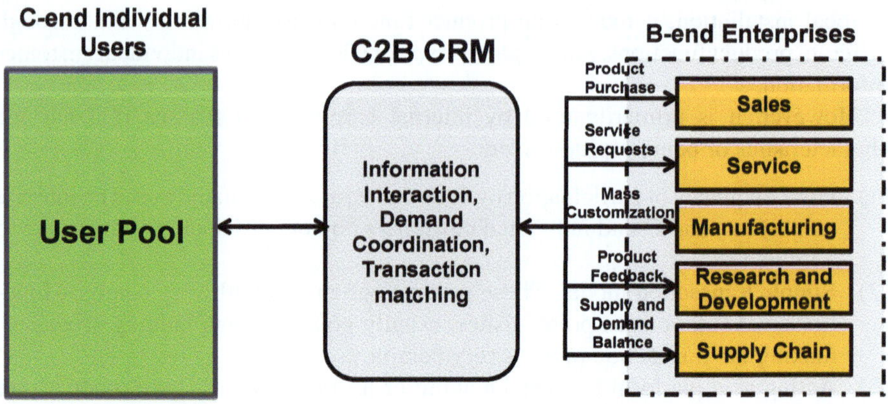

Fig. 1.12 C2B CRM

Many people may not think that e-commerce is customer relationship management. As I mentioned earlier, in a broad sense, CRM has two key points: one is related to the enterprise, and the other involves the market, sales, service, channels, and customers. As long as these two conditions are met, it can be considered as broad-sense customer relationship management.

C2B customer relationship management meets the characteristics of "high frequency of participation by C-end customers, simple transaction model, acting as a platform for matchmaking or as a connector, the key to competition lies in traffic and supply chain", so it believes that it can grow rapidly through capital-driven. JD.com and Pinduoduo have followed this model.

In addition to the docking of C-end individual users and business sales, there is also a huge market space in the fields of business services, manufacturing, research and development, and supply chain. I believe this is a blue ocean that can create "unicorn" companies through capital-driven.

(1) Docking with business services: This is the socialization of business service capabilities. For example, there are countless service outlets in society looking for customers, and countless users looking for service providers. The home appliance industry is a very typical example. We can find some service providers' contact information on the Internet, but just providing information cannot meet user requirements. The market needs a more professional platform, such as professionalizing and standardizing service standards, service norms, service content, service prices, etc., and then pulling all service providers who meet this standard into the platform, docking all demands in society, and becoming the Meituan of the service field.
(2) Integration with enterprise manufacturing, which is the socialization of enterprise manufacturing capabilities. This is similar to the integration with enterprise services. There are a large number of enterprises in society that have excess production capacity at certain times, especially with the emergence of smart factories, these capabilities can be digitized and output. Therefore, enterprises

need a platform to accumulate small orders from users and complete large-scale customization.

(3) Integration with the enterprise supply chain, which is about supply–demand balance and production based on demand. Due to inaccurate judgments of market demand, some enterprises produce products that cannot be sold, and the market needs cannot be produced in time. The reason for this is that if enterprises only predict current sales based on past sales and experience, the deviation will be very large. Enterprises must collect and summarize the demand of C-end users to achieve a balance of supply and demand.

(4) Integration with enterprise research and development, which is C2B research and development. We need the early participation of C-end users to possibly develop products that the market needs, not products that designers like.

All of these require the traffic of C-end and the joining of B-end enterprises, require a large amount of capital, but can also quickly occupy the market through capital, just like Meituan, JD.com, and Pinduoduo.

Focus on C2C2B Customer Relationship Management

Why is it C2C2B Customer Relationship Management, not C2C Customer Relationship Management? Because I always believe that the most important thing about customer relationship management is to be related to the enterprise. If it only happens between individuals, I don't think this is customer relationship management.

As shown in Fig. 1.13, I believe that C2C2B Customer Relationship Management mainly focuses on social, entertainment, work, and community circles.

(1) Social—The most typical is WeChat. Originally, WeChat was mainly used for communication between acquaintances, but with the widespread use of public accounts and mini-programs, the participation and involvement of enterprises

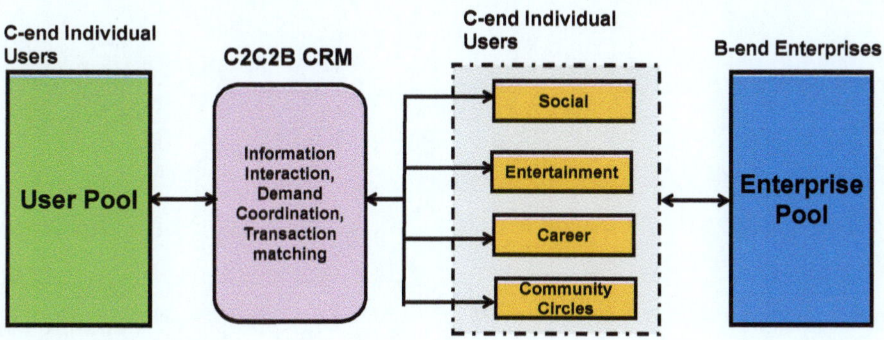

Fig. 1.13 C2C2B CRM

are getting deeper and deeper, and many interactions are ultimately for enterprise product sales and brand promotion.

(2) Entertainment—Short video platforms like TikTok and Kuaishou, as the ways of monetizing traffic gradually mature, the involvement of enterprises is getting deeper and deeper.
(3) Career—Platforms like LinkedIn have gradually become the main battlefield for enterprise and headhunter recruitment.
(4) Community Circles—I believe this is a very potential CRM market. The long tail effect of e-commerce has flattened the world and made it smaller. But it also has a problem, that is, it cannot effectively establish trust between people. Trust is based on knowing each other well, and it is often easier to establish trust the closer the distance. During the COVID-19 pandemic, everyone has become accustomed to group buying based on the community, that is, the dragon form in the neighborhood group of the community. Because it's tangible and visible, it's easier for each other to trust and make transactions. This is a blue ocean. Currently, there are hundreds of thousands of communities in China, and the main way of community group buying is still through WeChat, the market needs a platform that is more standardized in management, more intimate in service, more secure in funds, and more powerful in functions.

C2C2B Customer Relationship Management has the characteristics of "high-frequency participation of C-end customers, simple transaction mode, acting as a platform for matchmaking or connectors, and the core of competition lies in traffic and supply chain". It can achieve rapid growth driven by capital.

Summary > This section introduces the three types of customer relationship management in a broad sense, that is, CRM used internally by enterprises, C2B customer relationship management, and C2C2B customer relationship management. It also analyzes which type of customer relationship management can rapidly expand the market through the power of capital.

Chapter 2
CRM3.0's B2B Sales Digital Transformation

As I have introduced before, CRM3.0 involves five levels of innovation: ① theoretical system innovation; ② industry innovation; ③ value assessment innovation; ④ charging model innovation; ⑤ digital innovation. This chapter will introduce the theoretical system of B2B sales in CRM3.0.

B2B Sales Digital Transformation

Currently, digital transformation is in full swing among leading companies in various industries, with many digital innovation and transformation cases in B2C marketing, after-sales service, manufacturing, supply chain, and R&D. However, in the B2B sales field, the progress of digital transformation is relatively slow. Although there are some digital applications such as machine scoring of leads and opportunities, assessing win rates based on historical data, and automatically finding contacts, the effects are not significant. B2B sales, especially large customer sales, still use the traditional methods of maintaining good relationships (trust you) + making plans (move him).

B2B sales may be one of the hardest areas to be replaced by artificial intelligence. The difficulty of large-scale digital transformation in B2B sales is determined by its characteristics: many interactions and decision-making processes in B2B are invisible, customer decisions are influenced by various explicit and implicit factors, and the degree of influence changes with time and progress, all of which are difficult to describe digitally, and thus difficult to recreate through digitalization.

Before introducing sales process management, a problem needs to be clarified. Due to the special and complex nature of B2B sales, you cannot use digital tools to monitor the entire contact between sales and customers, to evaluate the customer experience, otherwise no one would dare to do business with you; nor can you evaluate the win rate based on a customer's feedback on your plan, because the

© China Science and Technology Press Co., Ltd. 2025

J. Yang, *Sales and Service Digital Transformation*,
https://doi.org/10.1007/978-981-96-5961-6_2

decision-making mechanism of B2B business is very complex. Therefore, it is not those B2B sales that use cool digital technologies that are called B2B sales in the digital age. In the digital age, we can innovate the theory of customer relationship management, so that B2B sales can meet the needs of enterprises and bring business value to enterprises, which is also a manifestation of B2B sales innovation in the digital age.

In the digital age, if we want to enhance the B2B sales capability of enterprises through digital tools, in addition to digital management and innovation of the part above the "iceberg" (i.e., the sales process), we also need to do digital management and innovation of the part below the "iceberg" (i.e., large customer management and sales support system management). Winning orders is about letting things take their course. Many of the tasks in the process of forming an advantage are invisible, such as large customer management and sales support system management, which are often overlooked, but are the most basic and core parts.

As shown in Fig. 2.1, B2B sales in the digital age can be summarized as three steps: defending the norm, surprising, and accumulating momentum. Defending the norm is large customer management, surprising is sales process management, and accumulating momentum is sales support system management.

(1) Key account management, also known as customer line management, emphasizes direction and strategy, not pursuing short-term goals. It values integrity, benefiting others to benefit oneself, and giving before receiving. If too much emphasis is placed on short-term returns in key account management, the relationship is unlikely to last, and business will fluctuate. The purpose of key account management is to continuously improve the quality and quantity of

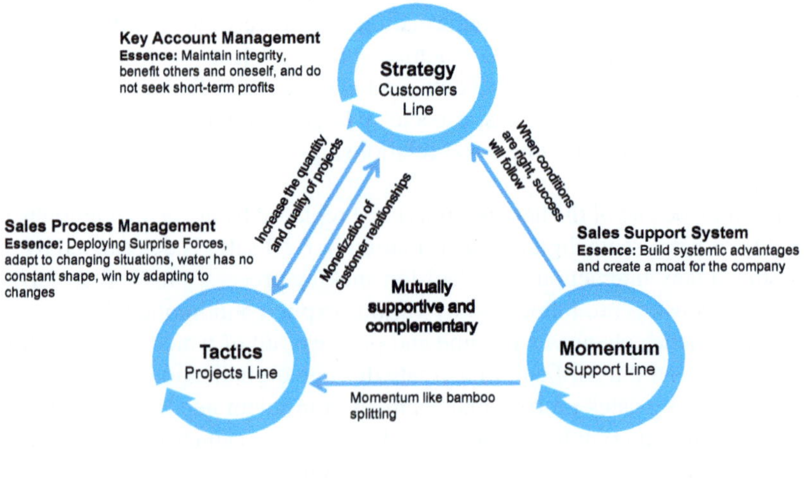

Fig. 2.1 B2B sales management model in the digital age

projects for this key account over a long period of time, thereby generating sustainable and maximized returns.

(2) Sales process management, also known as project line management, focuses more on short-term effects, with winning orders as the measurement standard. It values cunning, surprising strategies during the order process, the so-called "no constant tactics in war, no constant shape in water, winning by changing with the enemy". Sales process management is the process of monetizing the relationships and capabilities we have established in key account management and our own sales support system. There are many methods of sales process management, and they are quite complete, such as the TAS methodology, which has been successfully applied in practice.

(3) Sales support system management, also known as support line management. B2B sales, especially large orders, may take half a year, a year, or even several years, involving issues of support and cooperation from internal and external company executives, various proposal lines, delivery lines, product lines, testing lines, and external experts. A single mistake could lead to a total loss. If a large project cannot be won, the reasons can usually be found in inadequate relationships and support resources. The importance of support resources for winning orders is increasing, but companies often lack a mechanism for investing the best resources in the most valuable projects. Therefore, building the most reasonable and efficient sales support system is to establish a systematic advantage for the company and build the company's "moat".

Figure 2.2 is an example of the growth curve of the value output of the three main components of B2B sales as the company grows.

Sales process management is a technique, easy to master, but its effect will gradually weaken as the company grows; key account management is a principle, it can establish stable relationships and generate continuous income, and its effect will gradually strengthen as the company grows and time passes; sales support system management is a force, the larger the company, the greater the potential energy it generates, forming the company's "moat", subduing the enemy without fighting. Therefore, in the short term, sales process management is the most effective, and in the long term, sales support system management is the most core.

Summary > B2B sales can be summarized as three steps: integrity, surprise, and momentum. Integrity is key account management, key account management is a principle, also known as customer line management, emphasizing direction and strategy, not pursuing short-term goals. Surprise is sales process management, sales process management is a technique, also known as project line management, focusing more on short-term effects, with winning orders as the measurement standard. Momentum is sales support system management, sales support system management is a force, also known as support line management.

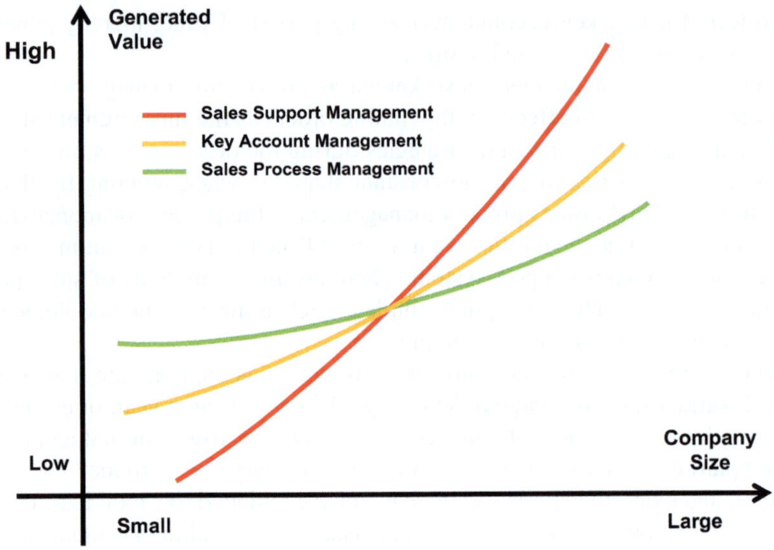

Fig. 2.2 Example of value output curves for the three major components of B2B sales

Key Account Management in B2B Sales

The previous section introduced the digital transformation of B2B sales in CRM3.0. It consists of three parts: namely, integrity, The Trilogy of Surprise and Accumulation. In the trilogy of B2B sales, key account management seems easy, but it is actually the most vague and difficult to implement. The reason why it is difficult to establish a key account management system is because it is hard to quantify and evaluate. Sales process management, which is the process from opportunity to contract, from contract to cash, can be fully evaluated by digital indicators such as contract amount, payment, profit, cost, project delivery quality, and cycle to assess input and output. However, it is difficult for key account management to have quantifiable measurement indicators, which makes it difficult to evaluate the relationship between the cost and output to be invested, thus making many companies hesitant to invest a lot of money and manpower. In addition, both key account management and sales process management involve customer management. Where the boundaries of the two are, how to allocate and connect in terms of organization, personnel, resources, and processes, and how to decompose performance and responsibilities, there is also a large vague space, causing many companies to be unable to establish a complete key account management system.

But key account management is the seed sown in spring, and the win rate is the fruit harvested in autumn. So if a company wants to reap a lot of fruit in a few years, it must establish a systematic, complete, and efficient key account management mechanism.

This section mainly introduces the elements and management model of key account management.

Five Elements of Key Account Management

To carry out key account management, you must first achieve three knowledges: know who the key accounts are; know who is responsible for the key accounts; know how to manage the key accounts. Then formulate strategies and tactics, and finally evaluate through a dynamic evaluation mechanism. In addition, you must achieve three observations: observe whether the key account is qualified; observe whether the sales are qualified; observe whether the management mechanism is qualified.

As shown in Fig. 2.3, the five elements of key account management (WHCSE) are introduced respectively: ① How to determine the key account (Who); ② How to manage the key account (How); ③ Who is responsible for the key account (Coverage); ④ Strategy and tactics (Strategy); ⑤ Dynamic evaluation (Evaluate).

How to Identify the Key Account

Many companies determine key accounts mainly by looking at sales. Because the customer produced many projects last year, this year the customer is positioned as a key account, and a higher sales target is given, causing the salesperson responsible for this customer to be unable to complete the task and forced to resign.

Key account management cannot pursue short-term benefits. The original intention of our key account management is: over a relatively long period of time, these customers will play a pivotal role in our company's performance, so we need to invest more resources and energy in these customers. And sales only represent yesterday, not the future, so based on this, resources will be misallocated, performance will fluctuate, and sales will keep changing.

As shown in Fig. 2.4, it is recommended to use the comprehensive scoring method when determining key accounts: calculate the total score of the customer based on

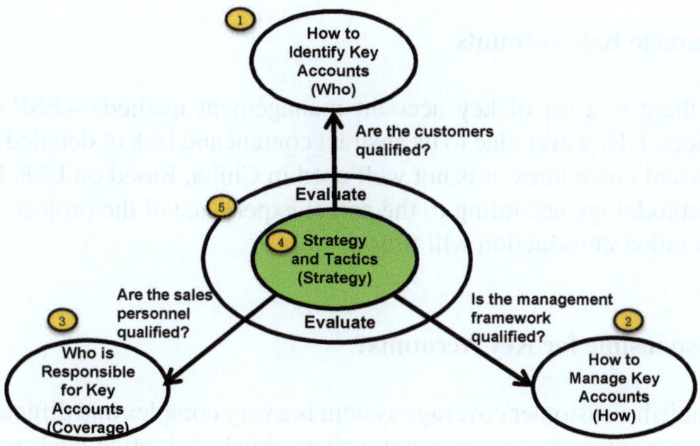

Fig. 2.3 Five key elements of key account management

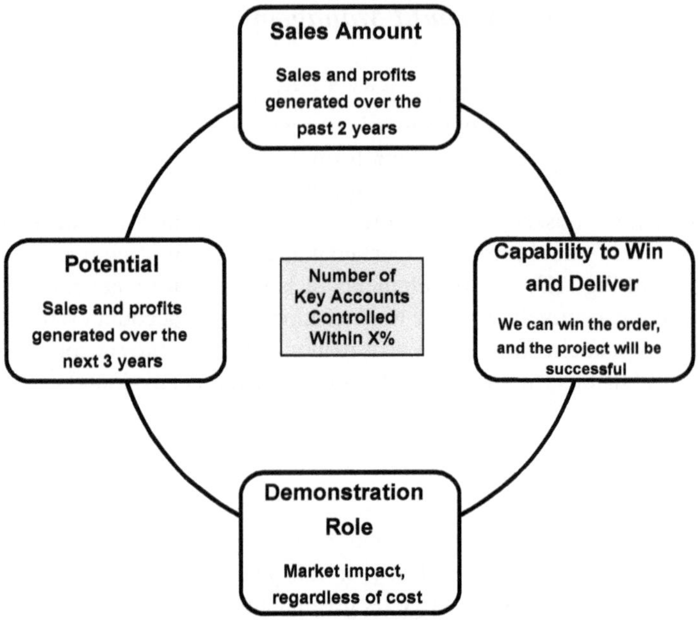

Fig. 2.4 Four key elements for determining key accounts using an integrated scoring method

the customer's scores in sales, potential, demonstration role, and ability to win and do, multiplied by the weight, and then rank according to the score, take the top x % as key accounts, that is, $\sum$ element interval score x weight.

Since different industries and different types of customers vary greatly, we can set different interval score thresholds for different industries or different types of customers, so as to be as fair as possible.

How to Manage Key Accounts

In Siebel, there is a set of key account management methods—ESP (Enterprise Selling Process). However, due to its abstract content and lack of detailed implementation steps and procedures, it is not well used in China. Based on ESP, I optimized the ESP methodology according to the actual experience of the project, and named it ESP+. Detailed introduction will follow.

Who is Responsible for Key Accounts?

How to establish a customer coverage system is a very complex and difficult problem. If the customer coverage system is not well established, it often leads to the consequence that major clients are not well managed, and small clients are neglected, greatly restricting the expansion of the company's market capabilities. I will give a detailed introduction in the content of the "Customer Coverage Effectiveness Model" later.

Let's start with a simple example. Whether major clients are managed by regional branches or offices, or by the headquarters' key account management department, this issue involves sales performance and personal income, so the dispute will be significant, and many companies are always adjusting. Personally, I suggest that at the beginning, existing major clients are still managed by regional sales; the headquarters of major clients focuses on resource support for major clients, dynamic evaluation and assessment, as well as task assignment, guidance, training and support for regional sales. As for sales performance, it can be double credit.

As shown in Fig. 2.5:

(1) Major clients are still directly managed by regional sales.
(2) Regional sales are directly managed by local or office managers, but need to report to the regional major client director in a dotted line, and the regional major client director assigns tasks, guides, trains and supports regional sales.

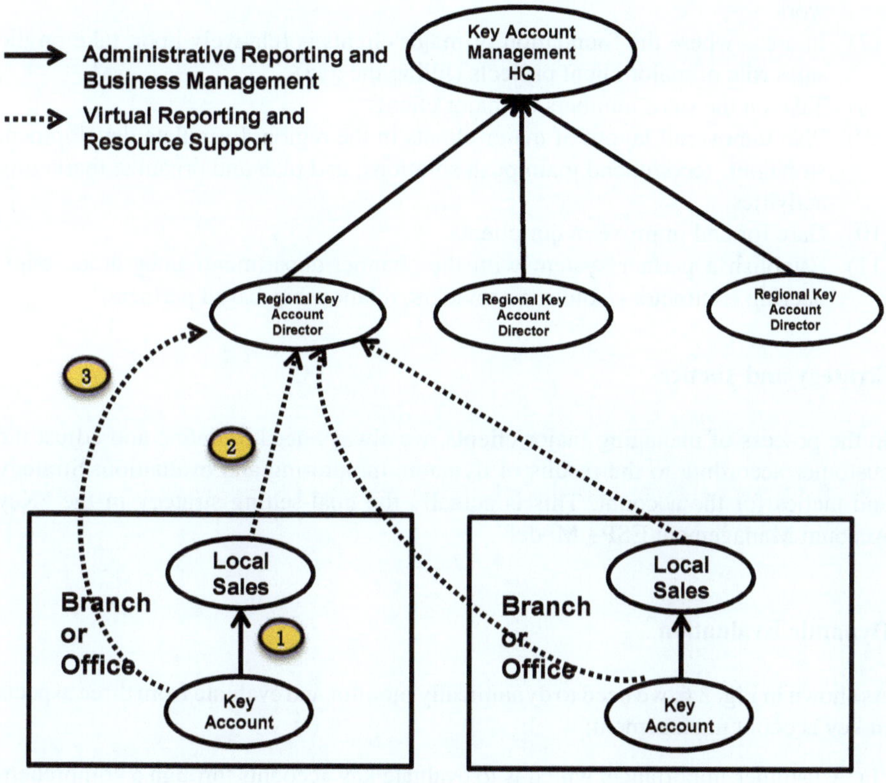

Fig. 2.5 Example of key account responsibility relationships

(3) The regional major client director does not directly manage major clients, but focuses on dynamic evaluation and assessment of major clients, as well as providing resources such as experts, plans, and budgets at various stages.

Below are the job responsibilities I defined for the regional major client director in a project, for reference:

(1) Evaluation and approval of major client-related projects, invocation of delivery resources, tracking of project progress in pre-sales and post-sales stages.
(2) Provide pre-sales support for major client projects at the request of office sales (for example, before the business opportunity is established and before the pre-sales expert of the delivery team is in place).
(3) Responsible for the overall layout of various partners such as engineering contractors, integrators, and design institutes in the region.
(4) Coordinate and arrange resources from the office and solution department to follow up and support important partners.
(5) Establish a close interactive relationship with the office, regularly train office sales, pre-sales and technical support personnel.
(6) Supervise the industry sales of the office, listen to their reports, and guide their work.
(7) In areas where the foundation of major clients is relatively poor, take on the sales role of major client projects (filling the gap).
(8) Take on the sales numbers of major clients.
(9) Plan the overall layout of major clients in the region, formulate development strategies, recommend main push solutions, and plan and organize marketing activities.
(10) Care for and improve major clients.
(11) Establish a partner system with the channel department: integrators, engineering contractors, solution providers, relationship-based partners.

Strategy and Tactics

In the process of managing major clients, we always need to define and adjust the customer according to the results of dynamic monitoring and evaluation. Strategy and tactics for the account. This is actually the goal-setting strategy in the "Key Account Management ESP+ Model".

Dynamic Evaluation

As shown in Fig. 2.6, we need to dynamically monitor and evaluate from three aspects in key account management:

(1) Customer Importance, which is to evaluate key accounts through a comprehensive scoring method. This evaluation frequency can be every three months or every six months.

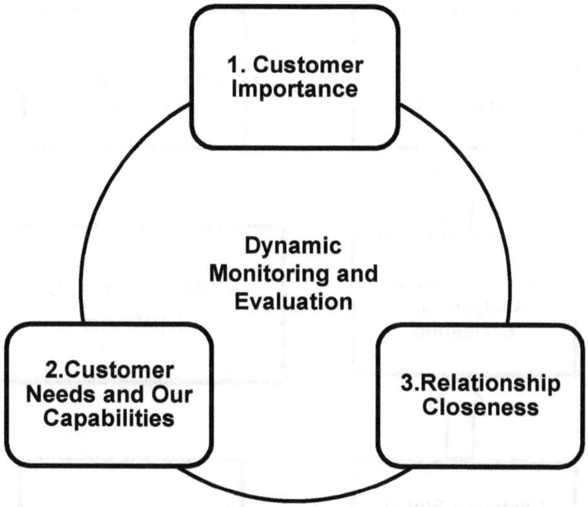

Fig. 2.6 Dynamic monitoring and evaluation

(2) Customer Needs and Our Capability, which is to analyze the customer's needs for related products, solutions, and services in three stages: within 3 months, 3–12 months, and 1–3 years, which are the business opportunities we are going to incubate, and the current company's capability and resource gap to meet these needs. The recommended evaluation frequency is once a month or once every three months.
(3) Relationship Closeness, which is used to evaluate the development of our relationship with customers. The later chapters on business relationship management and corporate networking resource management will detail how to evaluate relationship closeness. The recommended evaluation frequency is once a month, and some parts can be automatically counted by the software system.

Overview of Key Account Management

Before introducing key account management, let me briefly introduce the traditional key account management method.

As shown in Fig. 2.7, traditional key account management only provides a thought process for key account management, but does not have very specific implementation measures. Therefore, when I was designing key account management for some customers, it was much more difficult than sales process management, and it was very difficult to design specifically for implementation. I have contacted many companies, and they basically have very detailed and perfect sales process management designs, but very little planning for key account management.

As shown in Fig. 2.8, I believe that the core output of key account management is to incubate business opportunities. As long as we firmly grasp the three core tasks, we have a handle and can implement key account management.

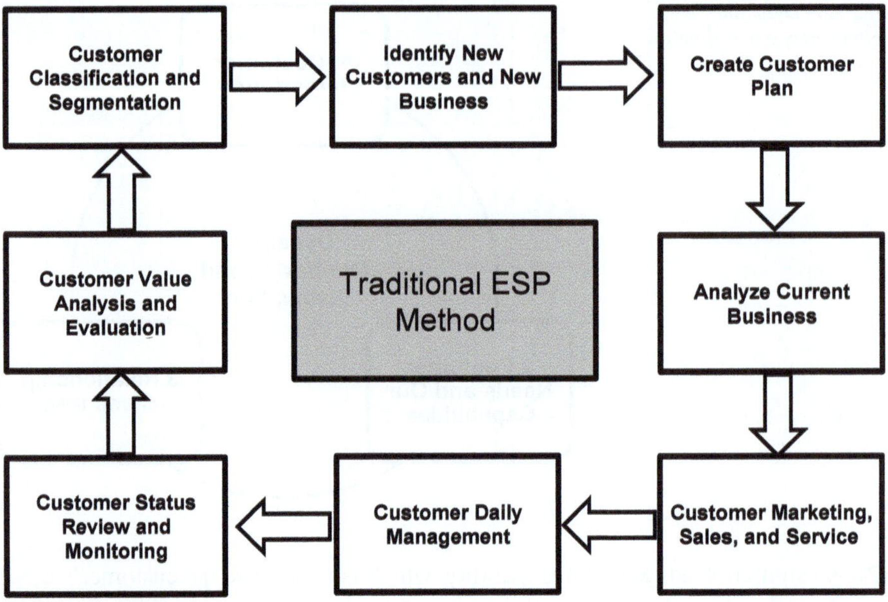

Fig. 2.7 Traditional key account management methods

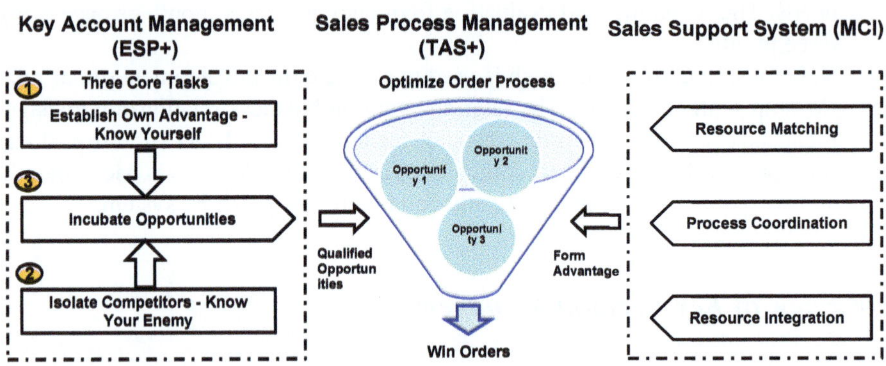

Fig. 2.8 Overview of three main lines in B2B sales

(1) Core Task 1: Establish Self-advantage. This task is divided into two parts, one is to establish your own relationship advantage, and the other is to establish your own solution advantage. This is knowing oneself, that is, understanding oneself, also understanding the relationship between the customer and oneself, and enhancing one's own advantages.

(2) Core Task 2: Isolate Competitors. This task is divided into two parts, one is to isolate the relationship between competitors and customers, and the other is to put the competitors' solutions at a disadvantage. This is knowing the enemy, that

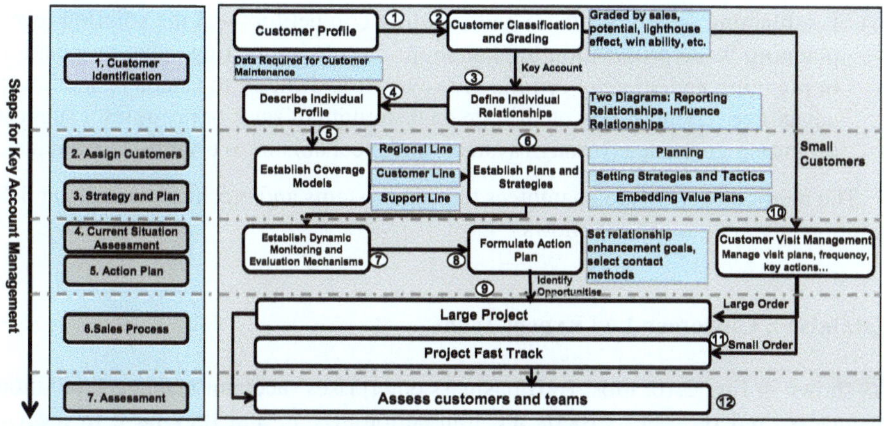

Fig. 2.9 Key account management (ESP+) Model

is, understanding the competitors, also understanding the relationship between the customer and the competitors, and putting the competitors at a disadvantage.

(3) Core Task 3: Incubate Business Opportunities. For existing leads, accelerate the project initiation to make them business opportunities; for potential leads, guide and catalyze them to initiate projects and become business opportunities.

As shown in Fig. 2.9, by optimizing the Key Account Management ESP model and focusing on the above three core tasks, I designed the Key Account Management ESP+ model.

The Key Account Management ESP+ model takes the three core tasks of key account management as the main line:

(1) Establish self-advantage and isolate competitors—Relationship level

   1) Define networking resources: Step 3, define individual relationships; Step 4, describe individual portraits.
   2) Plan how to establish an advantage in relationships: Step 6, make plans, set strategies.
   3) Execute actions to establish an advantage in relationships: Step 8, formulate action plans; Step 10, customer visit management.

(2) Monitor the status of self-advantage and isolation of competitors—Relationship and solution level Step 7, establish Dynamic monitoring and evaluation mechanism.

(3) Incubating business opportunities and integrating them with sales process management: Step 9, after discovering business opportunities, connect with key account management (and major project lines); Step 11, discover business opportunities during customer visits, and connect with small and medium-sized customer management (fast track for projects).

(4) Establishing own advantages and isolating competitors—at the solution level, planning value proposition implantation: Step 6, implanting value proposition in planning and strategy setting. However, it is difficult to establish a solution advantage relying solely on the personal strength of sales or pre-sales. I suggest providing guarantees through systems and mechanisms to establish advantages.

The methods to provide guarantees through systems and mechanisms to establish solution advantages are as follows:

Establish a Customer-Led Expert Team

As shown in Fig. 2.10, most B2B business enterprises' account managers, solution managers, and pre-sales experts are transaction-driven, and they have to meet a certain sales quota each quarter. They don't know if they will still be responsible for the customer next year. Therefore, whether from subjective willingness or objective ability, they cannot complete the tasks of early layout and customer guidance.

Therefore, for key account management, we have always lacked positions like customer guidance experts or customer mentors. Customer guidance experts can be internal experts or external experts; they can be individuals or teams. Their main

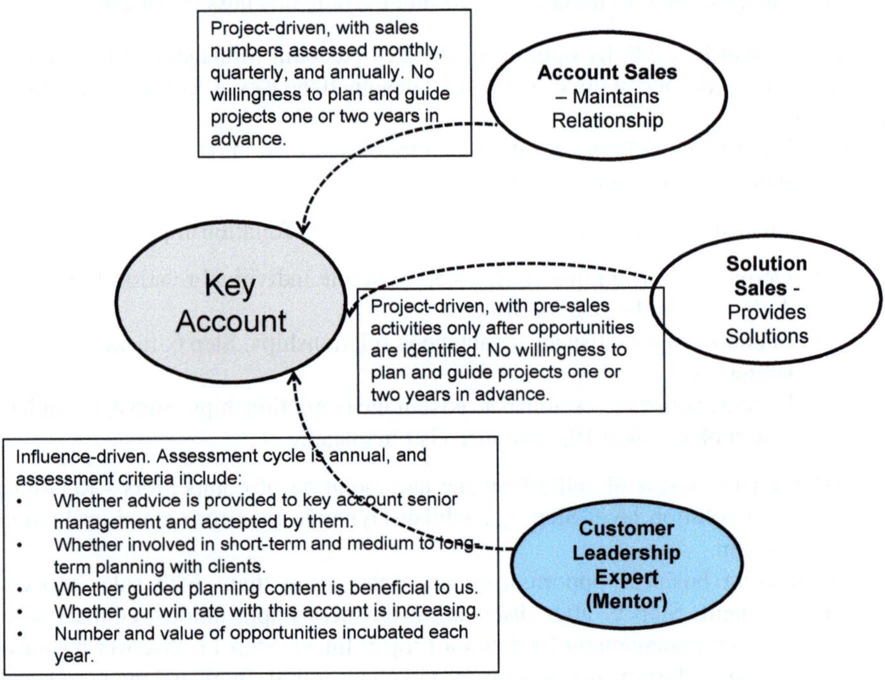

Fig. 2.10 Establish a customer-led expert team

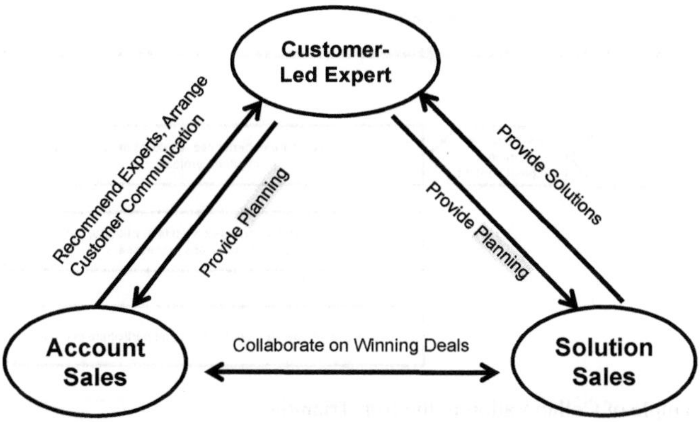

Fig. 2.11 Key account management iron triangle

role is to influence the top management of major customers in the long term at the solution level. The assessment cycle is annual, and the assessment indicators are:

(1) Whether they provide advice to the top management of major customers and get their approval.
(2) Whether they participate in the customer's short-term and medium-long term planning.
(3) Whether they guide the content of the planning to make the planning beneficial to us.
(4) Whether our win rate for this customer is increasing.
(5) The number and amount of business opportunities incubated each year.

The Customer Guidance Expert, Account Manager, and Solution Manager Form an "Iron Triangle"

As shown in Fig. 2.11, there were only account managers and solution managers before, and their basic job was to focus on making deals. With the customer guidance expert, through the expert's early layout, they can help the solution manager implant solutions and help the account manager incubate business opportunities.

The "Iron Triangle" Cooperates with Each Other for Mutual Benefit and Win–Win

As shown in Fig. 2.12, only with the customer-led expert and the position of customer early layout and planning guidance, we can lay out in advance and seize the initiative.

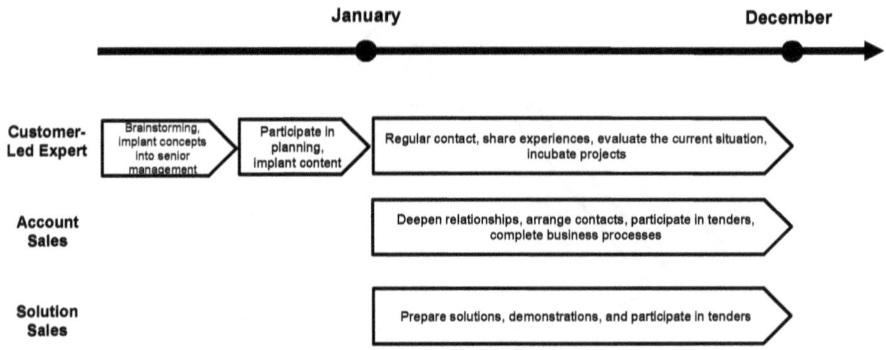

Fig. 2.12 Example of Collaboration in the Iron Triangle

Detailed Steps of Key Account Management

Customer Identification

Customer Profile

The company profile includes a 360-degree description of the company's customers. This information varies according to different industries and project requirements, so it will not be discussed in detail.

Customer Classification and Grading

There are three types of customer grading: ① based on the rights of customers to purchase products, that is, divided according to the Service Level Agreement (SLA), we call it rights grading; ② based on contribution, potential, ability to win and do, demonstration effect, etc., comprehensive scoring division, this method is often used to define the responsibility relationship, that is, which customer belongs to Which team is responsible for what, we call management grading; ③ divided according to the nine-grid, this is often to define customer tactics, such as which type of customers need to be prioritized, and which type of customers need to be maintained, we call tactical grading.

(1) Equity grading: Equity grading refers to the company giving customers different service levels based on the products they purchase and the sales they bring, through the form of a contract. The higher the equity level, the larger the service scope, the faster the service response time, and the shorter the resolution time.
(2) Management grading: In management grading, the customer grading method can refer to the comprehensive scoring method mentioned earlier, as shown in Fig. 2.4, which will not be repeated here.

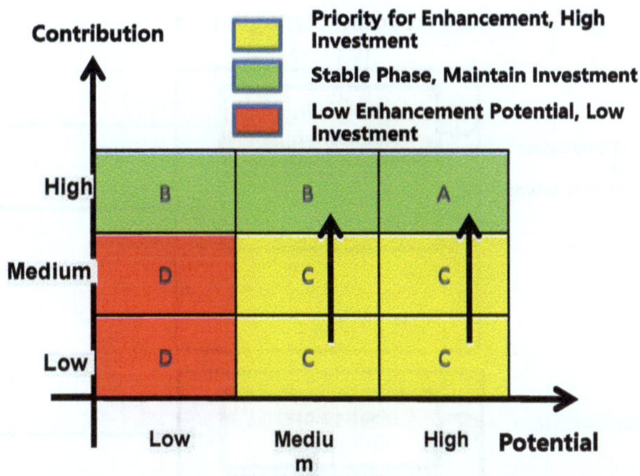

Fig. 2.13 Customer grading

(3) Tactical grading: Customers can be classified using the nine-grid method, and then different management strategies are used for different types of customers. As shown in Fig. 2.13, our focus is definitely on Class C customers, that is, those with great potential but low contribution; for Class D customers with little potential, we don't need to invest too much; for mature Class A and B customers, we need to maintain reasonable investment.

Define Individual Relationships and Individual Profiles

This step is an important one to achieve "establishing our own advantages and isolating competitors", it reflects our relationship advantage with competitors. This is also an important way to measure the closeness of the relationship with customers. How to establish our own advantages and isolate competitors in the relationship? In key account management, we need to clearly describe our own and competitors' two types of relationships with customers (reporting relationships and influence maps) and four types of individual profile dimensions of key customer roles (behavior orientation, relationship status, interaction level, and importance level), and through continuous efforts, make it develop in a direction that is beneficial to us. As shown in Fig. 2.14.

But this method is still preliminary. To truly build a company's core relationship capability (Enterprise Connections Management, ECM), four types of enterprise relationship capabilities need to be managed: customer relationship map, our company's relationship resource map, project decision chain, and competitor's relationship resource map. This part will be detailed in "Building the Core Relationship Capability of the Enterprise".

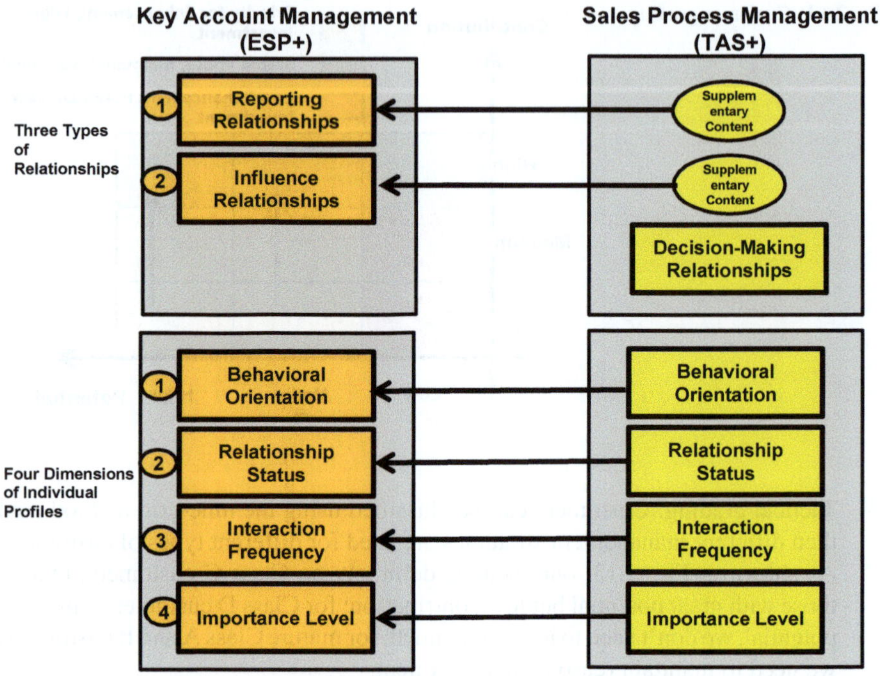

Fig. 2.14 Three types of relationships and four dimensions of individual profiles in key account management

Two Types of Relationships in Key Account Management

1) Reporting relationship The reporting relationship is explicit, it is relatively stable, and has nothing to do with the project, it should be managed in key account management (ESP+), and perfected through sales process management (TAS+).
2) Influence map The influence map built according to influence and belonging circle is implicit, it is relatively stable, and has nothing to do with the project, it should be included in key account management (ESP+), and perfected through sales process management (TAS+).

Four Types of Individual Profile Dimensions

1) Behavior orientation. It refers to the type of decision-making basis of this key person, such as professional type, pragmatic type, professional pragmatic type, pragmatic professional type, balanced type, etc. This is divided into two parts, one is the overall behavior orientation, the other is the behavior orientation in a certain project. Therefore, it is described in both key account management and sales process management.

2) Relationship status. It describes the attitude of this key person towards us, such as strong positive, positive, neutral, negative and strong negative, etc. This is divided into two parts, one is the overall attitude, the other is the attitude towards us in a certain project. Therefore, it is described in both key account management and sales process management.
3) Interaction level. It describes the degree of contact with this key person, such as no contact, occasional contact, frequent The level of contact, such as superficial contact and deep contact, etc. Here it is divided into two parts, one is the overall level of contact, and the other is the level of contact with us on a certain project. Therefore, the degree of interaction is described in both key account management and sales process management. This information can be automatically updated through the data in activity management, without manual selection.
4) Importance. It describes the importance of this key person in the company, such as the importance of the position, the importance of interpersonal relationships, the importance of both position and interpersonal relationships, and ordinary. Here it is divided into two parts, one is the importance in the company, and the other is the decision-making role in a certain project. For example, approvers, decision-makers, evaluators, and users, etc. Therefore, it is described in both key account management and sales process management, and can be mutually verified with the importance in the company through the decision-making role in the project.

Assign Customers, Make Plans, Set Strategies, and Implant Values

Establish a Coverage Model

The content about regional lines and customer lines (industry lines) has been introduced in "Who is responsible for key accounts (Coverage)", so it will not be repeated here.

Line management support will be introduced in the "Layered pre-sales resource scheduling mechanism" in "Sales Support System Management".

Make Plans, Set Strategies, and Implant Values

(1) Make plans. There is a standard method for making plans (GOSART): Ultimate Goal, Short-term Objective, Strategy, Action, Resource, and Test. When making plans, it is important to focus on how to establish your own advantages in relationships and solutions and isolate competitors.
(2) Set strategies and choose tactics. Here are five types of strategies and corresponding tactics:

    1) Customer acquisition. It is a strategy to convert important potential customers into formal customers. This strategy requires first identifying

important potential customers and using corresponding tactics to make them purchase products.

2) Customer upgrade. It refers to the strategy of upgrading customers with low contributions to high-contribution customers. This strategy requires understanding the customer's business situation and needs, laying out in advance, guiding customers, strengthening interaction, increasing pre-sales and solution input in the early stage, participating in project bidding within the year, and striving to win the project.
3) Customer retention. It refers to the strategy of retaining high-contribution customers and making them generate continuous income for the company. This strategy requires maintaining close contact with customers and having the ability to provide overall planning and advice for customers, the ability to provide cost-effective operation and maintenance services, prevent competitors from entering, and strengthen after-sales service to improve customer satisfaction.
4) Make up for the lost sheep. It refers to the strategy of gradually recovering high-value users who are gradually alienating us. This strategy requires understanding the real reasons why customers alienate us, formulating a recovery plan, investing corresponding resources to make customers feel our sincerity, and providing more favorable prices and more personalized services.
5) Use stillness to control motion. It is a wait-and-see strategy adopted for important lost customers that we can no longer recover. This strategy is not passive waiting, but maintaining a certain contact frequency with customers, understanding internal changes in customers, and waiting for opportunities.

(3) Value implantation. Explain the solution we use and the business value it can create for customers. Be sure to include a comparison with the top two main competitors—what advantages we have in terms of solutions, software and hardware strength.

Current Status Assessment and Action Plan

Establish a Dynamic Monitoring and Evaluation Mechanism

The "Dynamic Evaluation" (Evaluate) section of this chapter introduces specific evaluation methods in terms of customer importance, relationship closeness, and customer needs and self-capabilities. It will not be repeated here.

Formulate an Action Plan

For major customers, formulate measures to "establish own advantages, isolate competitors, and incubate business opportunities."

Customer Visit Management

The management process for major customers is more complex, such as setting strategies, planning, assessing the current situation, formulating action plans, etc. For small and medium-sized customers, due to the large number and small projects, it is generally necessary to formulate customer visit plans and manage customer visits.

Implementation

Major Customer Management (Major Project Line)

Implement the action plan formulated before managing major customers. If successful in incubating business opportunities, then enter the sales management process (TAS+).

Small and Medium Customer Management (Fast Track for Projects)

Manage the activities of the visit plan formulated for small and medium customers. If successful in incubating business opportunities, then enter the sales management process (TAS+).

Evaluation and Assessment

Evaluation and assessment refer to the annual evaluation and assessment of major customer management by enterprises. The specific content of the assessment of major customers is the same as the "establish dynamic monitoring and evaluation mechanism" in this section's "Current Status Assessment and Action Plan", but it also needs to assess major customer management from the two dimensions of sales personnel and sales organization.

Summary > This section mainly introduces the five elements of major customer management: ① How to determine major customers (Who); ② Who is responsible for major customers (Coverage); ③ How to manage major customers (How); ④ Customer strategy and tactics (Strategy); ⑤ Dynamic evaluation (Evaluate). And it introduces how to establish a program advantage in the mechanism, what is major customer management (ESP+), and with the three core tasks of major customer management "establishing own advantages, isolating competitors, and incubating business opportunities" as the main line, it details how major customer management (ESP+) is carried out.

Sales Process Management in B2B Sales

In CRM 3.0, B2B sales can be summarized as the trilogy of adhering to the norm, surprising, and accumulating momentum. This section focuses on the surprising part, that is, sales process management.

In B2B sales, there is a widely used sales process management model—TAS (Target Account Selling, sales process management). Many companies use this method to manage the LTC sales process in their CRM, that is, the process from sales leads to contract signing. Around 2013 when I was working at IBM, IBM also used this method to manage business opportunities internally. The TAS method is too theoretical, a "one-size-fits-all" method, but it lacks many elements that can be implemented and produce actual results.

Sales process management is a technique, also called project line management, which focuses more on short-term effects and whether it can win orders as a measure. Measurement standards. Based on my own consulting, implementation, and order-taking experience, I have designed an evolved version of the TAS methodology for the digital age, TAS+, to make it more practical and enhance the sales capabilities of enterprises, generating business value.

Before introducing TAS+, let me first analyze the traditional TAS methodology and its existing problems.

As shown in Fig. 2.15, I have summarized the traditional TAS methodology. It consists of the following parts:

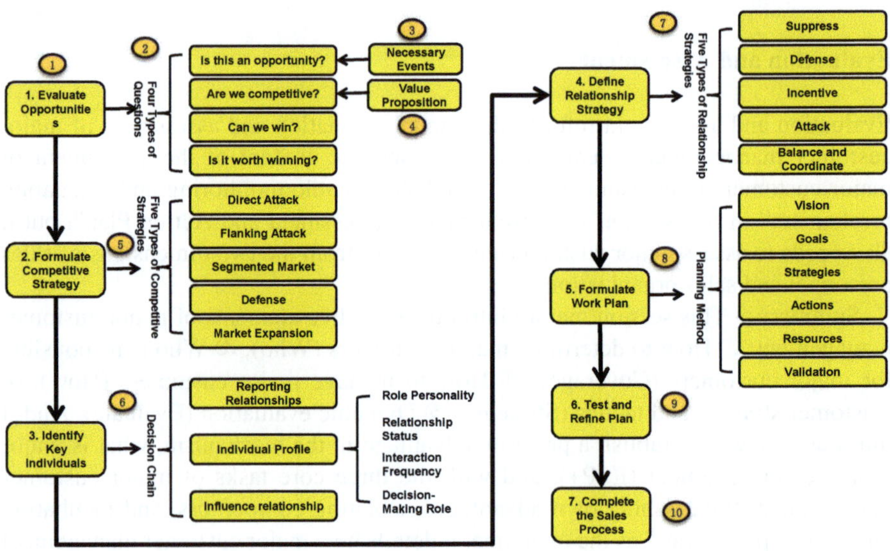

Fig. 2.15 Overview of Traditional TAS Methodology

(1) Seven main steps: Assessing sales opportunities, formulating competitive strategies, identifying key individuals, defining relationship strategies, devising work plans, testing and improving plans, and completing the sales process. This is the backbone of TAS. However, these are the seven steps of order-taking action, not the stages of order-taking divided according to the client's business opportunity stage. Therefore, the TAS methodology lacks a method for dividing sales stages.
(2) Questionnaire: There are four types of questions in the "Assessing Sales Opportunities" step: ① Is this an opportunity? ② Are we competitive? ③ Can we win? ④ Is it worth winning? Each type has a series of specific questions. These four types of questions can help salespeople clarify their thoughts, but these questions do not touch on the key points and are less practical. In addition, the questionnaire should not be a self-questioning and answering by the salesperson. The mechanism for the management and sales staff to complete the questionnaire interactively is the key, and TAS does not specify how this process should be done.
(3) Necessary events: In the "Is this an opportunity?" of "Assessing Sales Opportunities", the reality of the project is judged through necessary events. The method of judging necessary events is commendable because many projects have invested a lot of pre-sales resources before seriously judging whether the customer will really start this project.
(4) Value proposition: In the "Are we competitive?" of "Assessing Sales Opportunities", the advantages of our plan and the output of business value are given through the value proposition. The value proposition method is commendable. I have done sand table deduction for enterprises. Many salespeople of companies put all their energy into making relationships. It is very difficult for them to clearly state the advantages of their company's products or solutions and the business value brought to customers in two minutes.
(5) Five types of competitive strategies: The five types of competitive strategies are good, but lack specific tactics and methods.
(6) Decision chain: This is the highlight of TAS. It describes the decision chain in three parts, one is the administrative reporting relationship, one is the description of influence and the influence map of the circle, and the other is the portrait of each person in the relationship. Individual portraits are divided into four dimensions: role personality, relationship status, interaction degree, and decision-making role. The definitions of these three elements in traditional TAS have defects: they did not distinguish the boundaries between large customer management (ESP+) and sales process management (TAS+). I will introduce the new three relationships and four types of individual portrait dimension models in the upcoming TAS+ relationship map.
(7) Five types of relationship strategies: These are based on the five types of relationships with our customers, and adopt the five types of relationship strategies of suppression, defense, motivation, offense, and balance coordination. This is only directional and does not have specific implementation measures.

(8) TAS planning method: In the process of formulating a work plan, planning can be done through vision, goals, strategies, actions, resources, and verification. But this part of the content is too broad and not very practical.
(9) Test and improve the plan: TAS does not provide a practical method.
(10) Complete the sales process: TAS does not provide a practical method.

In addition to the issues present in the aforementioned ten elements of TAS, traditional TAS also lacks some requirements in sales process management. For example, how are project stages divided? How are business opportunities classified? How does the team collaborate in the project? How to manage and defeat competitors in the project? How to effectively implement TAS management methods? And so on.

I have optimized the TAS methodology, called TAS+, to make it more grounded, efficient, targeted, and easy to implement.

As shown in Fig. 2.16, TAS+ is divided into two major parts, internal and external collaboration, combining dynamic and static aspects. Against competitors, we need to be dynamic, ever-changing, and victorious; for internal sales personnel, we need to be calm, stable, efficient, fair, and transparent, so they can confidently charge into the fray.

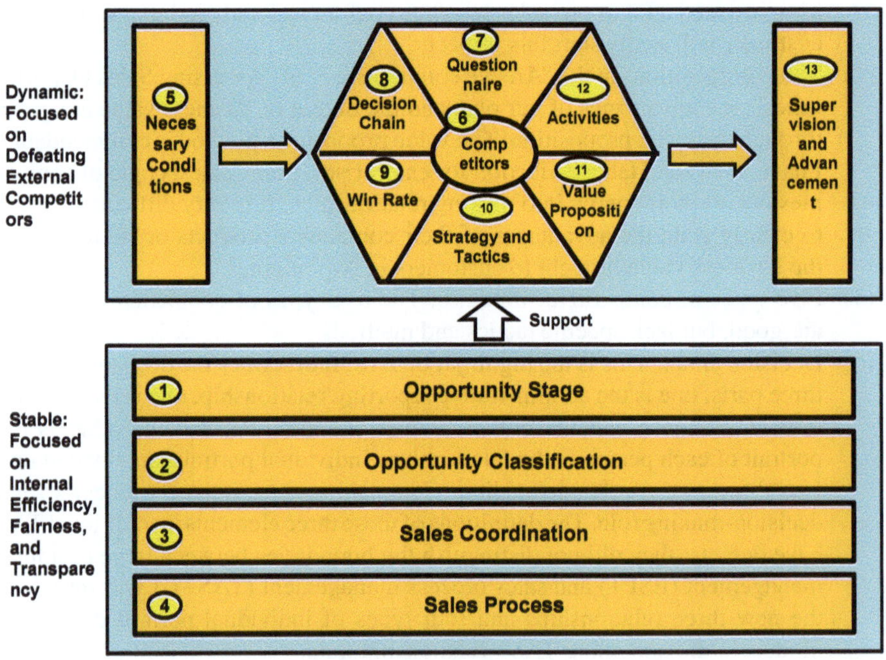

Fig. 2.16 Sales process management (TAS+)

Internal Part

This is the calm and stable part, which supports the dynamic part of defeating competitors. This part is based on efficiency, fairness, and transparency, and is designed to assist and motivate sales personnel to go to the front lines. Therefore, this part is relatively stable and cannot change every day, as frequent changes will leave sales personnel at a loss. The internal part consists of the following four elements:

(1) Business Opportunity Stage: The business opportunity stage refers to the stages into which a project is divided from sales lead to contract signing (LTC) according to the timeline. The business opportunity stage can be divided into seven stages, and different projects can modify and adjust based on this.

   1) Validate the opportunity. From the start of collecting sales leads to verifying that it is indeed a business opportunity, and then beginning to coordinate internal resources.
   2) Opportunity initiation. From the start of coordinating internal resources, through project initiation review, to the formation of the project team.
   3) Requirement analysis. From the approval of the project initiation review, the formation of the project team, to the determination of the value proposition, competitive strategy, and action plan.
   4) Value presentation. From the determination of the competitive strategy and action plan, striving for the dominance of the bidding proposal, to the customer beginning to draft the bidding documents.
   5) Bid preparation. From the customer drafting the bid documents to the official release of the bid by the customer.
   6) Organize bidding. From the official release of the bid by the customer to the generation of the bid result.
   7) Negotiation and signing. From the announcement of our company winning the bid to the signing of the contract.

(2) Business Opportunity Grading: Business opportunity grading is the main basis for division, but it can be manually adjusted according to the demonstration role or importance of the project. Below is the business opportunity grading template, different projects can modify and adjust based on this.

   1) Class A and B. Large orders, follow the large project order process, that is, go through all the sales stages of TAS+, using all sales methods.
   2) Class C and D. Small orders, follow the fast track for small orders, that is, they can directly skip the middle sales stages of TAS+ to the final stage, and in order to improve efficiency, many sales methods of TAS+ can be omitted.
   3) Class E. Business opportunities led by partners, follow the partner business opportunity reporting mechanism.

(3) Sales Collaboration: Winning B2B often requires a team from several different departments to collaborate, so the company needs to allocate effective resources

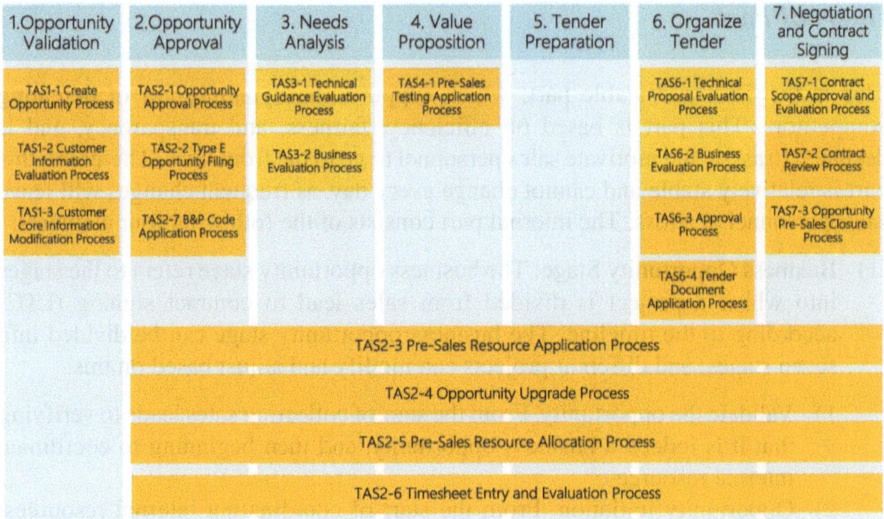

Fig. 2.17 TAS+ Process framework example

to the best projects in a reasonable and efficient manner. Most of the B2B companies I have come into contact with have some shortcomings in sales collaboration due to barriers and conflicts of interest between departments. These shortcomings seriously restrict the company's sales efficiency and sales capabilities. This part will be introduced in the management of the sales support system.

(4) Sales Process: The sales process involves five elements: sales model, department, position, assessment, and process. As shown in the template in Fig. 2.17, different projects can modify and adjust based on this foundation.

External Part

The external part is centered on defeating competitors. As introduced earlier, sales process management is an art that requires cunning, with the ability to win orders as the measurement standard. As the saying goes, "There are no constant tactics in war, just as water has no constant shape, victory comes from adapting to the enemy's changes.“ Therefore, this part is dynamic and needs to be adjusted according to the situation of the enemy. The external part consists of the following nine elements:

(1) Necessary Conditions: This refers to reasons that can confirm that the customer definitely needs to carry out this project, such as last year's budget has been made; or the main decision-maker has decided that the project must go live within a certain time limit, etc. This part is easily overlooked, and salespeople are reluctant to face it. I have encountered many such cases where the party B invested a lot of pre-sales resources in the early stage, but later the party A

customer did not proceed. Therefore, necessary conditions are very important, and we need to continuously evaluate them throughout the project process. If we cannot confirm that the customer's project will definitely be carried out, then we need to carefully consider the subsequent investment.

(2) Competitors: "Knowing yourself and your enemy, you can fight a hundred battles without danger; if you know yourself but not your enemy, you will win one and lose one." If we don't understand our competitors, winning or losing in some sense depends on luck. I have learned many lessons where I felt that the customer was very appreciative, but still lost the project, mainly because I did not understand the competitors. If we are bad, but the competitors are worse, we win; if we are strong, but the competitors are stronger, we lose. Therefore, we need to put more energy into studying competitors. As shown in Fig. 2.18, knowing ourselves is the way to understand the satisfaction of our solution to customer needs+ the closeness of the relationship, and knowing the enemy is to understand the satisfaction of the competitor's solution to customer needs+ the closeness of the relationship. In most cases, we only achieve self-knowledge, so we only have a 50% chance of winning.

As mentioned above, understanding competitors is as important as understanding ourselves. The competitor information we need to collect includes: basic information about competitors, the relationship between competitors and customers, core partners of competitors, important events of competitors, quotation history, competitor analysis library, etc.

(3) Questionnaire: In traditional TAS, questionnaire questions are divided into four categories: Is this an opportunity? Are we competitive? Can we win? Is it

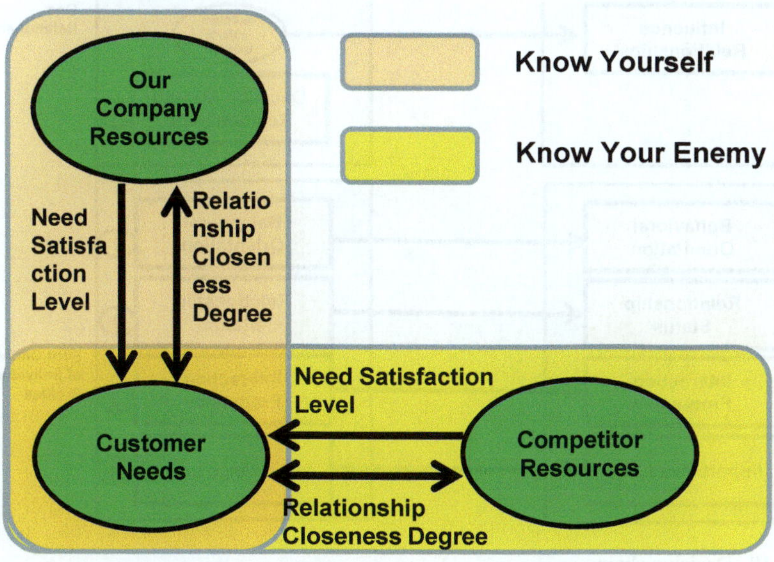

Fig. 2.18 Know yourself and know your enemy

worth winning? I think these questions are not very practical, and I suggest first confirming whether there is an internal news source. In the case of having an internal news source, the following four types of questions are more practical: To what extent do our resources meet customer needs? How close is our relationship with customers? To what extent do the resources of the top two competitors threatening us meet customer needs? How close is the relationship between the top two competitors threatening us and the customer?

(4) Decision Chain: As shown in Fig. 2.19, there is one type of relationship and four types of individual portrait dimensions in sales process management.

(5) Win Rate: Most of the companies I have seen calculate the win rate as higher the further along the sales stage. In the bidding stage, many times we know that we won't win this time, if we still calculate it as 80%, then the prediction through the sales funnel loses its meaning. In fact, during the order process, fluctuations in the win rate can reflect the real situation of the project and remind us of the measures we need to take. I suggest using the "Competitor Comparison Method" to calculate the win rate.

As shown in Fig. 2.20, it is best to update the calculation frequency weekly. In management, we can fully use the change in win rate as a trigger event and take corresponding countermeasures.

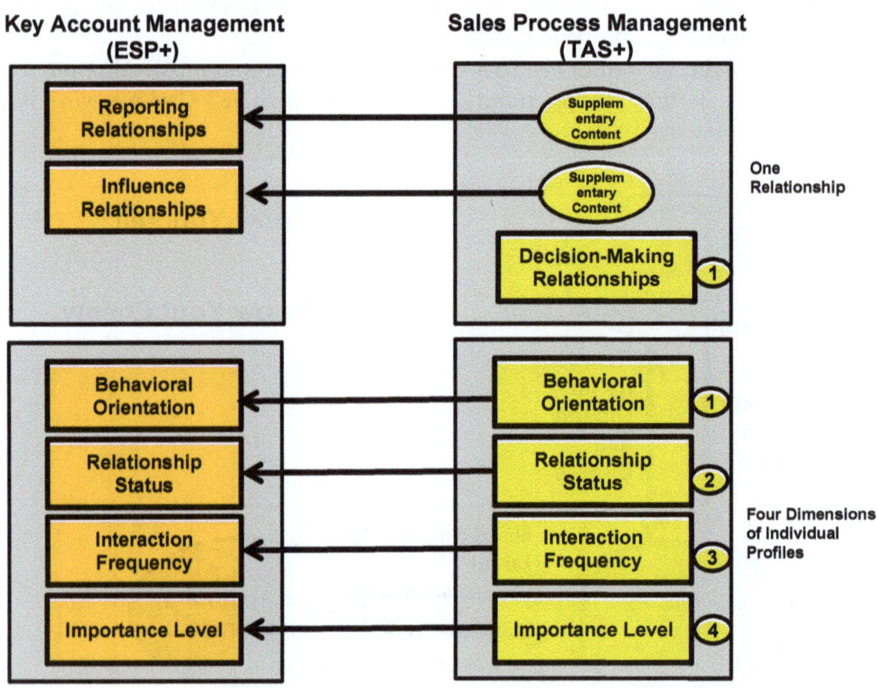

Fig. 2.19 Decision chain

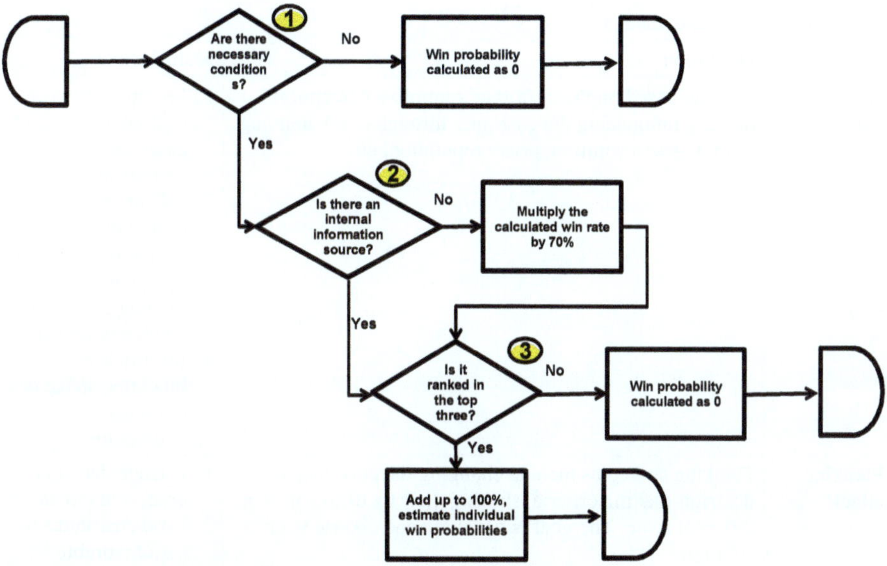

Fig. 2.20 Win rate calculation—competitor comparison method

1) If there is no necessary event, it means that we cannot confirm that the customer definitely wants to do this project, then there is no need to calculate the win rate.
2) If there is no internal news source to compare, we have to think about the worst, so after the results come out, discount it by 70%.
3) If we are not in the top three in the competition, then calculating the win rate is meaningless, just calculate it as 0.

(6) Strategy and Tactics
As shown in Table 2.1, I continue to use the original five strategies of TAS, but I have supplemented the tactics to make it easier to execute.
(7) Value Proposition In addition to using the TAS template, explaining what solutions we used and what business value we created for the customer, we must add a comparison with the top two main competitors, showing what advantages we have in terms of solutions, relationships, and hardware and software capabilities.
(8) Activities Activities refer to a series of improvement actions taken based on our strategy and tactics, as well as problems found in relationships, questionnaires, win rates, and value propositions. It is generally interactive with customers.
(9) Supervision and Promotion This involves a key issue, that is, sales process management is not a one-man show by the salesperson, not self-entertainment. If so, no sales method will be effective. To use TAS+ well, frontline sales managers need to coach salespeople based on the necessary conditions, questionnaires, relationship maps, win rates, strategic tactics, value propositions, and activities

Table 2.1 Strategy and Tactics

Strategy	Definition	Main Tactics
Direct attack	A tactic based on the customer's intuitive perception, directly influencing the customer through overwhelming advantages in solution, price, reputation, etc	1. Prominently lead customers to visit cases and companies 2. Influence customer's bidding standards 3. Speed up the bidding process for a quick decision 4. Information blocking, strike or eliminate major competitors
Flanking attack	Flanking strategies include changing the customer's decision-making criteria, shifting their focus to a new or different issue. The goal is to satisfy and choose your solution	1. Change decision criteria in our favor 2. Lead customers to visit favorable clients, cases, workshops, experience sharing 3. Avoid the introduction of stronger competitors 4. Find strong supporters among customers
Segmented market	Market segmentation strategy breaks down project opportunities into smaller, more detailed parts, allowing us to focus on each subset of the customer's concerns, thereby achieving breakthroughs in parts or segments	1. Find strong supporters among customers 2. Find strong reasons to support segmentation 3. Speed up or delay bidding process based on specific conditions 4. Find a balanced method of interest with competitors

(continued)

Table 2.1 (continued)

Strategy	Definition	Main Tactics
Defense	Defense strategy protects you from maintaining a solid position even when inevitably attacked by competitors	1. Keep a low profile, make customers believe in the strength of our solution 2. Eliminate hostile elements among customers 3. Timely understand real progress information of customers and projects 4. Consider delaying project decision progress
Market expansion	Market expansion strategy creates opportunites for future potential markets	1. Frequent contacts with customers to showcase solutions and strength 2. Learn more about customer's project planning during contact 3. Provide customers with feasible suggestions and services

of TAS+. To save time, you can only emphasize important projects and changes, once a week or once every two weeks.

Summary > This section introduces Sales Process Management (TAS+). The optimized TAS method Theory—TAS+ is more grounded, more efficient, more targeted, and easier to implement. TAS+ is divided into two major parts and thirteen elements, with internal and external coordination, and a combination of movement and stillness. Against competitors, we need to be dynamic, ever-changing, and victorious; for internal sales staff, we need to be calm, stable, efficient, fair, and transparent, so they can charge into the battle with peace of mind.

B2B Sales Support System Management

In CRM 3.0, B2B sales consist of three parts, namely, adhering to the norm, being innovative, and building momentum. This section introduces building momentum, that is, sales support system management, which can establish a systematic advantage for enterprises, build the enterprise's "moat", and the method used is sales support system management, which will be introduced in this section.

Figure 2.21 lists the problems I encountered when conducting a B2B sales process diagnostic project for a company. In general, there are three major types of problems in the B2B sales process:

(1) Resource allocation problem Basically, every company doing B2B business has this unreasonable phenomenon: the closer to the water tower, the first to get the moon. Many times, the quantity and quality of pre-sales resources that salespeople can get are not related to the quality of the business opportunities they are responsible for, but are related to their relationship with the resource department and the company's senior management. So The reason why a salesperson with good sales performance stands out may not be due to their strong sales ability, but rather the amount of pre-sales resources they can access. This issue greatly restricts the input-output ratio of the company, because many salespeople far from the power center of the company, even when encountering good large projects, may be unwilling to follow up due to the inability to apply for resources. Instead, they prefer to deal with small projects that they can handle. In this way, the company's resources will gradually be invested in salespeople with the most internal relationships, rather than the best projects, resulting in a "bad money drives out good" phenomenon.
(2) Process collaboration issue: Often, the larger the project, the more losses it incurs. Sales, pre-sales, solution products, and testing teams do not communicate with each other, everyone is responsible, yet no one takes responsibility, blaming each other during collaboration. When there is credit, it belongs to oneself; when there is a problem, it is the other party's fault. As a result, many projects lose due to the details of sales process collaboration. If the communication of information could be smoother, if the sense of responsibility of each team member involved in the project could be stronger, the probability of winning the order could be much higher.
(3) Resource capability issue: In B2B business, there are generally key industries and key solutions, which may account for 30%, or even more than 50% of the company's revenue. Key industries and key solutions usually have some large projects, which require the mobilization of the company's high-quality resources to win orders. But you will find that these resources are often scattered in many departments of the company: some are in regional branches, some are in the headquarters pre-sales, some are in the headquarters product and solution departments, and some are in the headquarters industry departments. Pulling a group of people from many departments to fight for a project, they do not understand each other and cannot form a tacit understanding, which easily leads

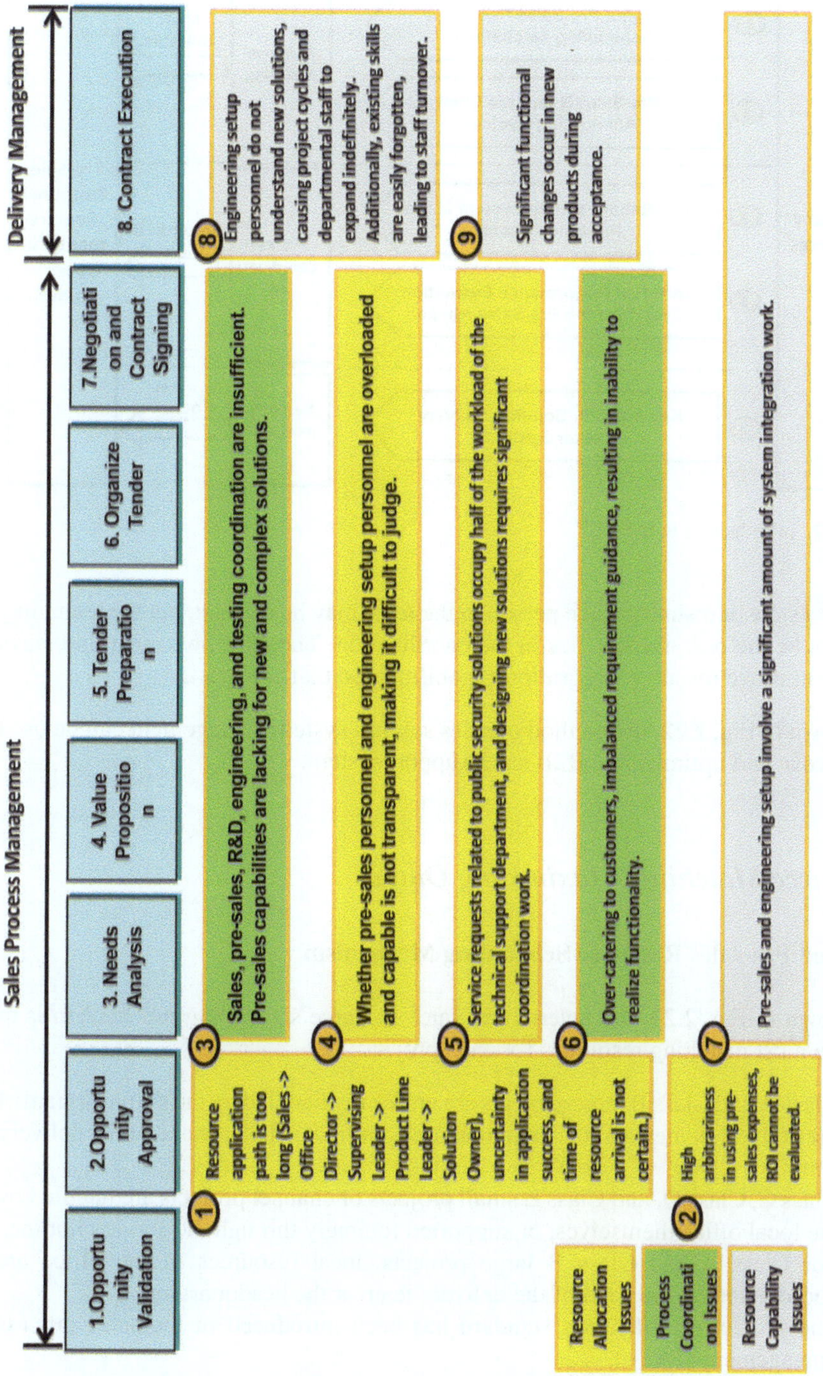

Fig. 2.21 Common problems in the B2B sales process example

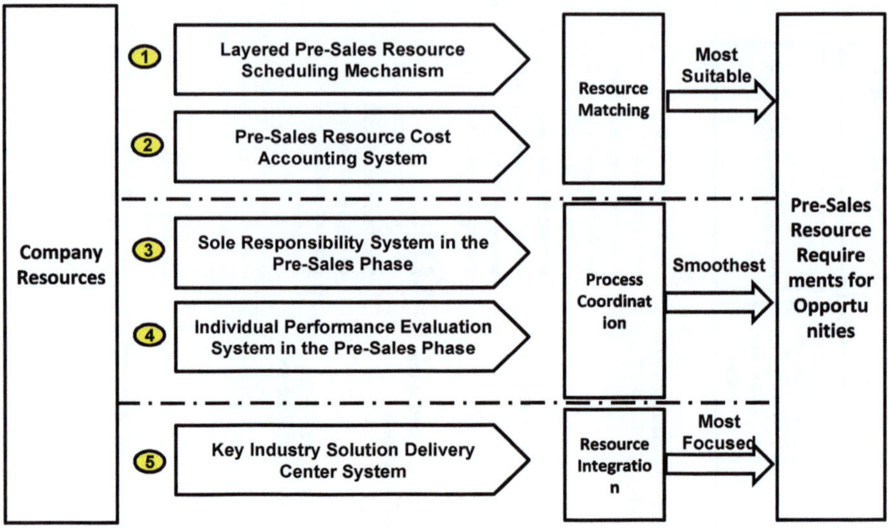

Fig. 2.22 Introduction to the MCI

to a state of disunity. Each person in the team may be the best, but the team may not be the best, the key lies in the coordination. Therefore, we must find ways to improve resource integration capabilities, so that $1 + 1 > 2$.

As shown in Fig. 2.22, the method of sales support system management can be used to improve and optimize the B2B sales support system.

Resource Matching, Maximizing Output

Layered Pre-sales Resource Scheduling Mechanism

As shown in Fig. 2.23, the layered pre-sales resource scheduling mechanism is to call the most matching resources for each project.

(1) Class A and Class B large projects are uniformly handled by the delivery team of the delivery center, and the resources are coordinated by the head of the delivery team.
(2) Class C, Class D, and Class E small projects or channel projects are handled by the local office themselves, or supported remotely through the service hotline.
(3) For Class A and Class B large projects, local resources of the office are coordinated by the head of the delivery team at the headquarters.
(4) The project classification standard has been introduced in the sales process management (TAS+).

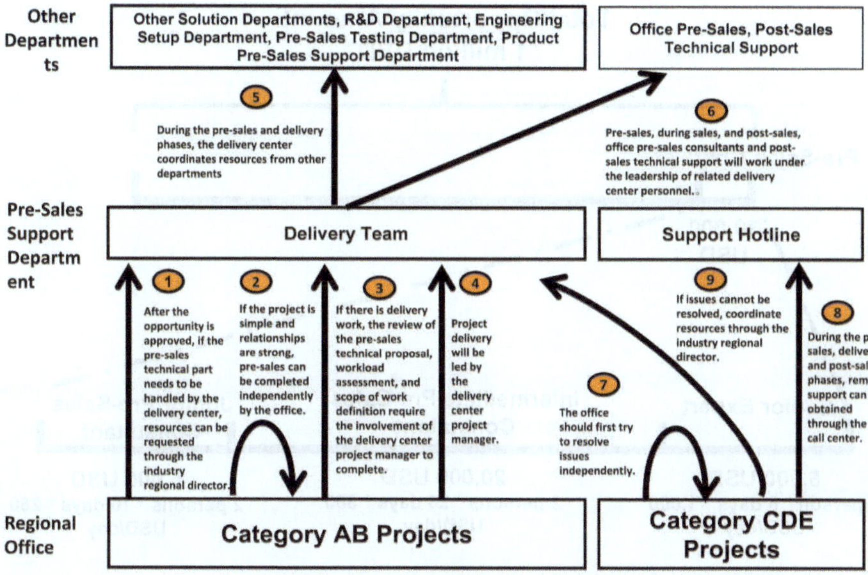

Fig. 2.23 Example of a layered pre-sales resource scheduling mechanism

Pre-Sales Resource Cost Accounting System

For any business opportunity, as long as you do not price and charge for pre-sales resources, pre-sales resources will always be insufficient. It will always be those who have relationships and can fight for resources who get the best and most resources, gradually forming a "bad money drives out good" internal sales atmosphere. Only by establishing a fair and reasonable pre-sales resource pricing and charging system can salespeople plan and use pre-sales resources reasonably, allowing the best resources to flow to the best projects.

As shown in Fig. 2.24, project sales should manage the project like living a life, arrange pre-sales resources reasonably on the project, be meticulous and thrifty, in order to achieve the maximum input-output.

Process Collaboration, Pulling Together

Sole Responsibility in the Pre-sales Stage

As shown in Fig. 2.25, a project involves many departments and many people. But "a thousand mouths in a family, one person in charge". In the example below, the person in charge is regional sales. At a certain stage, there can only be one person in charge, who has to take responsibility and also has the right to make decisions.

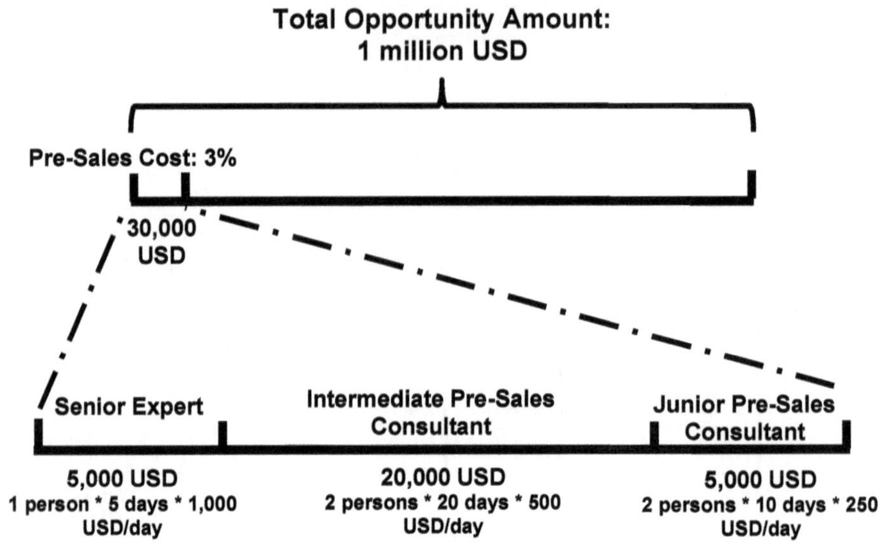

Fig. 2.24 Example of pre-sales resource cost accounting

Everyone is Assessed in the Pre-sales stage

With a person in charge, or a "leader", everyone involved in the project needs to be assessed, so that everyone can work together and pull together. There are two ways to assess a project:

1) Assess sales figures. For example, in addition to the person in charge assessing sales figures, pre-sales and project delivery managers also assess sales figures, which can be double counted. In this way, when a deal is won, sales, pre-sales, and future project delivery managers all have corresponding sales commissions, aligning everyone's interests.
2) The person in charge assesses and scores other project participants. For example, a large part of the performance salary of pre-sales and future project delivery managers is determined by the scores given by the main person in charge of the project, aligning everyone's interests and enabling everyone to pull together.

Resource Integration, Forming a Joint Force

This section adopts a key industry solution delivery center system. Figure 2.26 is an example of a delivery center organization position I designed for a client. In many B2B businesses, the best resources are scattered throughout the company, such as regional offices, headquarters pre-sales department, solutions department, key account department, product lines, etc. These resources belong to different departments and are difficult to integrate and form a joint force. For the company's key

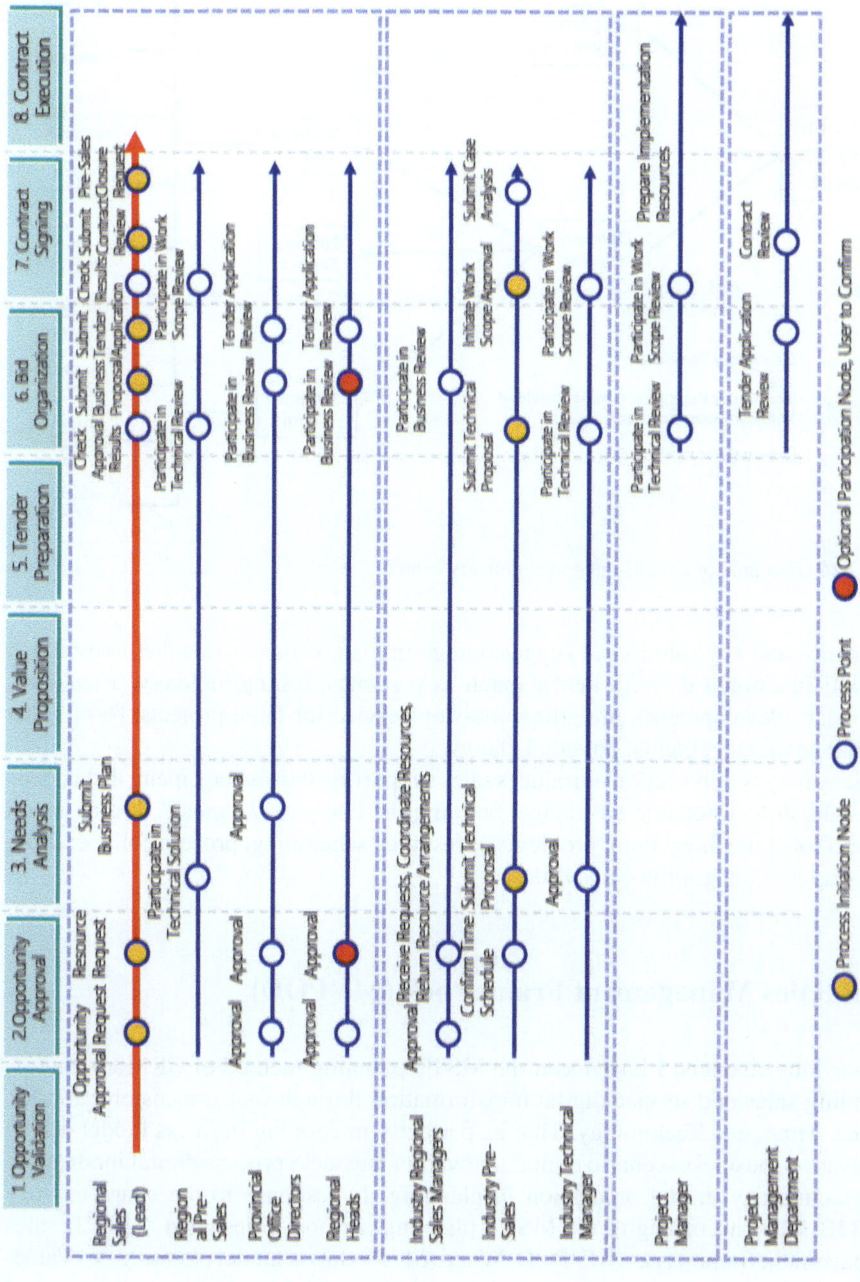

Fig. 2.25 Example of sole responsibility in the pre-sales phase

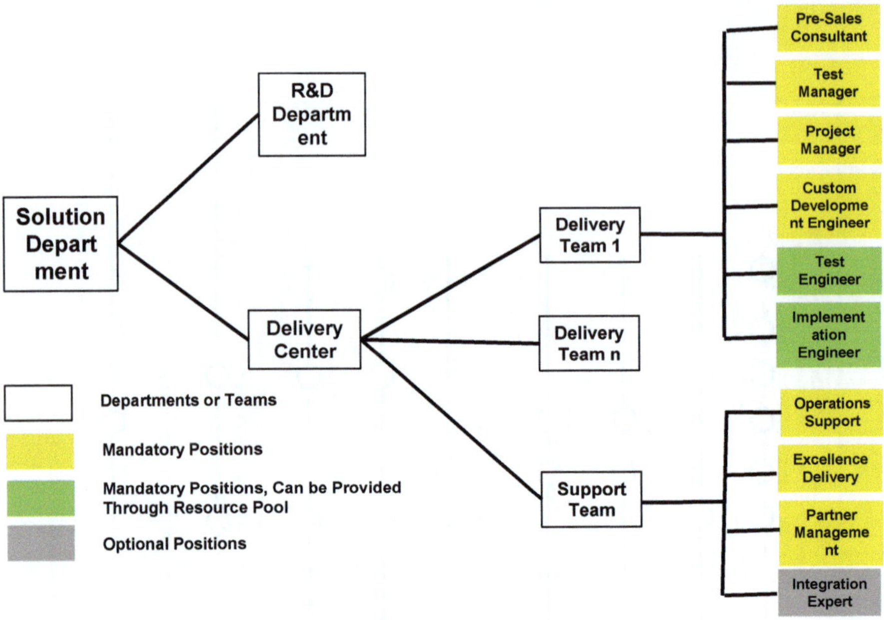

Fig. 2.26 Example of a multi-integrated delivery center

industries and key solutions, I suggest integrating all resources together to establish a multi-functional delivery center (such as pre-sales, testing, delivery, after-sales, secondary development), providing one-stop service for large projects, forming an overall advantage, that is, potential energy.

Summary > This section introduces sales support system management, that is, how to establish a systematic advantage, building the company's "moat". It focuses on how to solve the three major problems of resource scheduling, process collaboration, and resource integration capabilities.

B2B Sales Management Framework (MVPOD)

In previous chapters, I introduced the MSTT planning method of CRM3.0, that is, planning sales and service digital transformation through four dimensions: Model, Space, Time, and Technology. That is, perfectly integrating business model digital innovation, business scenario digital innovation, business process digital innovation, and technology digital innovation in planning. In response to the characteristics of B2B sales, according to the MSTT planning method, I designed the B2B sales management framework—MVPOD. Where M (Model) is model planning, V (Value) is value and innovation, P (Process) is process, O (Organization) is organization and position, and D (Digit) is digital support.

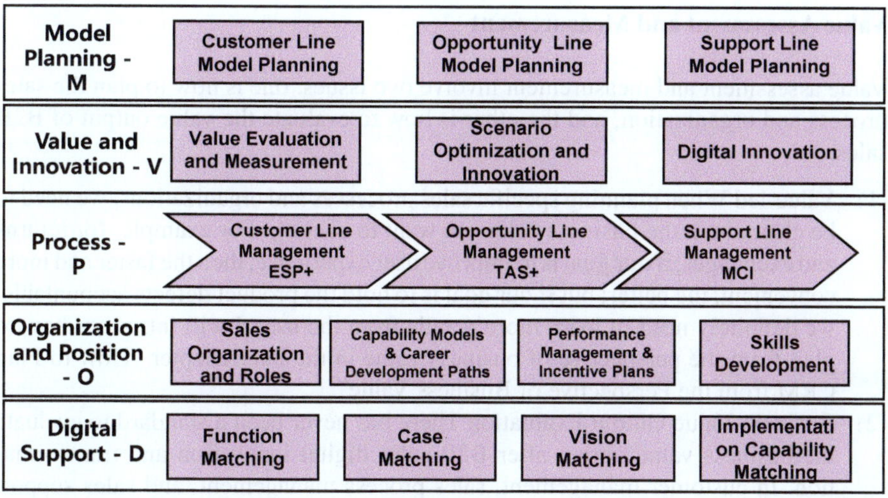

Fig. 2.27 B2B sales management framework—MVPOD

The B2B Sales Management Framework (MVPOD) is shown in Fig. 2.27 and consists of the following five parts.

Model Planning (Model)

B2B sales involve three types of model planning: customer line, order line planning, and support line. I have detailed the three models of key account management (ESP+), sales process management (TAS+), and sales support system management in previous articles. In addition, we need to focus on different models according to different market conditions (new market entry, rapidly growing market, and mature stable market). The later chapter "How to Choose Different Sales Strategies for Different Markets in B2B Sales" will provide a detailed introduction.

Value and Innovation (Value)

Traditional B2B sales planning focuses more on process design. In the digital age, we need to design business value output, business scenario optimization innovation, and digital integration before designing the process.

Value Assessment and Measurement

Value assessment and measurement involve two issues: one is how to plan the sales process and organization, and the other is how to evaluate the value output of B2B sales.

(1) Value-led When planning specific sales processes and organizations, we need to be clear about the business value we want to achieve. For example, for returns and exchanges, if our goal is to improve user experience, then the faster and more convenient, the better; but if our goal is to hold the product defects accountable, we definitely need to learn more details from the user. I will introduce how to plan from the perspective of business value in the later chapter "How to Plan CRM from the Perspective of Business Value".

(2) Business Value Output Evaluation There has never been a standard to evaluate the business value output after B2B sales digital innovation and transformation. In customer management, sales process management, and sales support management, there are many quantifiable indicators that can be used to evaluate business value output. Such as customer management ability, order processing control ability, resource scheduling and management ability, employee improvement ability, enterprise direction matching ability, etc. Through the trend curve of these indicators, we can make an overall prediction of the company's overall sales ability and future development trend. These indicators will be detailed in the later chapter "CRM Value Evaluation System".

Scenario Optimization and Innovation

Process and scenario are two different dimensions to view sales business. In the past, we mainly focused on designing the process because the business was relatively simple at that time. But a scenario often involves multiple processes, so it is impossible to describe and optimize the scenario based on the process alone. Therefore, we need to extract some important scenarios for separate design. For example, in the B2B sales process, conducting online workshops for customers, offline brainstorming, inviting customers to visit the company, etc., are all important scenarios. In the sales process, a series of important scenarios will be involved, and we need to design the participants, process, input and output, value evaluation, etc., centered on the scenario.

Digital Innovation

If we want to significantly improve sales efficiency and quality without changing the input resources, we must rely on digital empowerment. In traditional sales design, digital technology and tools are generally considered only in the delivery process, which is often too late. Because digital technology can often change business models and processes, if we don't consider it in advance, all the designed models and processes are based on the original business and digital technology. By the time the system is implemented, many new technologies can no longer be added. I believe we can first take out digital innovation technologies such as facial recognition, maps, machine deep learning, mobile positioning, etc., and discuss these. These technologies can change business models and business processes in various scenarios. Then, based on these scenarios, models, and processes, we can design accordingly.

Process

The direct sales process involves the processes mentioned in large customer management (ESP+), sales process management (TAS+), and sales support system management. I have provided a detailed introduction in the previous chapters, so I will not elaborate here.

Organization and Position

The sales organization and positions refer to "who is responsible for large customers" introduced in the previous large customer management. I will also provide a detailed introduction in the later chapter "Customer Coverage Effectiveness Model", so I will not elaborate here.

Digital Support

If we want our designed MVPOD sales management architecture to be implementable and digitally supported, we must consider the following four points during planning:

(1) Function matching: All designed models, scenarios, processes, etc. have corresponding digital system functions to match;
(2) Case matching: The chosen digital system is best proven by corresponding cases that it can be implemented;
(3) Vision matching: Consider whether the digital system has the ability to continuously introduce new technologies and new functions in the short term and medium and long term, and help customers grow continuously;
(4) Implementation ability matching: The most important thing for project landing is to choose people, so you need to find a team that matches the project's vision in terms of implementation ability and dedication.

Summary > This section introduces the B2B sales management architecture in the digital age—MVPOD: Model planning, Value and innovation, Process, Organization and position, and Digital support.

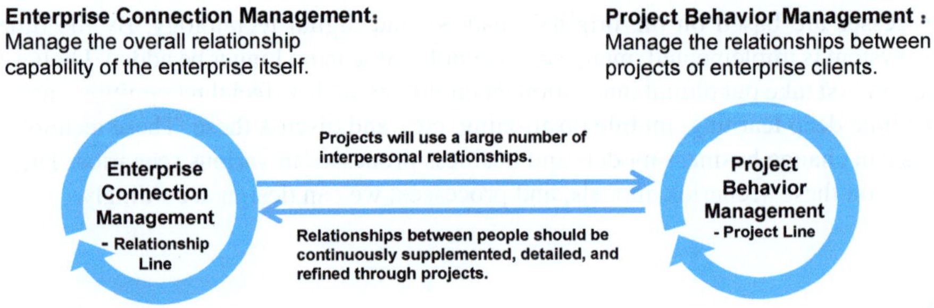

Fig. 2.28 Dual drivers of business relationship management

Business Relationship Management in B2B Sales

When I was developing CRM for a company in Canada in 1999, the company's motto was "Business is about relationship", which translates into Chinese as "Doing business is about handling relationships". This shows how important relationships are to a business.

I believe the three core capabilities of B2B sales are: 1. Relationship ability; 2. Solution ability; 3. Resource scheduling ability. Each accounts for one third of the importance. Among these three abilities, resource scheduling ability is the most stable; solution ability changes over time; relationship ability varies greatly for individual salespeople, but for the company as a whole, it is actually very stable, it's just a matter of how to use it.

BRM Definition

CRM 3.0, when building the B2B sales theory system, defined Business Relationship Management (BRM), that is, in the sales process, the company can collect, accumulate, analyze, optimize, and utilize the relationships between people, companies, and projects.

As shown in Fig. 2.28, Business Relationship Management (BRM) consists of Enterprise Connections Management (ECM) and Project Behavior Management (PBM). Enterprise Connections Management (ECM) and Project Behavior Management (PBM) will be detailed in the following chapters.

The Relationship Between BRM and CRM

Business Relationship Management (BRM) can be considered an extension of Customer Relationship Management (CRM). As shown in Fig. 2.29, in the digital

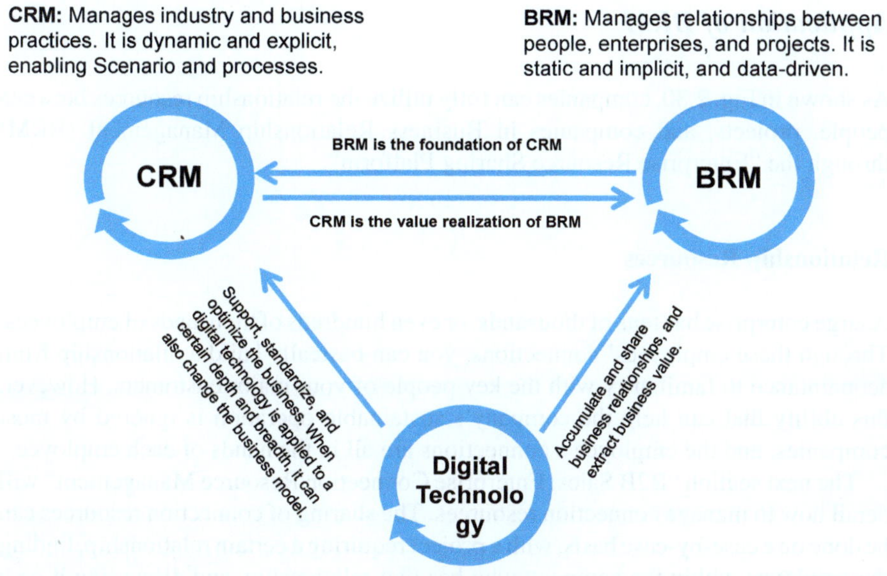

Fig. 2.29 The relationship among CRM, BRM, and digital technology

age, CRM, BRM, and digital technology are closely related. CRM is dynamic and explicit, often integrated with processes and scenarios; BRM is static and implicit, forming an accumulation of data assets, which are driven by data assets to empower scenarios and processes.

(1) CRM: CRM is closely related to sales and service business, it is very industry-specific and era-specific, reflected in business models, scenarios, organizations, positions, assessments, processes, etc., always emphasizing innovation and transformation, it is dynamic, constantly iterating and innovating.
(2) BRM: BRM defines the relationship between people, enterprises, and projects. BRM data has always been a private domain resource, always existing in the minds of salespeople, and companies have never had a good way to manage BRM data, let alone fully exploit and utilize its value. Much of the CRM data is temporary, and the data loses its value once the business opportunity is closed. But BRM data is the core data of the enterprise, the most valuable core data assets of the enterprise, and an important foundation for the enterprise to achieve business digitization.
(3) Digital Technology: In CRM, digital technology is generally used to support, standardize, and optimize business. When digital technology is applied to a certain extent, it can also change the business model. In BRM, digital technology is used to drive digitization, accumulate and inherit business relationships using digital technology, and excavate business value.

Application of BRM

As shown in Fig. 2.30, companies can fully utilize the relationship resources between people, projects, and companies in Business Relationship Management (BRM) through the "Enterprise Resource Sharing Platform".

Relationship Resources

A large enterprise has tens of thousands, or even hundreds of thousands of employees. Through these employees' connections, you can basically build a relationship from acquaintance to familiarity with the key people of your major customers. However, this ability that can help the company's sustainable operation is ignored by most companies, and the employee's connections are all in the hands of each employee.

The next section "B2B Sales: Enterprise Connection Resource Management" will detail how to manage connection resources. The sharing of connection resources can be done on a case-by-case basis, with a project requiring a certain relationship, finding the employee within the company who has that relationship, and discussing it on a case-by-case basis.

Project Resources

That is, there are projects that need to cooperate, take them out, and publish cooperation requirements on the resource sharing platform. In the form of grabbing orders,

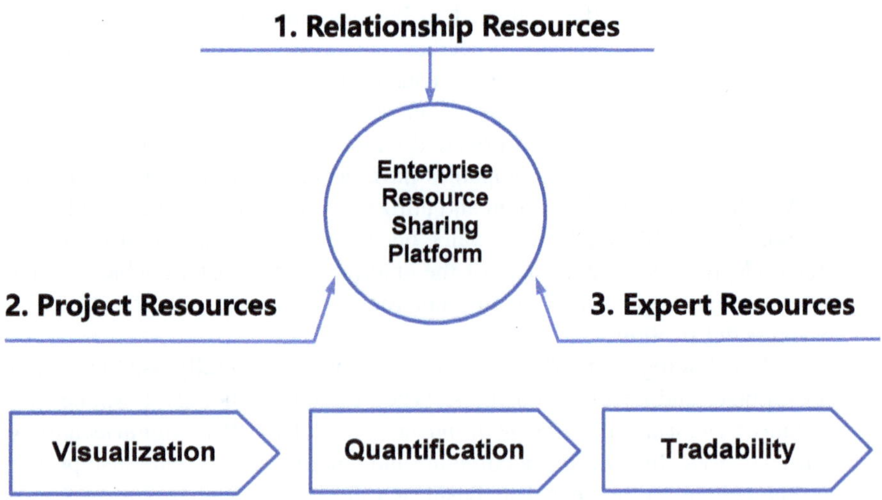

Fig. 2.30 Example of an enterprise resource sharing platform

employees or teams that meet the conditions compete, and ultimately the most suitable employees or teams are selected to participate in the project, achieving win–win cooperation.

Expert Resources

Expert resources can be internal or external. The company needs to have a dedicated person or team to maintain and operate these expert resource libraries. If it is internal, settle between departments; if it is external, pay the expert by the hour.

Having resources alone is not enough, we must have a mechanism to ensure that resources can be utilized. We can make the resource sharing platform operate through "three-ization", that is, making shared resources visual, quantifiable, and tradable.

(1) Visualization That is, sort out the resources owned by employees, put them in a digital system, so that relevant personnel can see them.
(2) Quantification All resources can be described in numbers, such as whether your relationship with Mr. Wang of Company A is very close or just general; whether this expert charges 500 yuan per hour or 1000 yuan.
(3) Tradable The resource provider and receiver can both settle. For example, this project cooperation Upon success, the resource provider can receive 10% of the project amount, etc.

Corporate Networking Resource Management in B2B Sales

In this section, I will introduce how to manage four core corporate relationship capabilities: customer relationship graph, our company's relationship resources, project decision chain, and competitor relationship resources.

I have used many CRM software, and the management of corporate networking resources is generally about managing the organizational structure and hierarchical relationships of customers. A better CRM can manage the influence relationships of customers. This management is too rough, difficult to utilize, and forms the core advantage of the enterprise, which can easily be taken away with the departure of sales, taking all the relationship secrets.

For B2B companies, relationship capability is one of the core capabilities of the company. It can serve as a digital asset of the company, driving the conversion rate and success rate of company sales. So why don't many companies carefully study relationship capabilities and invest resources to improve and operate this capability? That is, to build corporate networking resource management capabilities (CRM).

As shown in Fig. 2.31, for B2B companies, BRM needs to manage four types of relationship resources (customer resources, our company's relationship resources, project decision chain, and competitor relationship resources). They interact with each other and complement each other. As long as these four types of relationship

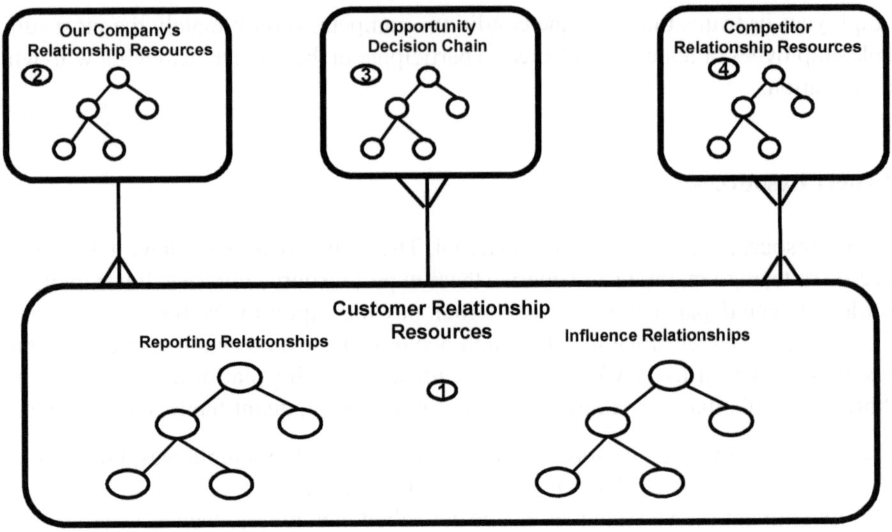

Fig. 2.31 Four types of relationship resources in BRM

resources are mastered and operated well, the core relationship capabilities of the enterprise can be built and improved.

Customer Relationship Graph

Customer relationships are divided into two types, one is the hierarchical relationship, looking for the decision center; the other is the influence relationship, looking for the influence center. Hierarchical relationships and influence relationships can be mixed and displayed on one graph. We can view it from two perspectives, one is the overall customer perspective, and the other is the key person perspective of the customer.

Overall Customer Perspective

As shown in Fig. 2.32, the customer relationship graph is composed of hierarchical relationships and influence relationships. We mainly focus on the following points:

(1) Overall Customer Relationship Density Assessment is to find out all the decision-making importance individuals and influence importance individuals in this customer, and score the overall customer relationship density based on the relationship density score of all individuals. The customer relationship density score in Fig. 2.32 is 62 points. With the overall score, we can make plans in large customer management to improve the overall customer relationship density.

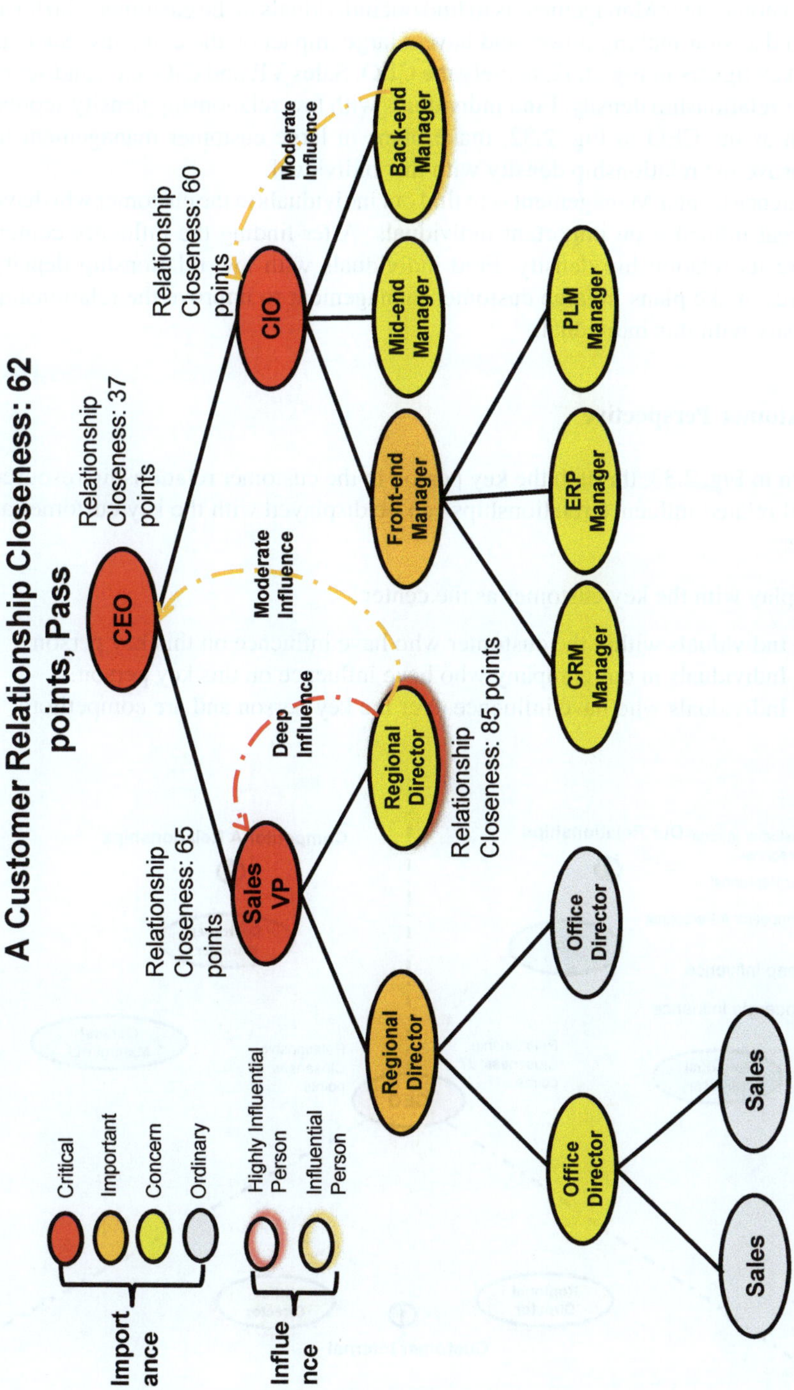

Fig. 2.32 Example of customer relationship resource map

(2) Decision Center Management is to find out individuals in the customer who have high decision-making power and have a large impact on the company. Such as the key figures in Fig. 2.32, namely the CEO, Sales VP, and CIO, etc., and score their relationship density. Find individuals with low relationship density scores, such as the CEO in Fig. 2.32, make plans in large customer management to improve the relationship density with this individual.
(3) Influence Center Management is to find out individuals in the customer who have a great influence on important individuals. After finding the influence center, score its relationship density. Find individuals with low relationship density scores, make plans in large customer management to improve the relationship density with this individual.

Key Customer Perspective

As shown in Fig. 2.33, through the key person in the customer relationship resource graph, all related influence relationships can be displayed with the key customer as the center.

(1) Display with the key customer as the center
    1) Individuals within the customer who have influence on this key person.
    2) Individuals in our company who have influence on this key person.
    3) Individuals who have influence over the key person and are competitors.

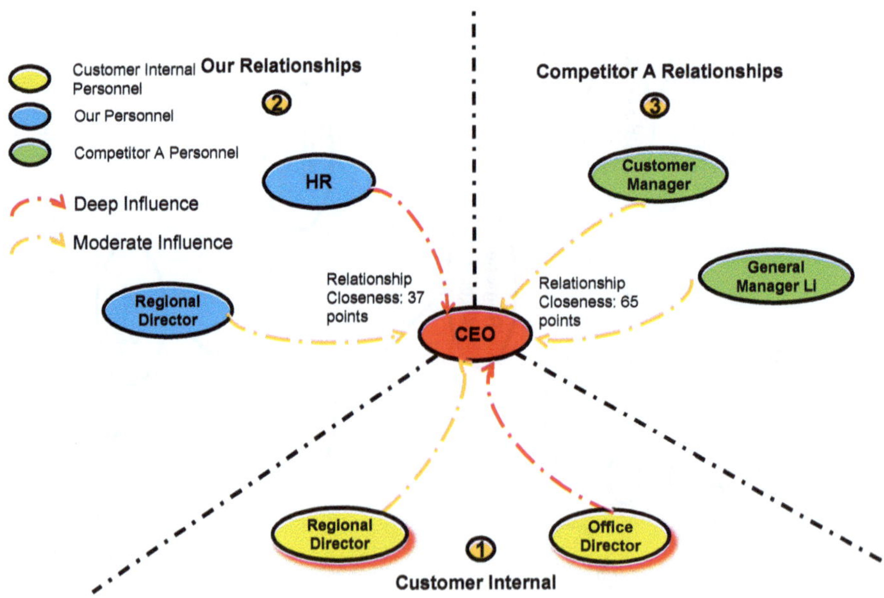

Fig. 2.33 Customer key person perspective

(2) Find the best path to influence the key person. As shown in Fig. 2.33, our company's closeness with the key person is relatively low. We can either deepen our relationship with them by finding our human resources, or we can influence the key person by strengthening our relationship with the customer's general manager.

Our Company's Relationship Resource Map

Our company's relationship resources are our core network resources. They can be divided into two perspectives: the company's perspective and the employee's perspective.

Company's Perspective

The company's perspective can be used to make an overall assessment of our network resources. If we want to grow our business, we need to continuously improve our overall core relationship capabilities, increasing the number of major customers with strong and medium relationships in the map.

Figure 2.34 shows an evaluation of a company's overall relationship capabilities, as well as the number of major customers with strong, medium, and weak relationships and the growth trend of each type of customer. This is the company's soft power and the foundation for continuously incubating business opportunities.

Employee's Perspective

The map shown from the employee's perspective can be used to evaluate and utilize the customer resources of the company's employees. This should also be an important indicator for employee performance evaluation, especially for sales staff. When making deals, companies currently rely mainly on individual salespeople, without fully utilizing the network resources of all employees. These network resources are the vast majority hidden "under the iceberg". If fully utilized, they can greatly expand the company's relationship resources and increase the win rate.

Figure 2.35 shows the relationship resource evaluation results of an employee of a company and the details of the key people he can influence. Companies should not only establish relationship resource maps for sales staff, but also for non-sales positions. If non-sales positions also contribute resources during the deal-making process, they should also be rewarded, achieving true company-wide sales.

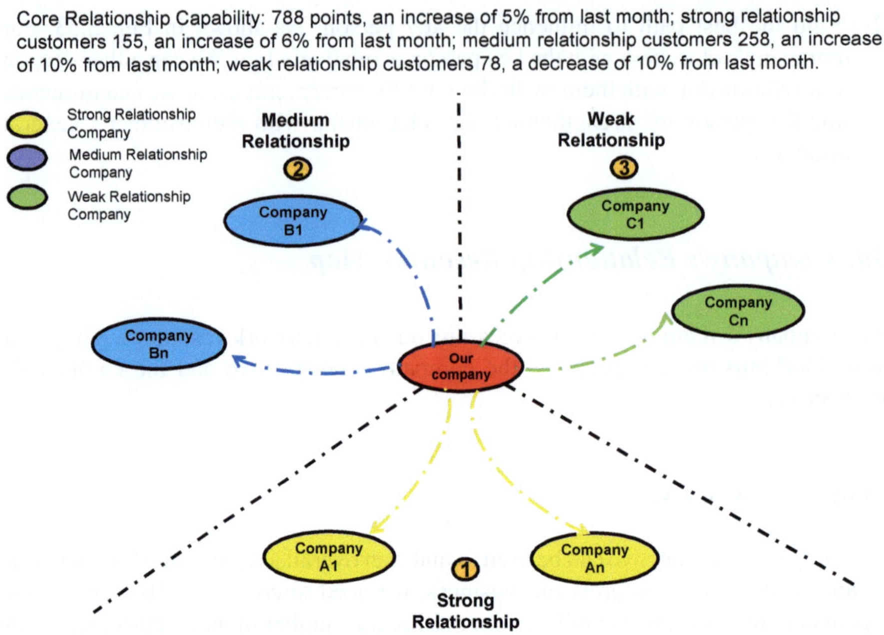

Fig. 2.34 Our company's core relationship capability map

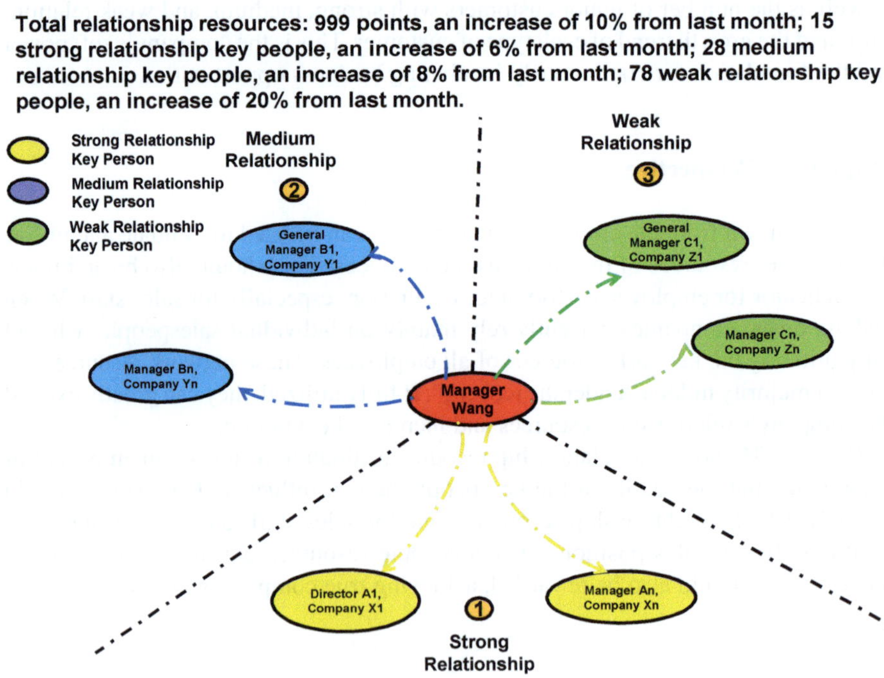

Fig. 2.35 Our employees' relationship resource map

Project Decision Chain Map

The project decision chain in Fig. 2.36 shows the relationship capabilities of a company in a specific project. With this decision chain, even if a salesperson is replaced temporarily, the company should be able to easily assess the probability of winning the relationship and find ways to improve it.

Project Decision Chain Display:

(1) Project Decision Relationship: Includes the relationship between the project approver, project decision maker, project evaluator, and project user, as well as information about each related person's closeness of relationship, personality, attitude towards our company, and level of contact.
(2) Influence Relationship: Shows who within the customer has influence over the key person, who is the center of influence, such as the regional director and the back-end person in charge in Fig. 2.36.
(3) Key Person Analysis: You can view the influence of the customer, our company, and competitors on the key person from the key person's perspective. That is, the customer's key person perspective in the customer relationship map. You can also view other project decision chains related to this key person to understand this key person's attitude towards our company in other projects.

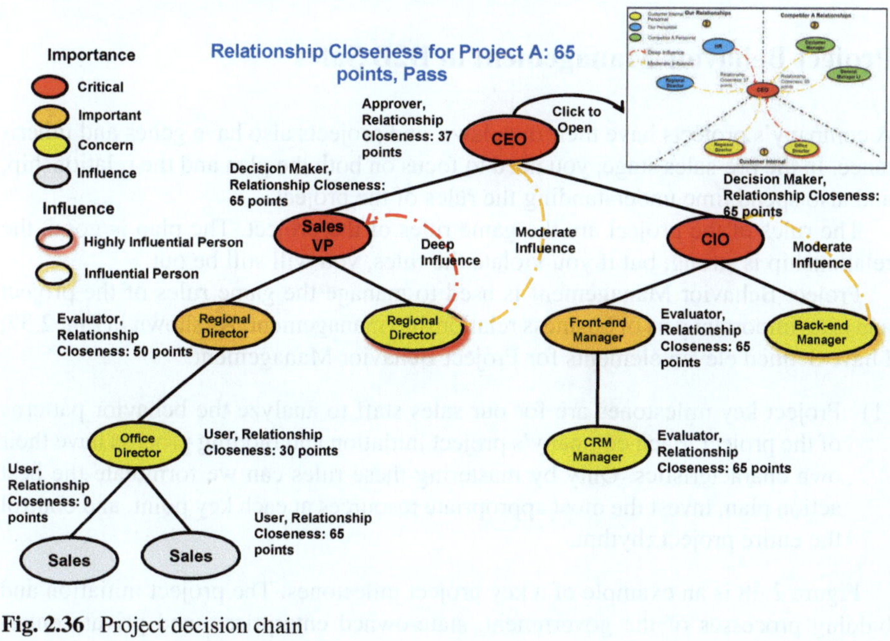

Fig. 2.36 Project decision chain

Competitor Relationship Resource Map

The competitor relationship resource map can display the relationship resources of a competitor, that is, the core The ability of relationship management. We can view this map from two perspectives, namely the competitor's enterprise perspective and the competitor's employee perspective. The presentation of this map is similar to our company's relationship resource map, but the content is definitely not as rich as our relationship resource map. The information in this map is mainly collected from the bidding process of each project.

Summary > This section introduces BRM, that is, how to manage four core business relationship capabilities: customer relationship resource map, our relationship resource map, project decision chain map, and competitor relationship resource map. Some people may worry about the difficulty of collecting these data, but if you are prepared, you will stand; if you are not prepared, you will fail. The core relationship capability of a company is the cornerstone of its success. Companies need to invest money and people, start managing, operating, monitoring, and assessing from today. Once this capability is successfully built, wealth will continue to flow, core competitiveness will be improved, and the company will be able to operate for a long time.

Project Behavior Management in B2B Sales

A company's projects have their own laws, and projects also have genes and inheritance. In the pre-sales stage, you need to focus on both the plan and the relationship, and also spend time understanding the rules of the project.

The rules of the project are the game rules of the project. The plan is good, the relationship is strong, but if you violate the rules, you will still be out.

Project Behavior Management is used to manage the game rules of the project and is an important part of business relationship management. As shown in Fig. 2.37, I have defined eleven elements for Project Behavior Management.

(1) Project key milestones are for our sales staff to analyze the behavior patterns of the project. Each company's project initiation and bidding process have their own characteristics. Only by mastering these rules can we formulate the best action plan, invest the most appropriate resources at each key point, and control the entire project rhythm.

Figure 2.38 is an example of a key project milestones. The project initiation and bidding processes of the government, state-owned enterprises, and private enterprises are different, and even for clients in the same industry and type, there may be significant differences. We can write different project key milestone models for each important client's project. Mastering the pace of a client's project can give them an advantage and put them in a competitive position.

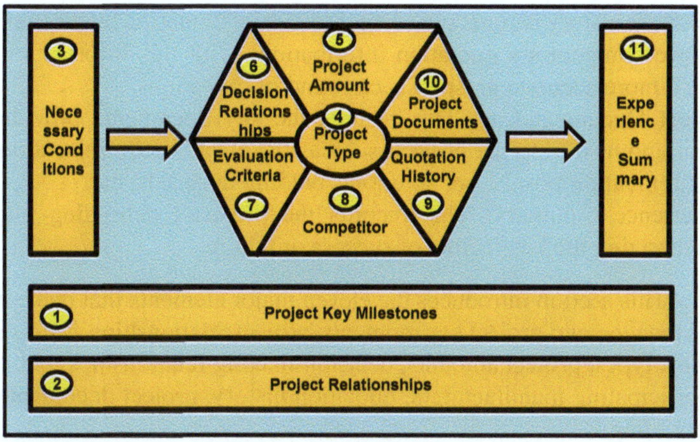

Fig. 2.37 Project behavior management composition

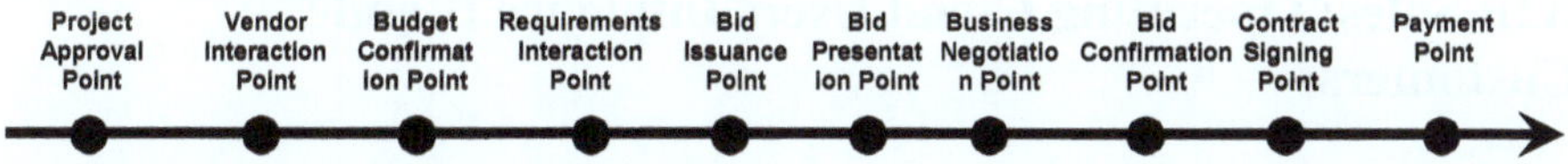

Fig. 2.38 Example of project key milestones

(2) Project relationships describe the relationship between each project, such as Project A is the second phase of Project B, Project A is the landing project of Project B, Project A is the replacement project of Project B, etc.
(3) Necessary conditions explain what key reasons make this project initiated, such as the old system cannot support business, senior leaders want to innovate, there is a fixed budget input every year, etc.
(4) Project type explains the nature of the project, such as consulting projects, implementation projects, hardware and software procurement projects, operation and maintenance projects, etc.
(5) Project amount includes the budget amount and the winning bid amount. With this information, we can make more accurate quotations in future projects.
(6) Decision-making relationship is the decision chain of this project that was introduced earlier.
(7) Evaluation criteria, that is, how this project selects the winning bidder. Whether it is open bidding, directed invitation to bid, or single source. The selection criteria are the lowest bid price, or priority is given to comprehensive scoring. It is best to have detailed scoring items and weights for this project. With this information, we can accurately assess the possibility of our winning bid from the beginning, and we can also layout early and guide related scoring standards in time.
(8) Competitors record the main competitor information.

(9) Quotation history records our several rounds of quotation history, and it is best to have competitor's quotation information. With this information, we will have a more accurate grasp of each round of quotations.
(10) Project Documentation: This records the key documents provided by the client and us during the project, such as the client's requirement documents, requirement proposals; our solutions, bidding materials, etc.
(11) Experience Summary: This records the project's debriefing information, summarizing the key factors of success or failure.

Summary > This section introduces the eleven major elements that make up Project Behavior Management: project key moments, project relationships, necessary conditions, project types, project amounts, decision-making relationships, bid evaluation criteria, participating manufacturers, quotation history, project documentation, and project debriefing.

B2B Sales: Operating C-end Users Influence B-end Customers

The B2B sales field should be one of the areas least affected by digital technology. B2B sales, especially large B sales, have the following characteristics:

(1) Behavior is mainly offline: A large amount of behavior, especially many key behaviors, are mainly offline and cannot be effectively tracked and recorded through digital tools.
(2) Key information cannot be entered: Many key pieces of information cannot be entered into the system, otherwise, there would be compliance risks.
(3) Key information cannot be confirmed: Many pieces of information in B2B cannot confirm their authenticity, such as "key people support us a lot," "customers prefer our plan," etc.
(4) The customer decision chain is very complex: Large projects may involve dozens to hundreds of people, and there are many key decision-makers. It is difficult to sort out the complete decision chain based on the information of individual customer contacts.
(5) Industry Taboos: If all contacts and interactions with customer-related personnel are recorded in a digital system, customers will be very cautious when contacting us.

Without complete and accurate decision-making information, even the strongest AI system cannot make accurate judgments. Therefore, the position of large customer sales is a position that is difficult to be replaced by AI. As long as you can withstand the physical demands, and your connections and industry experience continue to accumulate, you can keep going.

Most companies do not manage business relationships, that is, they do not manage corporate networking resources and project relationships, and business relationship management manages truly valuable corporate decision-making data. We need to implement large customer management, sales process management, sales support system management, corporate networking resource management, and Project Behavior Management in CRM3.0 through a digital system, perfectly integrating data, processes, scenarios, and digital technology. In this way, we can make salespeople more efficient and precise in the sales process through digital technology, and provide decision-making basis for salespeople throughout the sales process, making the win rate higher. The integration of sales methods, data assets, salesperson capabilities and experience, and digital technology can significantly improve B2B sales results.

Next, I will introduce the "Five-step Method for Efficiently Operating C-end Users to Influence B-end Business Behavior", which is to integrate sales methods, data assets, and digital tools to gain insight and control over the entire order process, firmly control the project leadership, and make the project win naturally.

Step One: Operate C-end Users, Build Trust

From the customer's perspective, we hope to establish trust with the customer, to achieve belief and dependence; from the perspective of employee expectations, employees must be able to be friends with customers, to be mentors to customers.

Trust is mainly based on four dimensions: frequency, professionalism, depth, and length, as shown in Fig. 2.39.

(1) Frequency: In the process of building customer trust, the frequency of contact is an element that sales often overlook. Trust is built bit by bit. If a certain contact frequency can be maintained, results will definitely be seen after half a year or a year. What if you have tens of thousands of customer contacts? At this time, you can use digital tools to establish a customer contact interaction plan, automatically generate personalized greeting content, and automatically complete the greeting action at key points, as shown in Fig. 2.40.

(2) Professionalism: Many brands' knowledge transfer, expert lectures, and company visits require the application and coordination of backend resources.

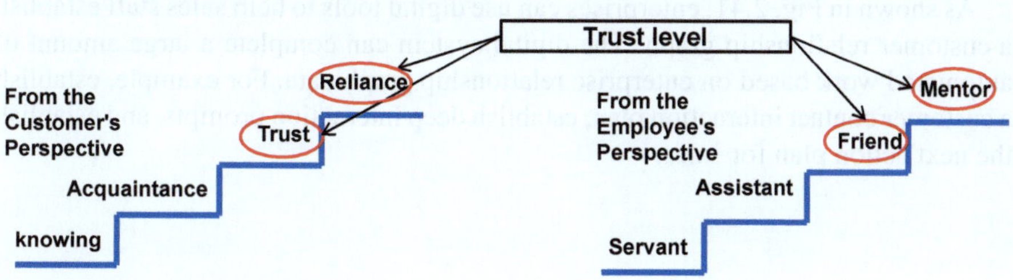

Fig. 2.39 Customer trust ladder

	Frequency				Professionalism			Depth	
	Holiday Greetings	House Visits	Birthday Greetings	Likes on Social Media	Knowledge and Brand Communication	Expert Advocacy	Company Tours	Dining Together	Family Contact
Critical Users									
Importa nt Users									

Fig. 2.40 Example of customer interaction plan

At this time, digital tools can help sales coordinate these resources. For the coordination mechanism, refer to the previously introduced sales support system management.

(3) Depth: Depth requires a lot of offline work, but you can use digital tools to find key figures in the customer relationship graph and project decision chain in Enterprise Contact Management (ECM), establish deep interaction prompts for sales, and establish action plans for sales.

(4) Length: A journey of a thousand miles begins with a single step. Enterprises should use digital tools as early as possible to improve the customer relationship graph and project decision chain, and establish a customer contact interaction plan. Figure 2.40 is a simple example of a customer contact interaction plan. Set the frequency of contact in the blank space, and the digital system can automatically generate plans and tasks, track execution, and provide dynamic evaluation and feedback.

Step Two: Network Expansion and Insight Analysis

In the process of building trust, enterprises should build network relationships and individual portraits. This includes relationships between customer departments, hierarchical relationships between personnel, influence relationships between personnel, and portraits of each person (importance, relationship closeness, degree of interaction, and behavioral tendencies). For a detailed introduction, see the content of the Enterprise Contact Management (ECM) section.

As shown in Fig. 2.41, enterprises can use digital tools to help sales staff establish a customer relationship graph. The digital system can complete a large amount of automated work based on enterprise relationship graph data. For example, establish a customer contact interaction plan, establish deep interaction prompts, and establish the next action plan for sales.

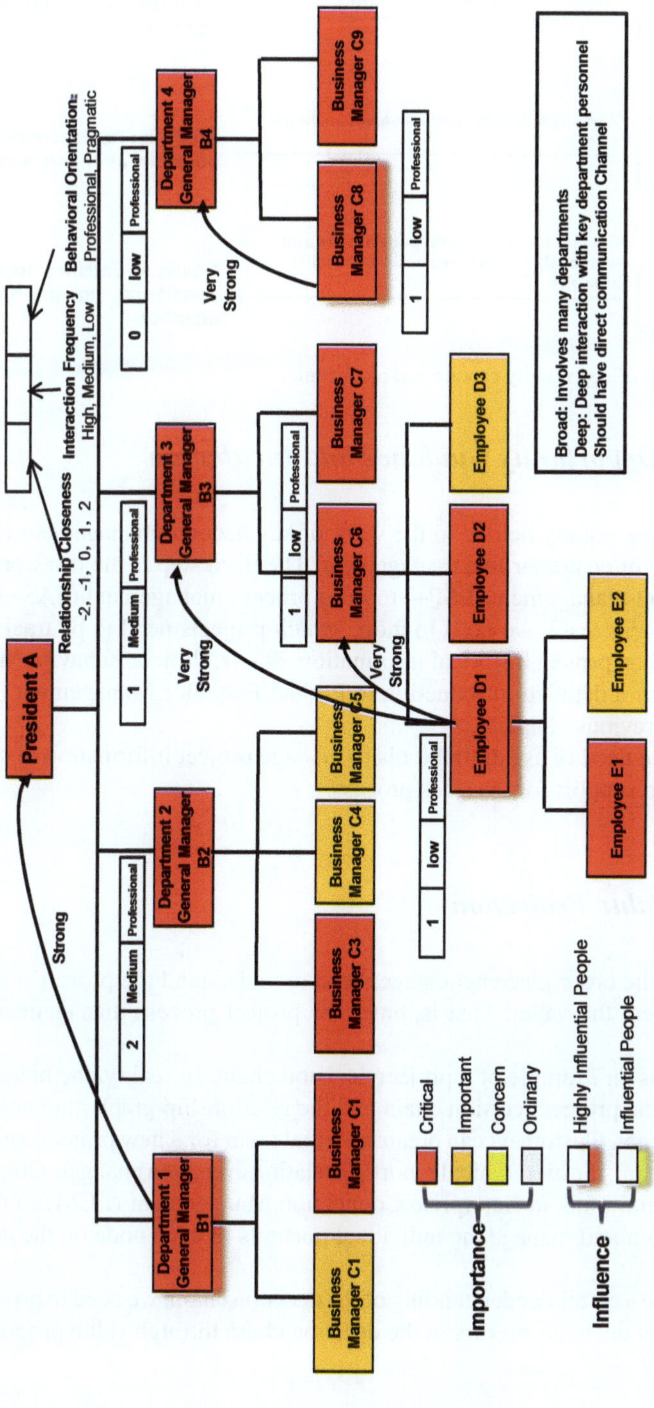

Fig. 2.41 Example of building relationship networks and individual profiles

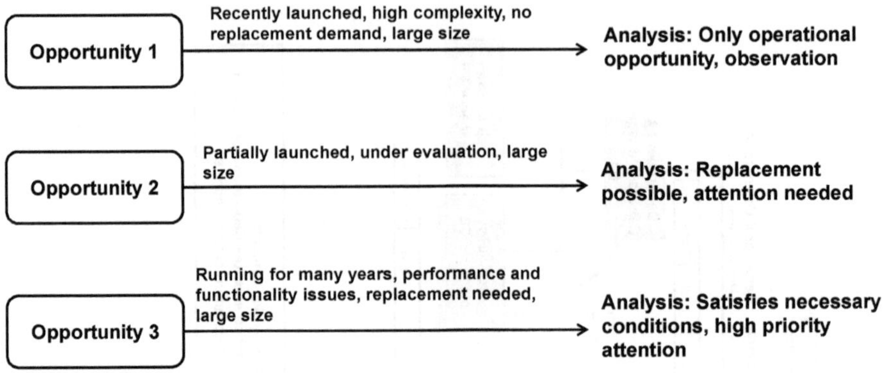

Fig. 2.42 Example of opportunity capture and incubation

Step Three: Opportunity Guidance and Incubation

The first two steps mainly belong to the work of key account management (ESP+), that is, the stage of customer line management. The third step is the transformation from key account management (ESP+) to sales process management (TAS+).

As shown in Fig. 2.42, we need to judge which projects need to be tracked and incubated based on project historical information, that is, Project Behavior Management (PBM). For a detailed introduction to Project Behavior Management (PBM), please see the previous chapters.

Therefore, we need to use digital tools to manage project information in order to provide decision support for the sales process.

Step Four: Value Projection

Next, we enter the order placement stage, need to understand the project's decision chain, and present the value. That is, enter the project process management stage (TAS+).

Figure 2.43 is an example of a project decision chain. In reality, the hierarchical relationship in the project decision chain and the relationship graph may not necessarily be consistent. Customers can create a virtual team for a new project, and in the virtual project team, the hierarchical reporting relationship often changes. Companies need to use digital tools in Enterprise Connection Management (ECM) to manage the decision chain and manage the individual portraits of each node on the decision chain.

Once we have a certain understanding of the decision chain, we need to project and influence the key decision-makers in the decision chain through value propositions.

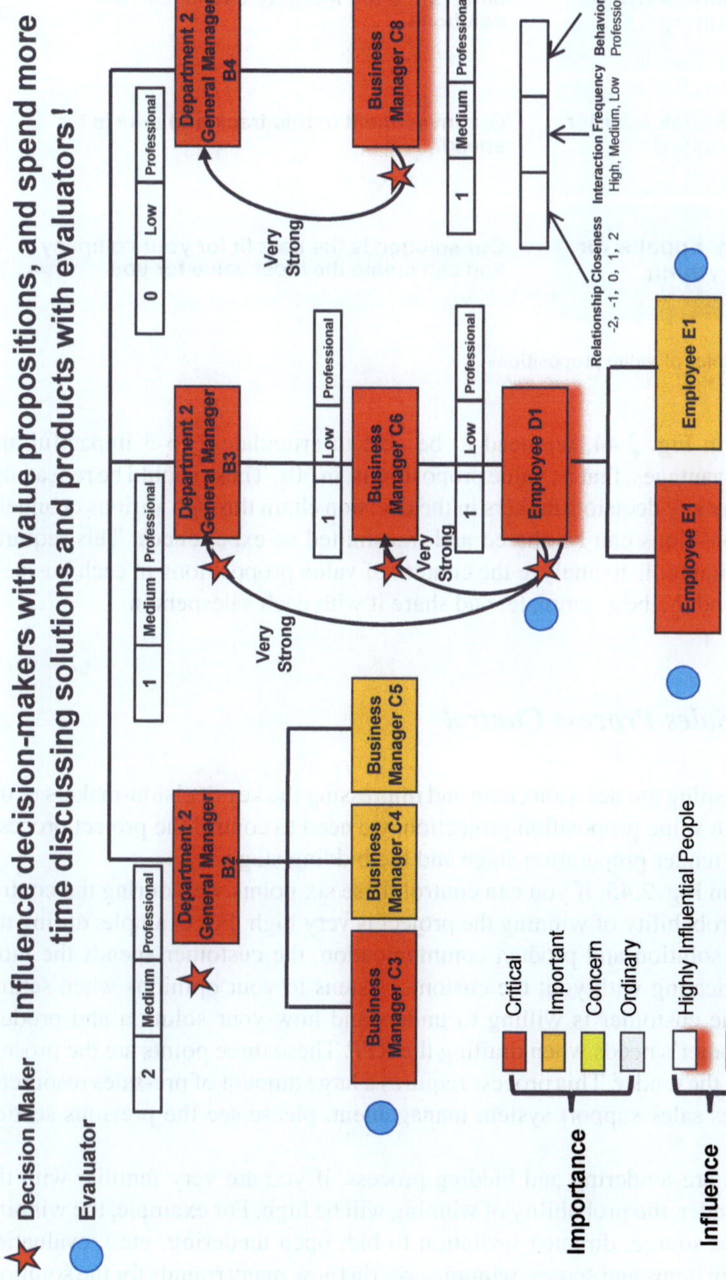

Fig. 2.43 Example of project decision chain

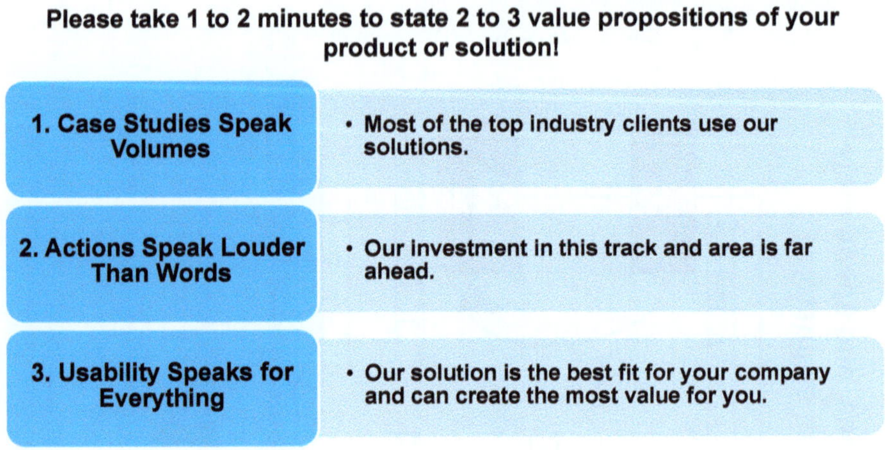

Fig. 2.44 Examples of value propositions

As shown in Fig. 2.44, we need to be able to articulate 2 to 3 impactful and memorable advantages, that is, value propositions, in 60s. These should be repeatedly conveyed to the key decision-makers in the decision chain through various channels.

Value propositions can be shared and transmitted as experiences. This requires us to have digital tools to analyze the content of value propositions in each business opportunity, find the best template, and share it with each salesperson.

Step Five: Sales Process Control

After fully grasping the decision chain and impressing the key decision-makers of the project through value proposition projection, we need to control the project process, especially the tender preparation stage and the bidding stage.

As shown in Fig. 2.45, if you can control these six points well during the control process, the probability of winning the project is very high. For example, during the pre-tendering solution and product communication, the customer spends the most time communicating with you; the customer listens to your opinions when setting the budget; the customer is willing to understand how your solution and product meet the customer's needs when drafting the RFP. These three points are the process control before the tender. This process requires a large amount of pre-sales resources, which involves sales support system management, please see the previous section for details.

During the pre-tendering and bidding process, if you are very familiar with the rules of this tender, the probability of winning will be high. For example, the winning method (single source, directed invitation to bid, open tendering, etc.), evaluation criteria, scoring items and scores, winning criteria (how many rounds for the solution,

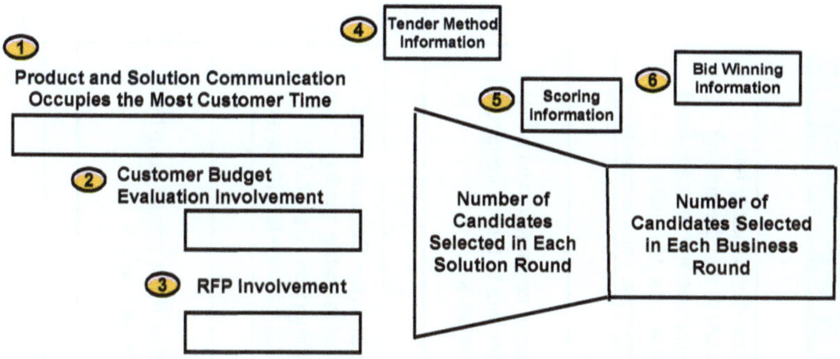

Fig. 2.45 Example of sales process control

how many rounds for the business, whether the lowest price wins, etc.). All this information, you need to obtain during the order process, and you need to infer based on the historical information of past projects, which requires the use of information in Project Behavior Management.

So in the fifth step of project process control, whether it is sales support system management or project behavior management, it needs to be supported by a digital system.

Summary > This section introduces how to efficiently operate the five steps of C-end user influencing B-end enterprise behavior and the digital tools involved in each step: (1) Operating C-end users, building trust; (2) Network expansion and insight analysis; (3) Business opportunity guidance and incubation; (4) Value projection; (5) Project process control.

Different Market Strategies for B2B Sales

B2B sales can be summarized as the trilogy of defending the norm, surprising, and accumulating momentum. Defending the norm is large customer management, surprising is sales process management, and accumulating momentum is sales support system management. These three parts are managed by large customer management, sales process management, and sales support system management methods respectively. This section will introduce how companies choose and apply these methods in different market environments.

As shown in Fig. 2.46, there is no constant strategy in warfare, and water has no constant shape. We need to adapt according to different market conditions (new Entering the market, rapidly growing markets, and mature stable markets), adopting different sales strategies, focusing on different sales areas.

	New market	Fast-growing market	Mature and stable market
Market description	The market of horse racing, such as the new entry of domestic enterprises into the market of a certain overseas country.	It has entered the market for a certain time, but the market capacity is still expanding, such as the domestic security market around 2013	The market capacity has stabilized, and the leading enterprises are basically fixed, such as the domestic commercial vehicle market.
Marketing strategy	Seize the opportunity and control the risk	The best sales support system, the best sales method, rapid replication, rapid expansion of the market	In-depth cooperation with major customers to form a community of interests
Key Account Management	**Non-focused.** Because I have just entered the market, I can't be sure who the big customers are	**Sub-emphasis.** Key account management requires a large investment and a long cycle, and we should start to increase capital and personnel investment	**Top priority**. Because when the market is stable, the big customers decide who the market balance tilts towards
Sales process management	**Focus.** Seize opportunities and control risks through sales process management	**Focus.** With a growing number of projects and sales personnel, successes must be replicated and managed quickly	**Focus.** But it should have been done well before
Sales support management	**Non-focused.** Because they have just entered the market, they often rely on a few people to work alone	**Top priority.** When there are enough market opportunities, focus on how to use resources efficiently to generate maximum return on investment	**Focus.** But it should have been done well before

New Market Entry

As shown in Fig. 2.47, in the newly entered market, we start from scratch. Because the base is low, opportunities are everywhere. Seizing one could potentially result in exponential growth in performance. At this time, companies should pay more attention to how to seize opportunities and avoid risks.

First, we need to care about how to act quickly, accurately, and heavily to seize market opportunities. But if we want to achieve this, we must give the sales manager enough power, that is, the integration of three powers: business rights, personnel rights, and distribution rights. After giving the sales manager enough power, we can let each region self-organize, self-drive, self-evolve, and self-profit through the system.

In the new market, the personal ability and vision of the leader play a big role, but corporate management is often imperfect and rough. How can the digital system empower sales management? I think we can start from the following four aspects.

Unification of Sales Terminology

When a company enters a new market, it is to achieve greater growth in its own business. But once the company grows, we will find that the inconsistency of sales terminology has greatly hindered the growth of the company. The same word, such as leads, opportunities, sales, costs, big projects, big customers, etc., everyone's understanding is completely different. Therefore, different business units, different regions, different teams, etc. cannot achieve effective communication, making it difficult to effectively execute coordination, management, and assessment. So first, we need to unify sales terminology through the digital system so that different departments and organizations can communicate in the same context.

Unification of Sales Management Methods

We can adopt personalized sales methods and sales processes according to the special circumstances of a certain region. However, the framework of corporate sales must be unified, with the premise of the overall corporate sales framework template. Each region or business unit can add its own personalized things to each process and function within the framework. For B2B sales, the sales frameworks of various industries at home and abroad are basically consistent. A unified, complete, and scientific sales management framework is the premise of unified control of the enterprise.

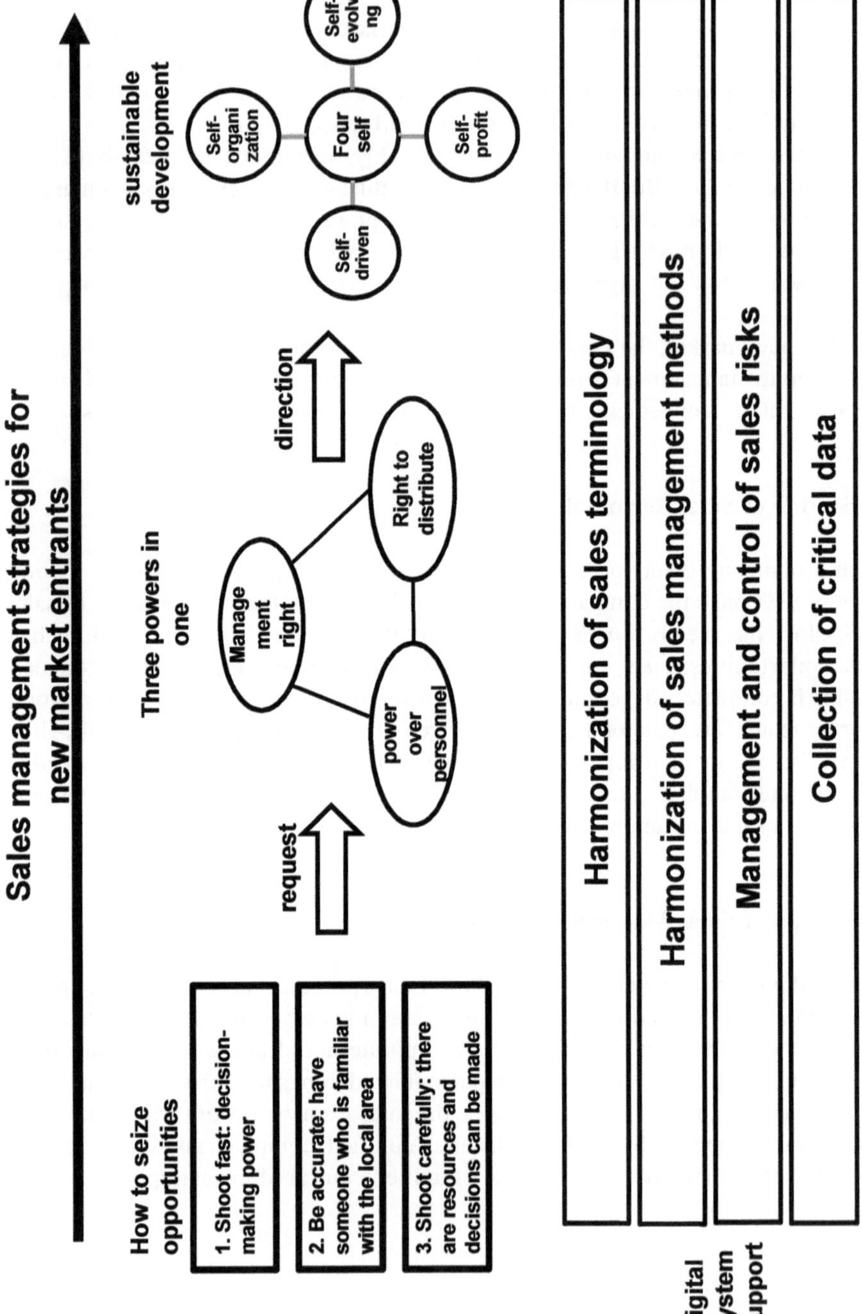

Fig. 2.47 Sales management strategy for new market entry

Control of Sales Risks

Before entering an unfamiliar market, we must understand and avoid risks, such as legal risks, tax risks, operational risks, ethical risks, market risks, etc. We can completely solidify the methods of avoiding risks in the processes and functions of the digital system, set various rules and reminders, to help companies avoid risks.

Collection of Key Data

Just entering a market, no matter how busy the salesperson is, they need to collect some key data through the digital system to form the company's data assets and lay a solid foundation for future business expansion and strengthening. For example, opportunity information, project information, partner information, customer information, key people of customers, decision chain information, etc. are all needed for daily accumulation.

Below are the application suggestions for key customer management, sales process management, and sales support system management in this market environment:

(1) Key Customer Management

Not important. The company cannot effectively evaluate who is a key customer because we only know the potential of the customer, not knowing The customer's contribution to us, we do not know whether our plan can meet the customer's needs, and whether the customer's attitude towards us is friendly, etc.

(2) Sales Support Management

Not important. Because the newly entered market often does not have too many sales support resources, it depends on a few people to develop the market.

(3) Sales Process Management

Important. The four main tasks of unifying sales terminology, unifying sales management methods, controlling sales risks, and collecting key data are achieved in sales process management. Sales process management has been detailed in previous chapters, so it will not be repeated here.

1) Unification of sales terminology: Implemented in opportunity grading, opportunity stages, win rate, and sales process.
2) Unification of sales management methods: Implemented in sales process, necessary conditions, value proposition, questionnaire, competitors, strategy and tactics, activities, and supervision and promotion.
3) Control of sales risks: Implemented in sales process and activities.
4) Collection of key data: Implemented in sales process, relationship graph, questionnaire, activities, and value proposition.

Rapidly Growing Market

In a rapidly growing market, although the company has been in the market for a certain period of time and has a considerable scale. But because there is still a large market increment space every year, everyone is eager to grab the territory, so companies usually focus on the process of grabbing the territory (sales process management), and how to reasonably allocate resources in the process of grabbing the territory (sales support system management). Because large customer management investment is long and the effect is slow, but for the future, it has to be done, so at this time the company can start to prepare and start to increase capital and personnel investment.

The following are the application suggestions of large customer management, sales process management, and sales support system management in this market environment:

(1) Large Customer Management

Secondary focus. The company's top management can generally realize that large orders are often laid out 1–2 years ago. If you start preparing when bidding, the chance of winning the bid will be much smaller; but on the other hand, there are plenty of incremental opportunities in the market, and large customer management requires large investment and long cycle, so the company can start to prepare and increase capital and personnel investment.

(2) Sales Process Management and Sales Support System Management

In a rapidly growing market, both sales process management and sales support system management are key points, especially sales support system management, which is often overlooked by companies.

Figure 2.48 lists the key issues that sales management needs to solve in a rapidly growing market. They are basically related to sales process management and sales support system management.

1) Establish a unified and replicable sales management mechanism. The company should establish the best structure and process for the sales management of the marketing unit, making the management unified and replicable. That is, it does not depend on individuals, just follow the management mechanism, and the front-end sales activities can operate effectively. This is what sales process management needs to achieve.
2) Optimize the mode of matrix industry and regional cooperation, and optimize the method of industry resource scheduling. For matrix industry projects in the region, the company should adopt different resource scheduling strategies based on different business opportunity levels, and strengthen the cooperation between the matrix industry and the region. This is what sales support system management needs to achieve.
3) Clarify the responsibilities and rights of relevant roles in the sales process. Based on different business opportunity levels and collaboration models, define the

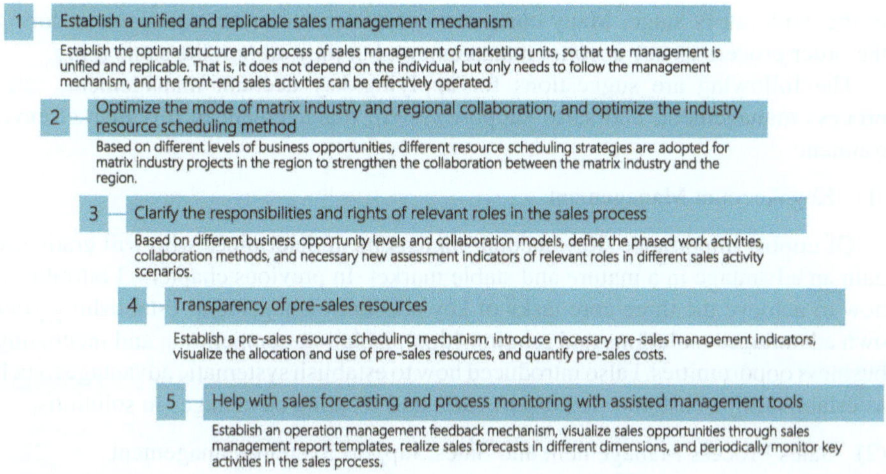

Fig. 2.48 Examples of common problems to be addressed by sales management in a fast-growing market

phased work activities, collaboration methods, and necessary new assessment indicators of relevant roles in different sales activity scenarios. This is what sales process management aims to achieve.

4) Pre-sales resource transparency. Establish a pre-sales resource scheduling mechanism, introduce necessary pre-sales management indicators, make the allocation and use of pre-sales resources visible, and quantify pre-sales costs. This is what sales support system management aims to achieve.
5) Use auxiliary management tools to help companies achieve sales forecasting and process monitoring. Establish an operation management feedback mechanism, visualize sales opportunities through sales management report templates, achieve sales forecasting in different dimensions, periodically monitor key activities in the sales process, and use digital tools to achieve the analysis and statistical functions of sales process management and sales support system management.

For how to apply sales process management and sales support system management, please refer to the corresponding chapter introductions.

Mature and Stable Market

When the market capacity has stabilized and the competition pattern of leading companies in the industry is basically clear, key account management becomes increasingly important. Because at this time, whoever the key accounts lean towards, the balance of victory in market competition will tilt towards them. However, in the field of key account management, both management methods and practices are still in the exploratory stage. Many companies consider customer management during the order process as key account management, but they are not the same thing.

The following are suggestions for applying key account management, sales process management, and sales support system management in this market environment:

(1) Key Account Management

Of utmost importance. Key account management determines who will gradually gain an advantage in a mature and stable market. In previous chapters, I introduced how to achieve the three core tasks of key account management: establishing your own advantages (solutions and relationships), isolating competitors, and incubating business opportunities. I also introduced how to establish systematic advantages, such as establishing a customer-led expert team and creating advantages in solutions.

(2) Sales Process Management and Sales Support System Management

Important. The content of sales process management and sales support management is the same as in rapidly growing markets.

Summary > There is no constant strategy in war, and water has no constant shape. This section introduces how to apply key account management, sales process management, and sales support system management in three types of markets: new markets, rapidly growing markets, and mature and stable markets.

B2B Market Management

In B2B business, management related to sales plans, budgets, costs, promotions, and activities all belong to market management.

As shown in Fig. 2.49, B2B market management consists of five parts: ① sales plan management; ② market budget management; ③ cost management; ④ market activity execution management; ⑤ market activity evaluation management.

Sales Plan Management

As shown in Fig. 2.50, sales plan management is divided into four parts: basic plan, assessment plan, challenge plan, and rolling plan.

Basic Plan

If sales targets are directly assigned from top to bottom, there can be significant deviations during the execution process. Therefore, before setting the assessment plan at the end of the year, the company should first issue a preliminary plan to

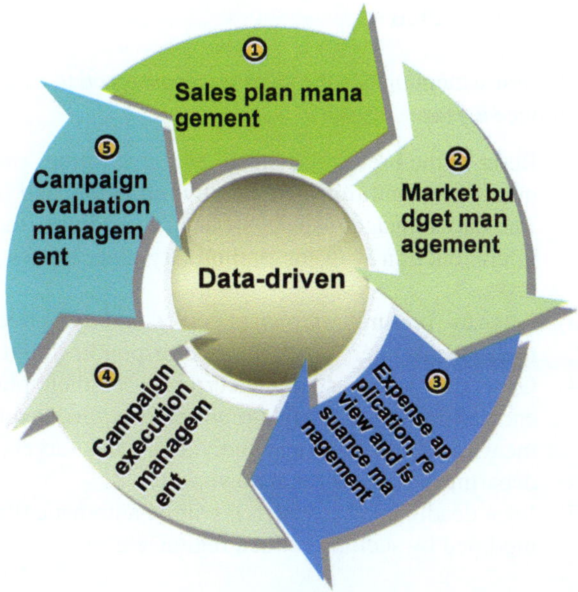

Fig. 2.49 B2B market management

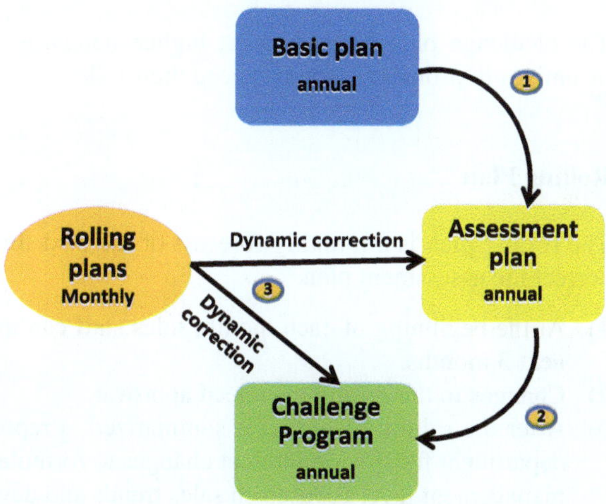

Fig. 2.50 Sales plan management

understand the sales staff's forecast for next year's performance from the bottom up, once a year.

1) To save sales time, a draft can be prepared based on data from recent years.
2) Sales staff can individually or in batches modify their forecasted sales and volumes.
3) Each key customer must be manually confirmed.
4) Set a deadline, after which it will be automatically locked.

Assessment Plan

The assessment plan is the sales target assigned to each salesperson for the next year, set once a year.

1) Refer to the preliminary plan, and give formal annual assessment targets based on market conditions, competitive situation, and investor requirements.
2) The sales management department, according to the company's requirements and in conjunction with the preliminary plan, breaks down the targets and assigns tasks.
3) After the preliminary plan is copied and converted into an assessment plan, the relevant sales personnel make corresponding adjustments.
4) Generate a summary of the current assessment plan every day, check the difference with the company's requirements, and require the relevant sales department to adjust team and individual sales targets at any time to complete the department's target breakdown.
5) Set a deadline, after which it will be automatically locked. It can be locked and modified by sector, product, region, etc.

Challenge Plan

The challenge plan is used to set higher standards for sales and provide higher incentives to promote sales to exceed their tasks.

Rolling Plan

The rolling plan is a monthly forecast of the next three months' figures, a plan to correct the assessment plan.

1) At the beginning of each month, sales staff can modify the rolling plan for the next 3 months.
2) Changes to the rolling plan need approval.
3) After the rolling plan data is summarized, a report is generated. The business department focuses on product changes to formulate production plans; the sales management layer focuses on sales trends and deviations from the annual plan.

Market Budget Management

As shown in Fig. 2.51, market budget management is divided into annual budget, monthly budget, and quota control:

1) The annual budget is generated based on the annual assessment plan.
2) If the assessment plan changes, the annual budget also needs to be adjusted.

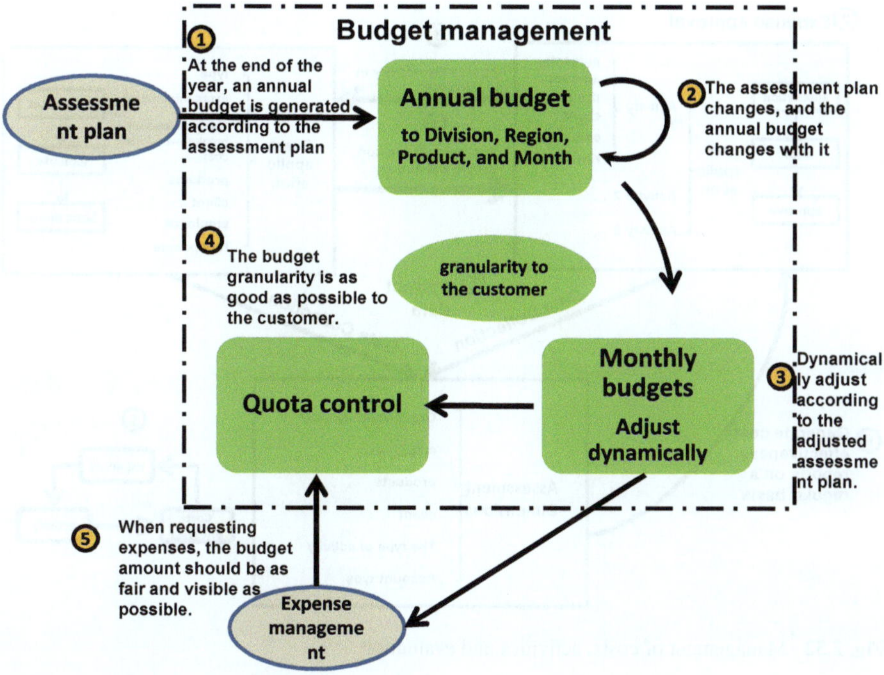

Fig. 2.51 Budget management

3) The annual budget needs to be broken down into a monthly budget, and the monthly budget needs to be dynamically adjusted with the adjustment of the assessment plan.
4) The granularity of the budget should be as detailed as possible to the customer.
5) When units and employees apply for expenses, they should be able to see their own quotas as much as possible to ensure fair resource allocation.

Expense Management, Market Activity Management, and Evaluation Management

As shown in Fig. 2.52, expense management, market activity management, and evaluation management are closely related, forming a closed loop.

1) In the expense application, list each activity, preferably detailed to the customer, which is conducive to subsequent cost-effectiveness analysis.
2) Once the expense application is approved, all related activities can be found in the activity management, where activities can be activated and carried out.

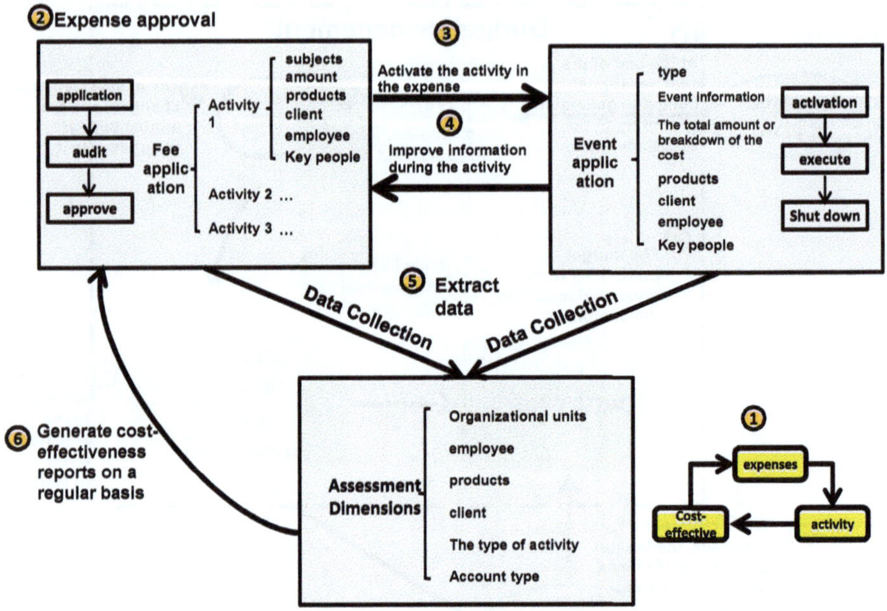

Fig. 2.52 Management of costs, activities and evaluation

3) In the activity, it is necessary to complete all related information and associate it with the expenses, so that cost-effectiveness analysis can be carried out for each dimension.
4) All related data will be extracted to the evaluation system for analysis. The evaluation analysis can be carried out from five dimensions: sales, cost-effectiveness, customers, key persons, and employees.
5) The related evaluation reports can help guide and improve the direction of expense allocation.

Summary > This section introduces the five main components of B2B market management: ① Sales plan management; ② Market budget management; ③ Expense management; ④ Market activity management; ⑤ Market activity evaluation management.

Chapter 3
CRM3.0's Service Digital Transformation

B2C Basic Service Innovation

When it comes to services, people generally think of call centers, but call centers are just one access channel for services. The scope of B2C services is much larger. This section introduces how to achieve innovation in B2C basic services.

As shown in Fig. 3.1, B2C services include nine aspects: ① User experience; ② Omnichannel; ③ Work order management; ④ Service network management; ⑤ Spare parts management; ⑥ Defective product management; ⑦ Quality management; ⑧ Technical support and training; ⑨ Settlement management.

User Experience Innovation

The most basic mission of service is to improve user satisfaction, so one area of service is user experience. As shown in Fig. 3.2, user experience innovation includes but is not limited to the following content:

(1) Community and Ecosystem Operation Innovation: In the digital age, the web-like many-to-many user interaction replaces the linear one-to-one user interaction. Innovating the operation of user communities and introducing stakeholders and social resources is an irreversible trend. This is introduced in the later section "Six Types of Innovation Supporting Service Digital Transformation" under "Community and Ecosystem Operation Innovation".
(2) Service Method Innovation: Service is not only a continuation of sales, but also the beginning of sales. Therefore, another important purpose of service is to create entrances, form stickiness, and generate trust. This is introduced in the later section "Six Types of Innovation Supporting Service Digital Transformation" under "Service Method Innovation".

© China Science and Technology Press Co., Ltd. 2025
J. Yang, *Sales and Service Digital Transformation*,
https://doi.org/10.1007/978-981-96-5961-6_3

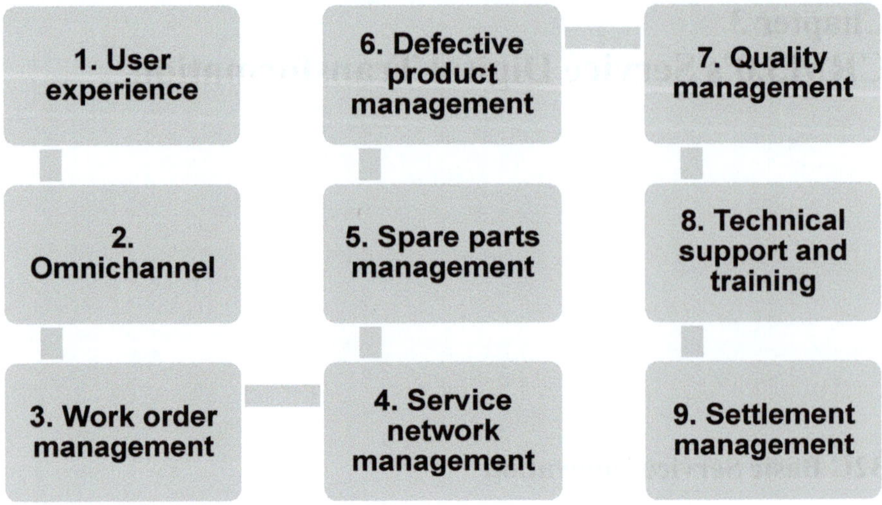

Fig. 3.1 Nine areas of B2C services

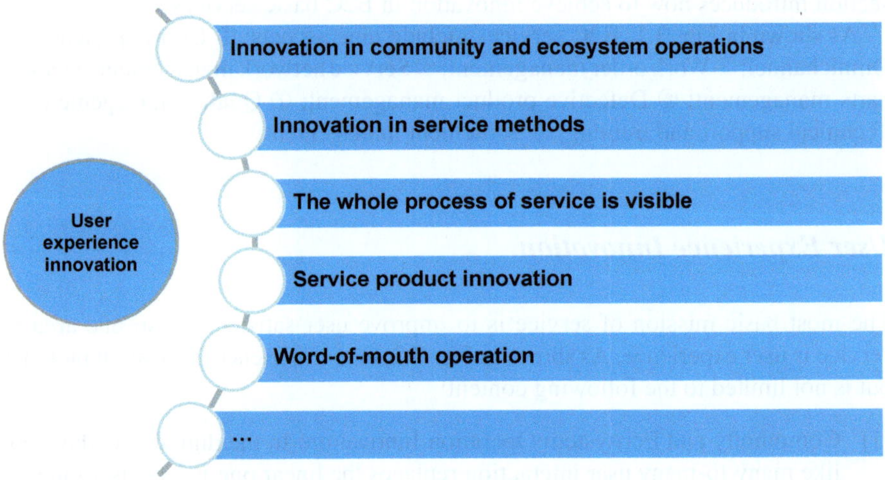

Fig. 3.2 User experience innovation

(3) Full Process Visibility of Service: Only when the service process is fully visible to users can users understand and feel at ease, reducing complaints; only when the service process is fully visible to service managers can they correct deviations and allocate resources during the process, improving service satisfaction. Full process visibility of service can be broken down into many key points,

and different industries have their unique needs, such as dispatch information, appointment information, service engineer location information, estimated arrival time, reassignment information, etc.

(4) Service Product Innovation: Relying solely on basic services such as installation and maintenance is difficult to significantly improve user stickiness. Indeed, we also need more service product innovations such as value-added services, ecological services, knowledge and platform services. More details can be found in the later chapter "Six Types of Innovation Supporting Service Digital Transformation" under "Innovation of Profit Models".

(5) Word-of-mouth operation: Service requires a transition from reducing user complaint rates to operating user word-of-mouth. The main difference is that reducing user complaint rates is passive, defensive, and merely meets the minimum demands of users; word-of-mouth operation is proactive, doing everything possible to impress users and encourage them to actively spread word-of-mouth about our products and services. This also requires us to change user evaluation indicators, such as from customer satisfaction index (CSI) to net promoter score (NPS). In addition, we can transition from focusing solely on individual satisfaction to focusing on the satisfaction of the entire community. More details can be found in the later chapter "Value Output Evaluation of Customer Satisfaction" under "Community Reference Value Evaluation Method of CRM3.0".

Omnichannel Innovation

In the digital age, omnichannel innovation includes not only access channel innovation, but also the empowerment of all-media interaction, machine learning and experience accumulation, voice and image AI applications, and IoT application technologies.

As shown in Fig. 3.3, omnichannel innovation includes but is not limited to the following:

(1) Touchpoint Integration: In today's digital age, we must ensure that services are ubiquitous, and users can communicate with the company in any way they have at hand. In addition to the customer service center, there are life touchpoints, such as cars and large-screen home appliances; application demand touchpoints, such as various company applications; social demand touchpoints, such as WeChat, Weibo, short videos, etc. in China, and Facebook, Twitter, WhatsApp, etc. overseas; usage demand touchpoints, such as official websites, instruction manuals, etc.

(2) Intelligent All-Media: Use various multimedia and artificial intelligence technologies to provide services, such as intelligent response, 360° portraits, remote resolution, automatic care, public opinion monitoring, etc.

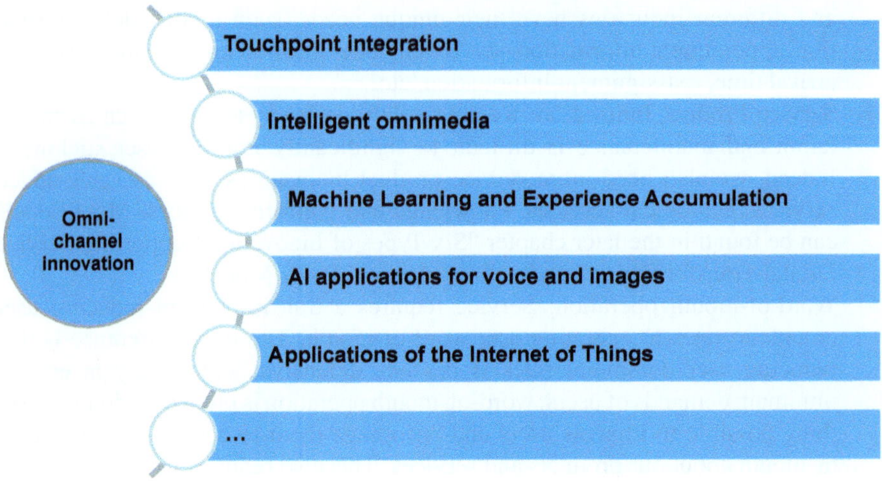

Fig. 3.3 Omni-channel innovation

(3) Machine Learning and Experience Accumulation: Currently, customer service center agents or robots often act as "intermediaries", recording customer problems and forwarding them to service engineers for resolution. This not only reduces service timeliness and customer satisfaction, but also increases time and monetary costs for both companies and users. Therefore, we need to accumulate service experience on the digital asset platform through machine learning to help service engineers and robots improve the first-time resolution rate of services.
(4) Voice and Image AI Applications: In the digital age, we can greatly improve service efficiency by using voice and image technologies, such as using image recognition technology to replace manual work in automatically completing service engineer photo identification tasks, and using voice robots to replace manual work in completing incoming installation and maintenance orders and outgoing return visit services, etc.
(5) IoT Applications: Provide automatic detection, automatic diagnosis, automatic repair, and automatic feedback services for products through IoT technology.

Work Order Management Innovation

The work order is the main line of the entire service, from receiving orders, dispatching orders, service engineers visiting, to closing orders, return visits, and settlements are all based on the work order. Therefore, work order management innovation is crucial for service efficiency and improving user satisfaction.

As shown in Fig. 3.4, work order management innovation includes but is not limited to the following:

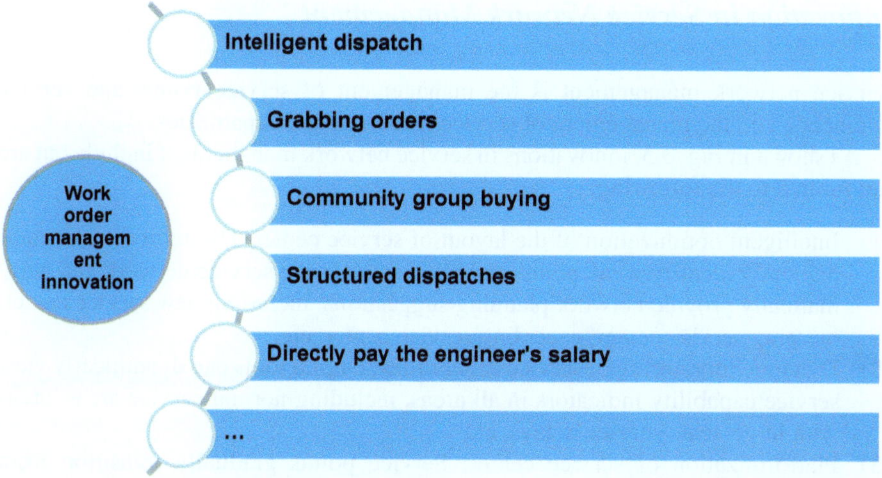

Fig. 3.4 Work order management innovation

(1) Intelligent Dispatching: Many people think that dispatching work orders to service engineers is a simple task, but for a company with tens of thousands or even tens of thousands of service engineers, this process can be very complex. It requires consideration of many factors such as distance, route, skills, types of services, installation and maintenance duration, etc. Moreover, it is necessary to establish different personalized models for each service engineer based on the products they are responsible for, their mastery of different types of services, and the duration of resolving different types of product failures. Currently, there are no particularly good digital tools that can perfectly solve this problem. Therefore, the service department will have a large number of roles such as service dispatchers, who are responsible for manually dispatching orders two or more times.
(2) Grabbing orders: For areas with insufficient service coverage, a model similar to ride-hailing or food delivery apps can be considered.
(3) Community group orders: For communities, a group order model similar to group buying can be adopted before providing door-to-door service, to meet as many community user service needs as possible at once.
(4) Structural dispatching: The rules for dispatching will often be adjusted. CRM companies need to support configurable dispatching rules, which can be configured based on many dimensions such as product, skills possessed by the service point, the block where the service point is located, different sources of work orders, user requirements, etc.
(5) Directly pay the engineer's salary: There needs to be the ability to directly pay service engineers, which is the only way to effectively manage them. However, this involves many issues such as invoices, third-party payments, profit-sharing ratios, mobile terminals, etc.

Innovation in Service Network Management

Service network management is the management of service points and service engineers, i.e., the management of service resources and capabilities.

As shown in Fig. 3.5, innovations in service network management include but are not limited to the following:

(1) Intelligent optimization of the layout of service center: Digital tools can automatically identify weak points and blind spots in the service network and automatically provide network planning suggestions, including new service center, merging service center, canceling service center, etc.
(2) Dynamic monitoring of service capabilities: Digital tools can dynamically view service capability indicators in all areas, including normal service areas, areas with large-scale service delays, etc.
(3) Platformization of service center: Service points gradually transition from focusing on work order execution to focusing on the operation of the entire regional service system, earning income based on operational indicators and customer satisfaction. This is further discussed in the later section "Contradictions between Service Business Models and Customer Satisfaction".
(4) Introduction of socialized services: The introduction of socialized service teams and personnel. Digital tools are needed to support processes such as certification, dispatching, assessment, settlement, etc.
(5) Transformation of service engineer capabilities: Service personnel transition from installation and maintenance engineers to product stewards, then to home stewards, and finally upgrade to life mentors. This transformation is achieved through changes in the positioning of on-site engineers, upgrades in the service

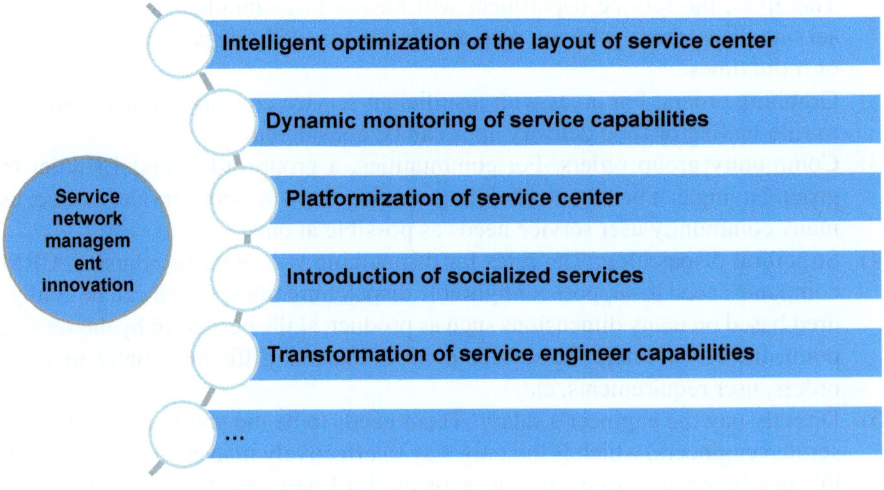

Fig. 3.5 Innovation in service network management

capabilities of on-site engineers, and changes in the assessment of on-site engineers. This is further discussed in the later section "Six Types of Innovations Supporting the Digital Transformation of Services" under "Transformation of Service Personnel Positioning and Capabilities".

Innovation in Spare Parts Management

Spare parts management mainly involves managing several levels of warehouses and spare parts, such as park warehouses, central warehouses, distribution warehouses, network point warehouses, service engineer warehouses, etc.

As shown in Fig. 3.6, innovations in spare parts management include but are not limited to the following:

(1) Intelligent prediction of spare parts: For large warehouses like central and park warehouses, the hit rate of spare parts can generally reach a high level through algorithm optimization. For warehouses with sparse data samples like service points, and also Service outlets are generally reluctant to tie up a lot of capital in stock, which often results in a less than satisfactory hit rate. Service engineers, unable to resolve issues in one visit due to lack of spare parts, often have to make a second visit, which is a major cause of complaints. This is where digital tools come in, using machine learning capabilities to continuously optimize the hit rate of spare parts at each outlet.

(2) Intelligent order matching: When an outlet is out of stock, the company needs to use digital tools to search the entire sales and service digital transformation spare parts network, including the surrounding service outlets, to provide the

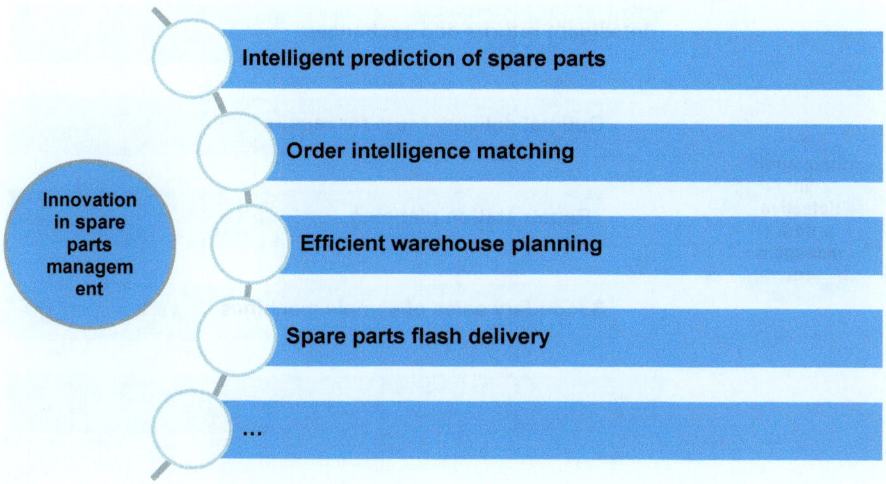

Fig. 3.6 Spare parts management innovation

most cost-effective and timely solution, and lock in the spare parts, rather than searching and locking in linearly from the lower-level warehouse to the upper-level warehouse.

(3) Efficient warehouse planning: By using digital tools to rationally plan the layout of the warehouse and the placement of goods, the efficiency of warehousing, outbound, and picking can be maximized.
(4) Spare parts flash delivery: When the service engineer arrives on site and finds that they have not brought spare parts, they can use digital tools to find available spare parts nearby (including from other service engineers, mobile spare parts warehouses, etc.) and have them quickly delivered to the site, effectively reducing the rate of second visits.

Innovation in Defective Product Management

Defective product management mainly includes returns and exchanges and the management of sample machines.

As shown in Fig. 3.7, innovations in defective product management include but are not limited to the following:

(1) Intelligent returns and exchanges: During the return and exchange process, digital tools can help users complete the entire process in the shortest possible time.
(2) Optimal delivery route for repairs: In some areas, due to the lack of repair capabilities for defective products and insufficient storage capacity of defective

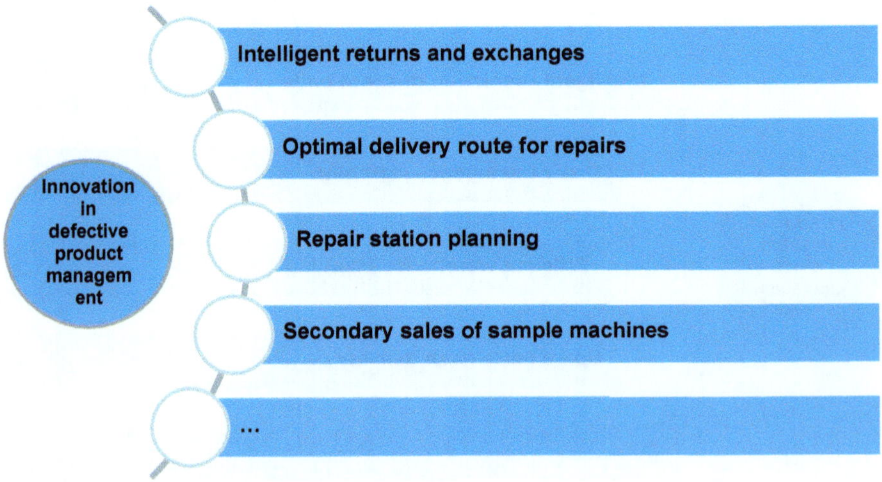

Fig. 3.7 Innovation in defect product management

product warehouses, losses are incurred due to warehouse explosions of defective products. Companies can use digital tools to adjust the rhythm and destination of defective product shipments, effectively reducing the rate of warehouse explosions of defective products.

(3) Repair station planning: Through digital tools, areas with weak repair capabilities for defective products can be automatically identified, and new repair stations can be planned.
(4) Secondary sales of sample machines Under the premise of legality and compliance, and without affecting the sales of genuine products, innovative models and allocation mechanisms can be used for effective sales of sample machines.

Quality Management Innovation

Quality management refers to the analysis, positioning, accountability, and improvement of product quality. As shown in Fig. 3.8, innovations in quality management include but are not limited to the following:

(1) Multi-tree integration: Through digital tools, diagnostic trees, quality improvement trees, fault logic trees, etc., can be combined into a simplified tree. The content of the simplified tree allows service engineers to quickly locate the cause of the fault and efficiently select repair measures and close orders through their mobile phones.
(2) Quality to person: Through digital tools, the workstation number and operator number that caused the product failure, as well as the model designer, can be quickly located.

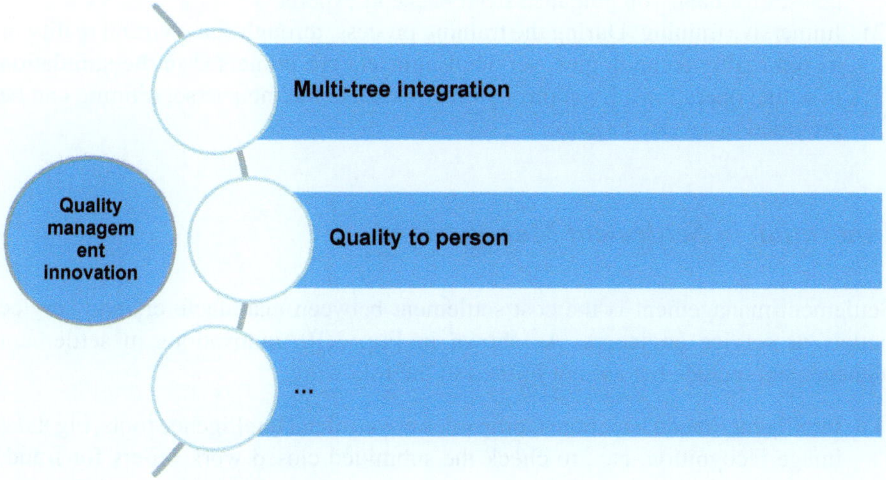

Fig. 3.8 Quality management innovation

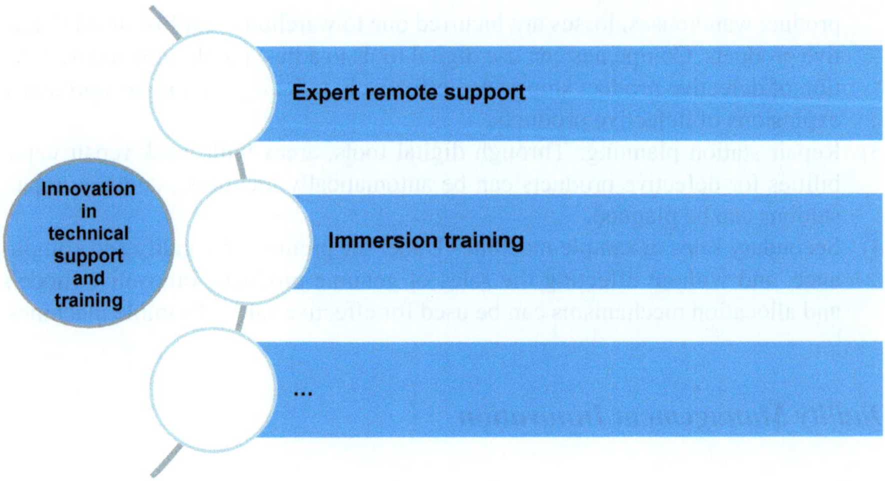

Fig. 3.9 Technical support and training innovation

Innovation in Technical Support and Training

Technical support and training refer to the support and training of service engineers.

As shown in Fig. 3.9, innovations in technical support and training include but are not limited to the following:

(1) Expert remote support: When service engineers are unable to solve problems on site, they can complete their work under the guidance of backend experts through remote video and other digital tools. They can even use mixed reality glasses for hands-on guidance from backend experts.
(2) Immersive training: During the training process, through some virtual reality or mixed reality technologies, service Engineers are immersed in the simulation of actual operations. Even through methods like the metaverse, training can be provided to service engineers.

Innovation in Settlement Management

Settlement management is the cost settlement between manufacturers and service outlets or service engineers. As shown in Fig. 3.10, innovations in settlement management include but are not limited to the following:

(1) Intelligent Fraud Detection: Companies use artificial intelligence tools, big data, image recognition, etc., to check the submitted closed work orders for fraud, greatly improving the efficiency and accuracy of fraud detection.

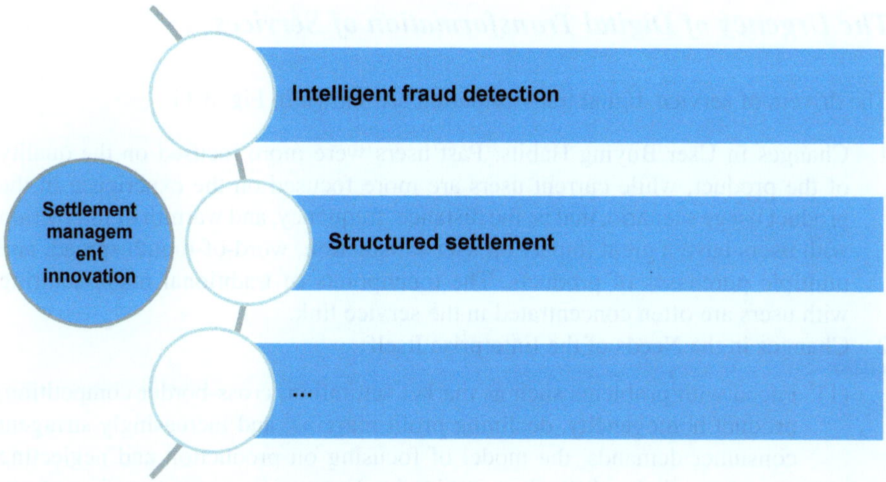

Fig. 3.10 Innovation in settlement management

(2) Structured Settlement: The settlement between manufacturers and service providers can sometimes be very complex. The settlement scheme is generated based on many factors such as the level of the service provider, product type, type of repair and installation, current incentives, distance to the site, service evaluation, etc., and these evaluation elements and payment standards often change. Therefore, digital tools are needed, which can support the dynamic configuration of settlement rules.

Summary > This section introduces nine aspects of B2C basic service innovation: ① User experience; ② Omnichannel; ③ Work order management; ④ Service network management; ⑤ Spare parts management; ⑥ Defective product management; ⑦ Quality management; ⑧ Technical support and training; ⑨ Settlement management.

Breaking Through the Transformation, Adding Wings

This section focuses on how to position and plan the digital transformation of services, and will introduce six aspects: ① The urgency of digital transformation of services; ② Liberating thoughts, repositioning services; ③ The aspects involved in the digitalization of services; ④ Positioning of service digitalization: innovation or transformation; ⑤ The planning method for the digital transformation of services (RMB-PT); ⑥ The six types of innovation that support the digital transformation of services.

The Urgency of Digital Transformation of Services

The drivers of service digital transformation are shown in Fig. 3.11.

1. Changes in User Buying Habits: Past users were more focused on the quality of the product, while current users are more focused on the experience in the product usage scenario, that is, the distance, frequency, and warmth of interaction with users have a great impact on user satisfaction, word-of-mouth spread, and multiple purchases of products. The touchpoints of traditional manufacturing with users are often concentrated in the service link.
2. Changes in the Needs of the Enterprise Itself:

   (1) Faced with problems such as market saturation, cross-border competition, product homogeneity, declining profit margins, and increasingly stringent consumer demands, the model of focusing on production and neglecting services will be difficult to maintain. Enterprises must transform from product-driven to user demand-driven, and must achieve three changes: ① From one-time income to continuous income throughout the user's life cycle; ② From a partial understanding of users to a comprehensive understanding of users; ③ From simple interaction with users to deep and high-frequency interaction. Service has become the best handle for all these changes.

   (2) The valuation of enterprises now is not only affected by sales and profits, but also by the integration of digital technologies, the stickiness and frequency of interaction with users, and the establishment of the ecosystem, among many other factors. For many enterprises, the best handle for digitalization

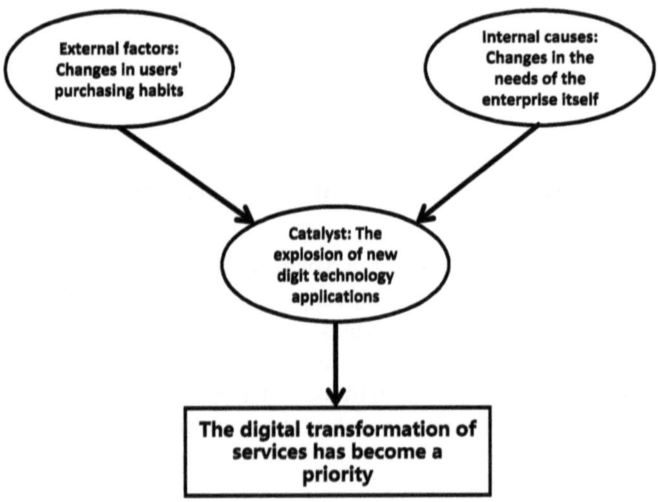

Fig. 3.11 Drivers of service digital transformation

and the establishment of the ecosystem is in the service link. Because this part is the easiest to improve user experience, cultivate multiple purchase habits, and form their own ecosystem through traffic.

3. The explosion of digital technology applications: With the popularization and promotion of technologies such as mobile tools, the Internet of Things, big data, artificial intelligence, social tools, maps, facial recognition, cloud computing, edge computing, mixed reality, blockchain, etc., it has become possible to create new service models through digital technology.

Freeing the Mind, Repositioning Services

For decades, we have always believed that the best service is no service (good product quality), or timely home visits, time-limited completion, one-time success, creating touching moments, etc. are the best services.

"An egg broken from the inside is rebirth; broken from the outside is abandonment." In today's digital age, we must free our minds and redefine what good service is. I believe that the best service in the digital age is like water, air, and sunlight. You use it every day and can't get rid of it, that is, users form a habit of the service. Good service has three main features:

(1) Service is everywhere.
(2) Service as you need.
(3) Service subtly influences.

As shown in Fig. 3.12, services in the digital age will consist of 1 person, 1 station, multiple screens, and 2 networks.

(1) 1 person: Service steward, that is, the creator, self-driven, evolving, and self-profitable;
(2) 1 station: Micro station, which is the interactive platform for users and stewards;
(3) Multiple screens: Multiple screens are the interface for information interaction, in order to achieve service everywhere, including mobile phones, TVs, car screens, home appliance screens, computer screens, etc.;
(4) 2 networks: 2 networks are the carriers of information transmission, namely the Internet of Things and the mobile Internet.

Aspects Involved in Service Digitization

When many companies talk about digital transformation, the first thing they think of is digital technology. Service digital transformation is not just the introduction of digital technology. Simply using new digital technology can be considered digital empowerment, but it is not considered digital transformation.

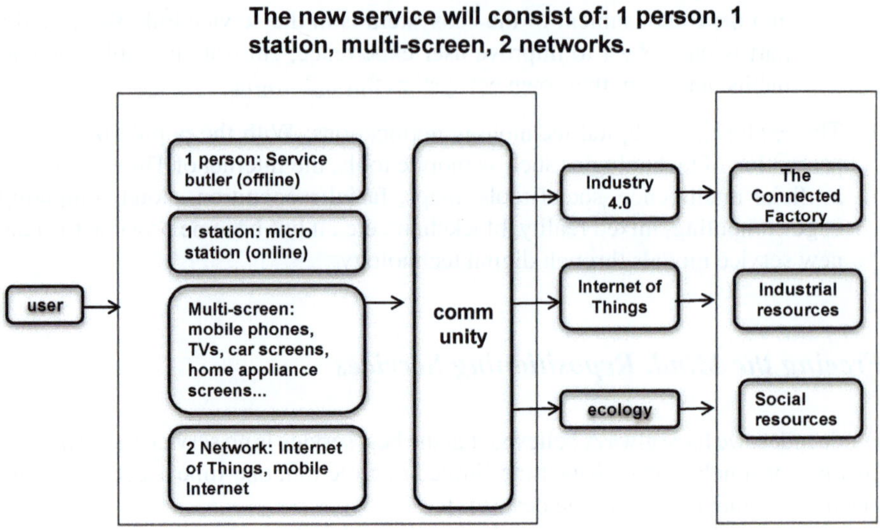

Fig. 3.12 Good services in the digital era

As shown in Fig. 3.13, if a company wants to do service digital transformation, it needs to consider the following issues:

(1) The company should consider in advance whether to do service digital transformation or service digital innovation. If you want to do service digital transformation, the top level of the company needs to plan and design service digital transformation from the company's positioning and corporate strategy.

Fig. 3.13 Aspects of service digitalization

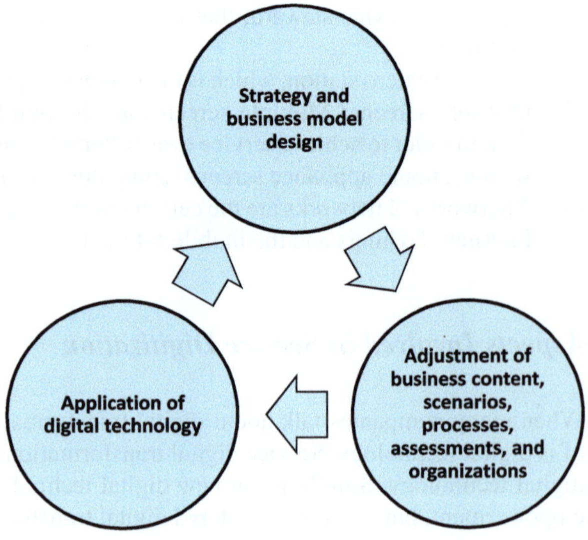

(2) Then carry out model design, such as business model, profit model, and operation model, etc. Afterwards, in order to support the model, various innovations and detonations are designed, followed by the design of organization, position, assessment, scene, process, etc. The RMB-PT method that will be introduced later can be used.
(3) When designing the process, companies need to consider how to empower and drive through new digital technologies.
(4) To achieve service digital transformation, there will be many obstacles in the original traditional corporate structure, and the company needs to have the courage and determination to establish a self-evolving organization that drives digital transformation.

Service Digital Positioning: Innovation or Transformation

In the process of service digital transformation, each company's starting point and current situation are different, and each company's demands are also different. Therefore, companies can choose to do a comprehensive and thorough service digital transformation according to their own situation; or focus on a certain point, do local improvement and improvement, that is, digital innovation.

As shown in Fig. 3.14, the different positioning of services by companies determines the different directions of service digitization, Strategies and implementation paths. There is no right or wrong, it's just different future positioning of services by the top management of the company.

Service Digital Transformation Planning Method (RMB-PT)

As shown in Fig. 3.15, if a company is determined to carry out service digital transformation, that is, it wants to make service digital changes from a strategic and business model perspective, it can use the RMB-TP model to plan the implementation strategy and steps.

Step 1: First, analyze and understand the industry direction and competitors. Companies can learn from benchmark companies, but they don't have to completely imitate them. Because each company has its own genes, it is difficult to emulate the success of other companies. What companies really need to think about is how to be the best version of themselves. Next, look at your own resources and see what the company's greatest strengths and usable resources are. The most important point in model design is to design a service digital transformation path that has the characteristics of the company based on its own resources and features.

Step 2: Based on market insights and the situation of own resources, design a service digital transformation model that suits the company's own characteristics. This will involve six aspects: ① Innovation in service methods; ② Innovation in

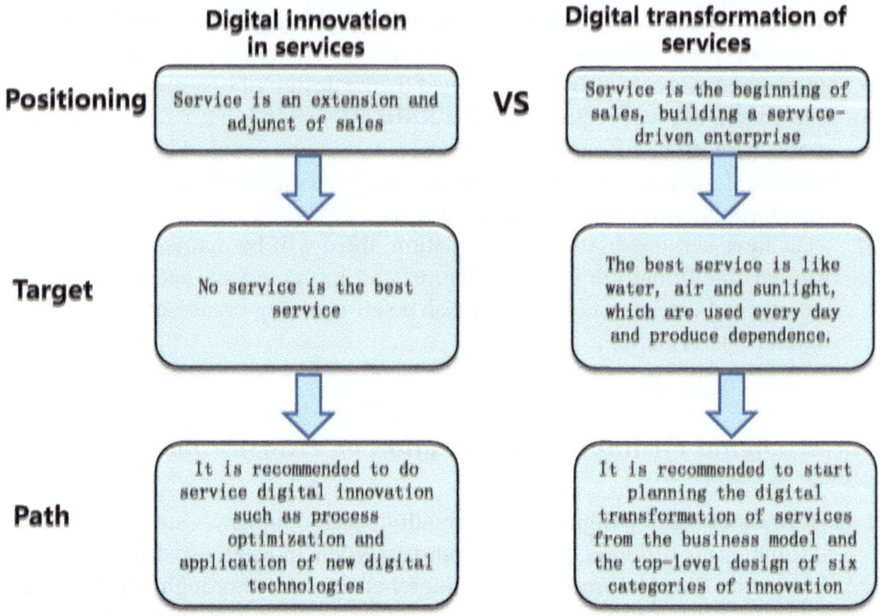

Fig. 3.14 Service digitalization is positioned in two ways

profit models; ③ Transformation of service personnel positioning and capabilities; ④ Innovation in service support systems; ⑤ Innovation in community and ecosystem operations; ⑥ Innovation in digital tools.

Step 3: In the service digital transformation, the company needs to set short-term goals. That is, within half a year and a year, we can achieve quantifiable improvements in which businesses, and reach a consensus with the top management of the company on short-term goals and assessment indicators.

Step 4: After the model and ignition points are determined, the company ensures the landing of the model and ignition business indicators by optimizing or reconstructing scenarios, processes, organizations, positions, and assessments.

Step 5: Finally, develop corresponding tools through current digital technology to accelerate the implementation of service digital transformation.

Six Types of Innovation Supporting Service Digital Transformation

As shown in Fig. 3.16, the digital transformation of enterprise services can be considered from the following six aspects: ① Innovation in service methods; ② Innovation in profit models; ③ Innovation of service personnel positioning and capabilities; ④

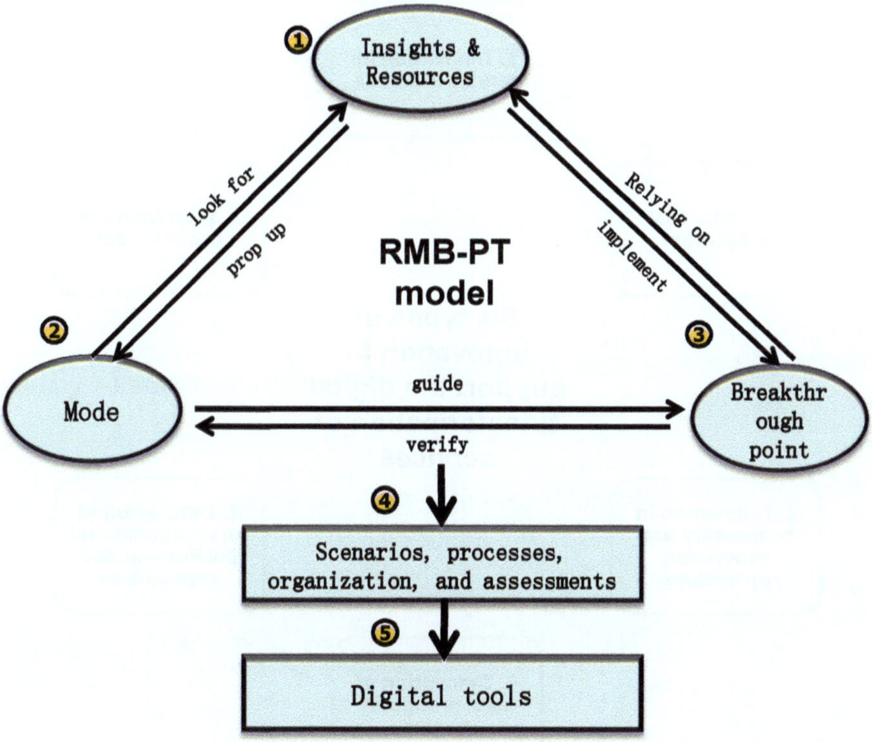

Fig. 3.15 RMB-PT planning model for digital transformation

Innovation in service support systems; ⑤ Innovation in community and ecosystem operations; ⑥ Innovation in digital tools.

Summary > This section is mainly for companies that want to carry out service digital transformation, including: ① Service digital transformation has become a top priority; ② Liberate thinking and reposition services; ③ The aspects involved in service digital transformation; ④ Service digital positioning: innovation or transformation; ⑤ Service digital transformation planning method (RMB-PT); ⑥ Six types of innovation supporting service digital transformation.

Six Types of Innovation Supporting Service Digital Transformation

As mentioned in the previous section, if a company wants to plan service digital transformation from the perspective of strategic and business model innovation, in order to support the transformation model design, CRM companies need to consider six types of innovation: ① Innovation in service methods; ② Innovation in profit models; ③

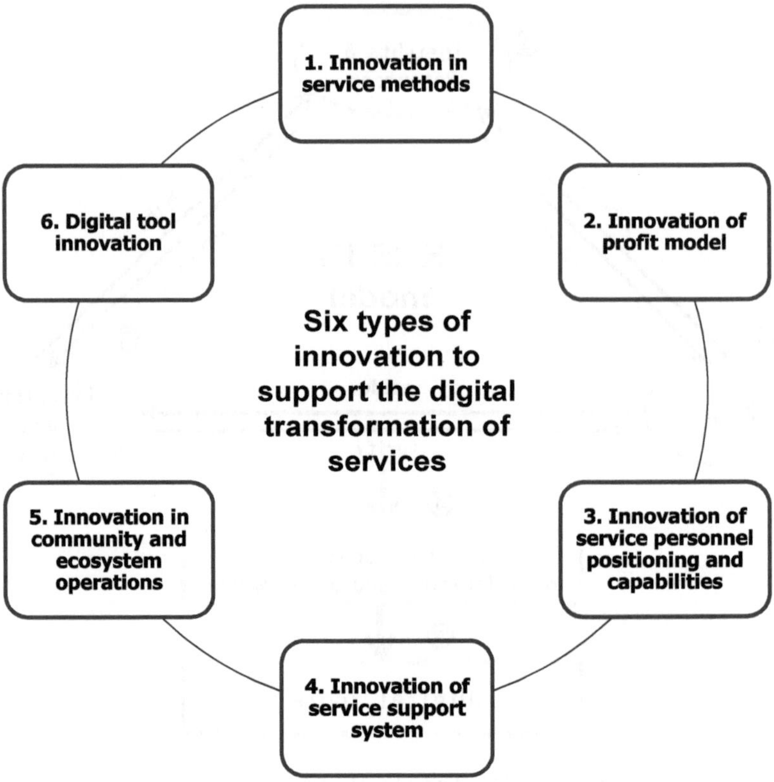

Fig. 3.16 Six types of innovations that support the digital transformation of services

Innovation in service support systems; ④ Transformation of service personnel positioning and capabilities; ⑤ Innovation in community and ecosystem operations; ⑥ Innovation in digital tools.

This section mainly introduces how to implement these six types of innovation.

Innovation in Service Methods

As shown in Fig. 3.17, the innovation of service model generally needs to go through five stages:

Change Service Positioning

This requires a change in concept, in a sense, it requires an internet mindset. Service is not the end, it is not just making the product available through installation and

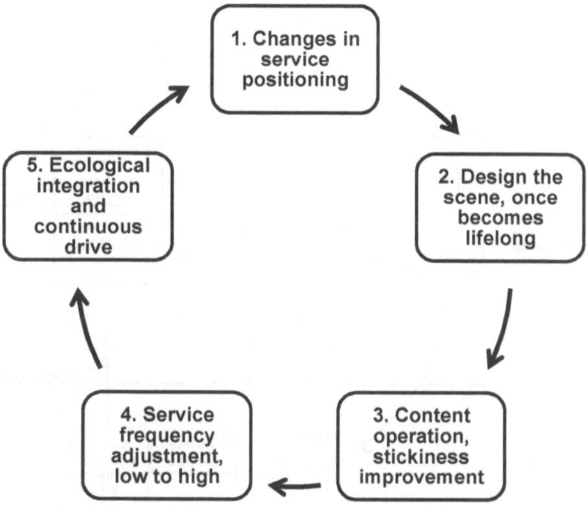

Fig. 3.17 Five steps of service model innovation

maintenance, but the starting point of continuous sales. The important mission of service is: ① to create an entrance; ② to form stickiness; ③ to generate trust.

Design Scenarios, Once Becomes Lifelong

Design service scenarios, transform one-time services into long-term interactive channels through service touchpoints. Because the content and process of services in each industry are different, it is difficult to have a unified planning and design for scenarios. The following is an example of a home repair service as a scenario design.

As shown in Fig. 3.18, in order to achieve the expected effect when designing service scenarios, the following points need to be paid attention to:

(1) Digital tools: In order not to affect the user experience, users need to complete the binding of the housekeeper and establish a lasting association through their mobile phones, in order to establish a lasting user interaction channel and provide housekeeper services. Therefore, it is not recommended to use an app on the client side, and WeChat public account and mini programs can be considered first.
(2) Pay attention to user experience: Don't bind for the sake of binding, be sure to integrate this process into the service scenario, so that users feel that all their operations are to improve their experience. For example, companies can use user evaluations, user viewing service content, etc., to achieve seamless binding and docking.
(3) Win–win with on-site engineers: Even the simplest binding process will delay the time of on-site engineers, companies must design a good benefit distribution mechanism, let on-site engineers benefit, this is crucial.

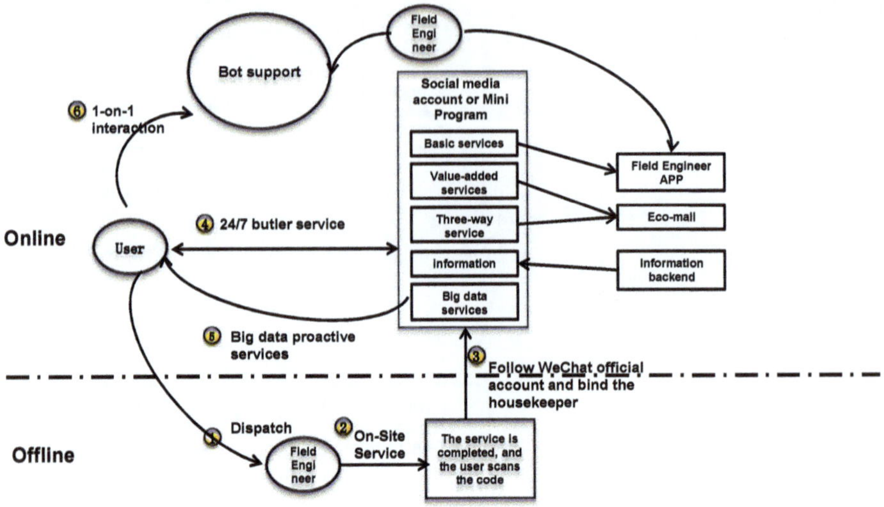

Fig. 3.18 Example of a service touchpoint scenario

(4) Introduce new digital technologies: For example, introduce robots and human operators to take over online user services, use data artificial intelligence and other technologies to establish proactive service models, etc. This can greatly improve interaction efficiency, reduce interaction costs, and achieve ubiquitous services.

Continuous Content and Activity Operations to Increase User Stickiness

After establishing a stable user interaction channel in the previous step, companies need to carry out continuous and stable content and activity operations, so as to gradually establish user trust. Trust is the cornerstone of interaction value-added, so in content operations, we need to have enough guarantees in terms of personnel and funds. In "Community and Ecological Operation Innovation", we will introduce how to integrate touchpoints, ignite communities, and parallel ecosystems.

Service Frequency Adjustment: Converting Low-Frequency Services into High-Frequency Services

Most companies' services are low-frequency services, which require service only once every few months or even years. Due to the characteristics of the product itself, no matter how we design value-added services based on the product, it is impossible to become a high-frequency demand like catering or socializing. Low-frequency services limit the on-site engineer's deep understanding of user needs and are not conducive to users' strong dependence and trust in on-site engineers.

So we can change our thinking, the service object changes from 1 user to 1 community. China's 1.4 billion population is distributed in 300,000–500,000 communities and about 700,000 villages. Services for individuals are low-frequency, but for communities, they are high-frequency. Services for communities have the following characteristics:

(1) Demand consistency Residents in the same community have similar income levels, home environments, etc., so they often choose similar products and services.
(2) Fast dissemination Each community has its own homeowner group, second-hand goods group, interest group, etc., so Related products and services are highly susceptible to word-of-mouth propagation.
(3) Service convenience: The cost of having on-site engineers continuously serve the same community is the lowest, and the service is the fastest.
(4) Maximum output: The service demand that can be generated by a community of thousands or tens of thousands of people is huge and continuous, enough to allow on-site engineers to devote themselves fully to their work.

We do not have the ability to meticulously cultivate every single one of the 1.4 billion users, but we do have the ability to meticulously cultivate every single one of the 300,000–500,000 communities. We can take the community as the basic unit, our goal is not to satisfy every user, but to satisfy every community as a whole. We can establish a new model of service and assessment centered on the community. Figure 3.19 shows a proposed design for a high-frequency interaction model centered on the community. More content can be found in the next section "Guiding C-end users to irrigate B-end everything".

Ecological Integration, Continuous Driving

Through the continuous import of traffic and demand, integration with offline and online ecosystems, companies can form new profit models, providing continuous support and driving force for the digital transformation of services.

Figure 3.20 shows how companies can establish community operations through service touchpoints, connect with IoT information, promote interactive value-added, and collaborate with offline stores to promote the closed-loop of product sales. The specific methods are detailed in the next section "Guiding C-end users to irrigate B-end everything".

In the 5th step of interactive value-added, the company will complete the transformation from a cost center to a profit center. The following will introduce how companies can innovate their profit models.

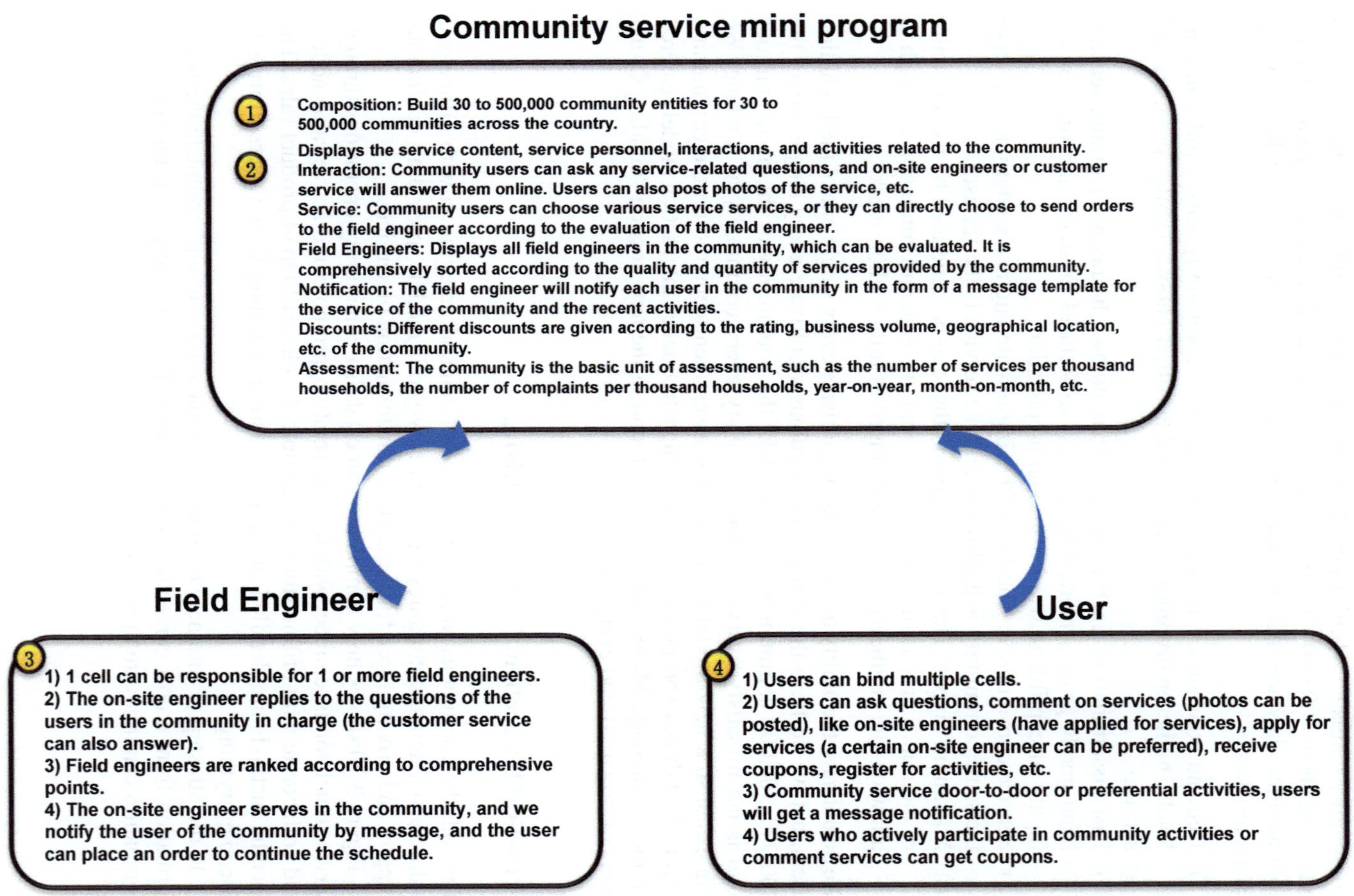

Fig. 3.19 Design of a community-centric high-frequency interaction mode

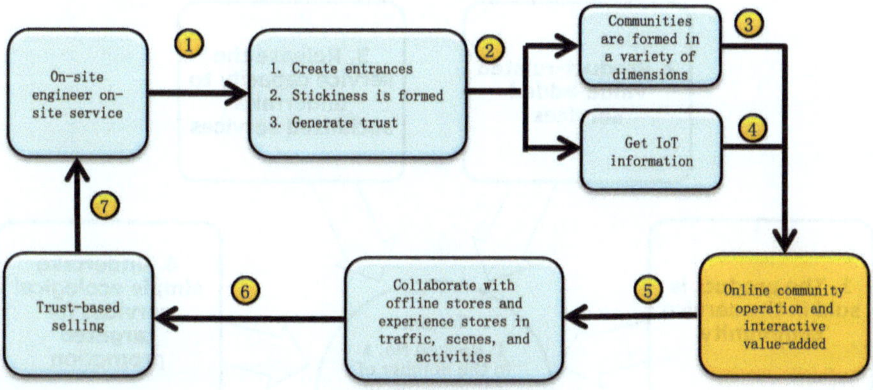

Fig. 3.20 Closed-loop digital service process

Innovation of Profit Models

The topic of how services can transform from a cost center to a profit center has been discussed for a long time, but few have succeeded. Digital technology provides strong support for accelerating service profitability.

As shown in Fig. 3.21, basic services are often in-house services, which are costs for companies. Knowledge and platform services have high profits, but they are difficult, require huge construction costs, and need to avoid the crush of internet giants.

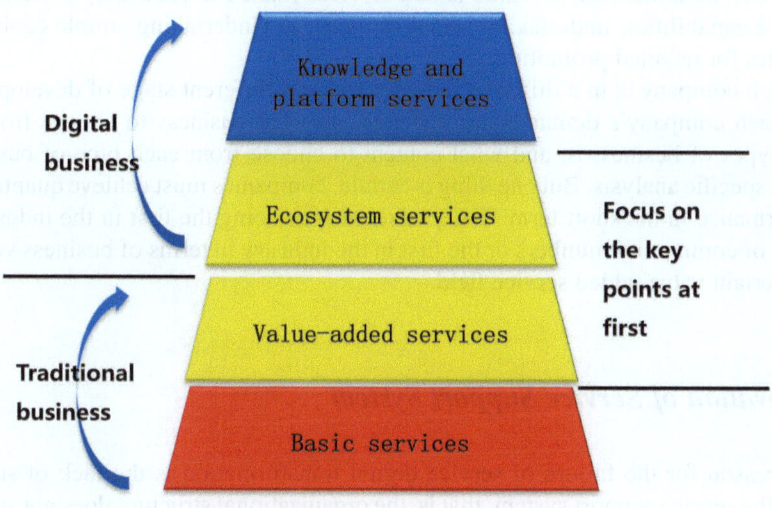

Fig. 3.21 Service monetization method

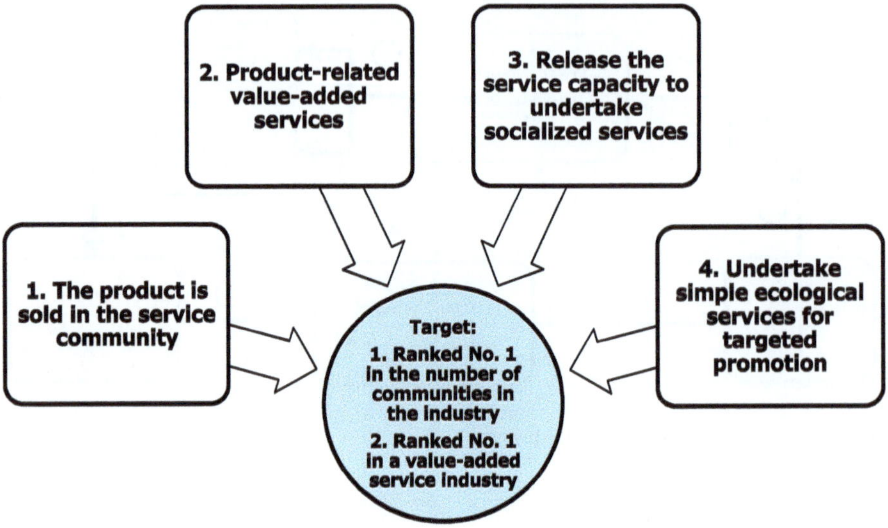

Fig. 3.22 Selecting a service profit method

Therefore, traditional companies can start with value-added services and simple ecological services. If you want to achieve a breakthrough quickly and rank in the top three in the industry, you must rely on your core products, and it is easier to succeed from product value-added services.

As shown in Fig. 3.22, in the early stage of service digital transformation, companies can choose from the following four relatively easy businesses: ① Product sales in service communities; ② Value-added services related to products; ③ Release of service capabilities, undertaking social services; ④ Undertaking simple ecological services for targeted promotion.

Each company is in a different industry and at a different stage of development, and each company's demands are different, so what business to choose from the four types of businesses, and what content to choose from each type of business, needs specific analysis. But one thing is certain, companies must achieve quantifiable performance in the short term (1–2 years), such as being the first in the industry in terms of community numbers or the first in the industry in terms of business volume in a certain value-added service field.

Innovation of Service Support System

One reason for the failure of service digital transformation is the lack of support from the service support system, that is, the organizational structure does not support service digital transformation.

It is very difficult to carry out strategic and model service digital transformation within traditional companies, because the concepts and management mechanisms within traditional companies are like defense systems, which will reject and expel this kind of transformation. We can Viewing the digital transformation of services as a new venture, the more and deeper a company does, the greater the impact on the company's internal operations, the more problems are exposed, and the greater the resistance and criticism it faces. Therefore, if a company wants to successfully transform its services digitally, it must nurture it in the right soil and environment.

Figure 3.23 is an example of the organizational structure of a company's digital transformation of services. There are two core points:

(1) Establish a new service value-added company or department, positioned as a profit center, including departments such as product value-added, community operations, ecological cooperation, and marketing, which are primarily responsible for revenue and user experience. Grant the new company management rights, personnel rights, and distribution rights, enabling it to be self-driven, self-organized, self-profitable, and self-evolving.
(2) Provincial-level service organizations adopt a dual reporting system, reporting to both the original service platform and the new service value-added company, so that the new service value-added company or department has the ability to use the original company's service resources when starting.

Transformation of Service Personnel Positioning and Capabilities

The company's existing on-site service engineers basically have the ability to install and maintain the company's existing products, but if we want to do interactive value-added and ecological income, these abilities are far from enough. Sales skills, communication skills, and community promotion abilities are must-haves for on-site engineers. This requires a certain change in the positioning and capabilities of on-site engineers. Therefore, we will face three problems: ① changes in the positioning of on-site engineers; ② upgrades in the service capabilities of on-site engineers; ③ changes in the assessment of on-site engineers.

As shown in Fig. 3.24, on-site engineers need to gradually complete the transition from the current on-site engineers to product stewards, to home housekeeper, and then to life coach, which is what the consulting field always says from being a customer's apprentice, to assistant, to friend, and then to mentor. We do not require every on-site service engineer to be able to advance to the later stages, as long as a certain proportion of personnel can successfully transition. In addition, we can recruit some elite teams from society to quickly complete the transformation process of the service team.

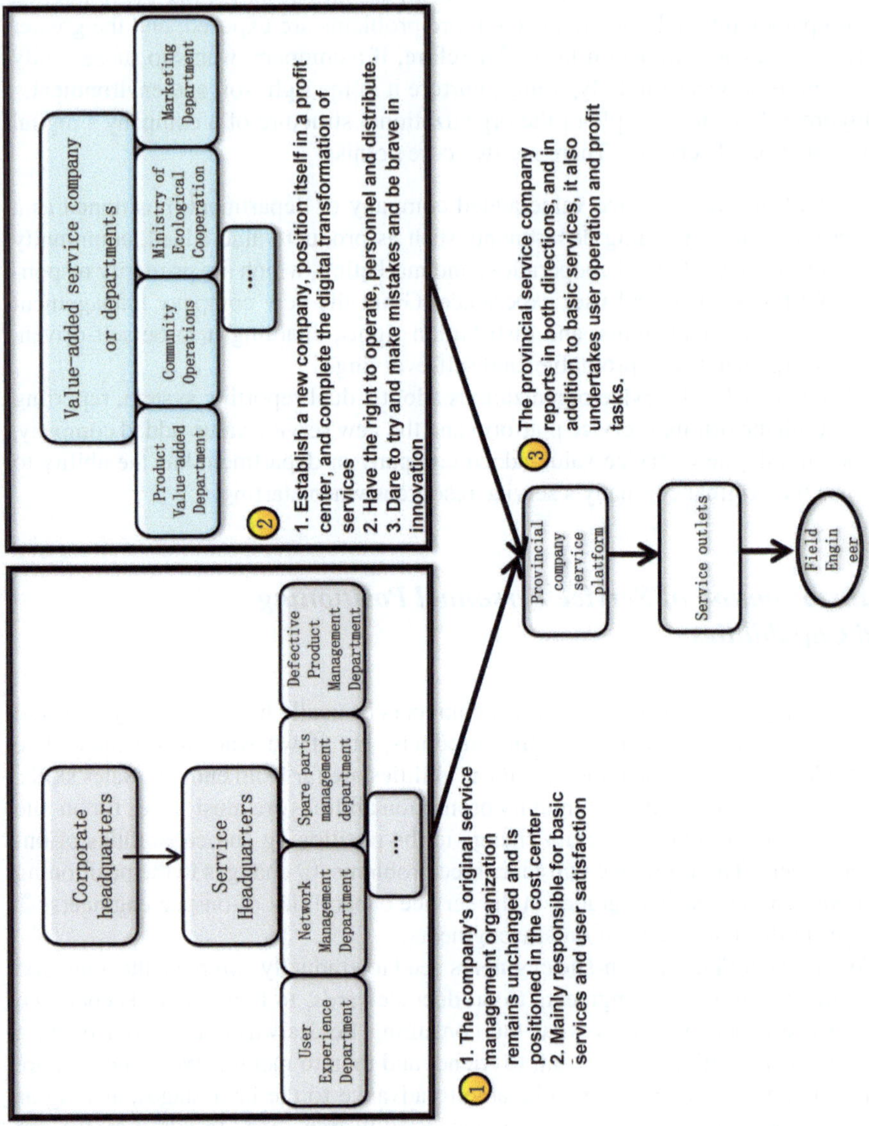

Fig. 3.23 Organizational structure for driving service digital transformation

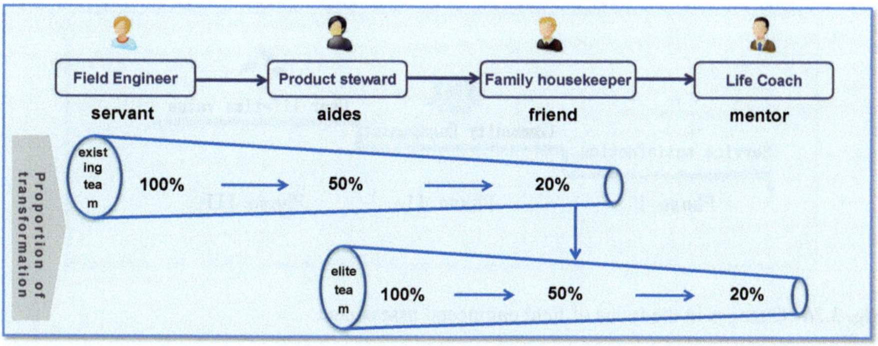

Fig. 3.24 Transformation of field engineer positioning

As shown in Fig. 3.25, the field engineer team can gradually complete the improvement of service capabilities through four ways to meet the transformation requirements: ① introduce new people, build an elite team; ② establish a powerful empowerment mechanism and training team like insurance companies; ③ guide field engineers to self-improve through career development paths; ④ change the assessment method, guide on-site engineers to transform through the baton of assessment.

As shown in Fig. 3.26, through the baton of assessment, we want to gradually guide on-site engineers to shift their energy from one-time service to sustainable management, and the assessment method also shifts from only focusing on service satisfaction, upgrading to community activity, and then upgrading to user lifetime value.

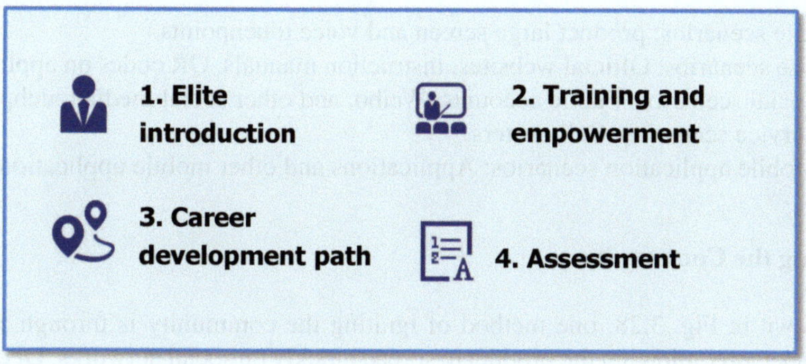

Fig. 3.25 Ways to improve the service capability of field engineers

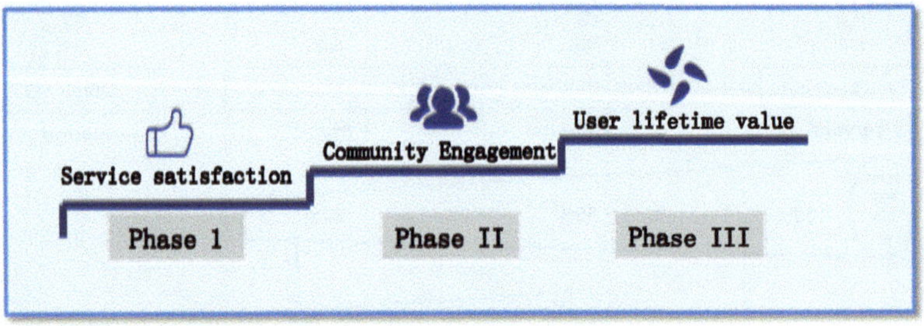

Fig. 3.26 Changes in the focus of field engineers' assessment

Innovation in Community and Ecological Operations

Innovation in community and ecological operations is generally achieved in three steps: ① integrate touchpoints; ② ignite the community; ③ parallel the ecology.

Integration of Touchpoints

Some companies can integrate as many as hundreds of touchpoints, spanning many departments, so it is recommended that companies develop interface application packages, provide standard interfaces for various touchpoints, and touchpoints can be directly integrated by calling the interface.

Figure 3.27 introduces the five types of service touchpoints that need to be integrated.

(1) Life scenarios: product large screen and voice touchpoints.
(2) Use scenarios: Official websites, instruction manuals, QR codes on appliances.
(3) Social scenarios: Public accounts, Weibo, and other social media touchpoints.
(4) Service scenarios: Call centers.
(5) Mobile application scenarios: Applications and other mobile applications.

Igniting the Community

As shown in Fig. 3.28, one method of igniting the community is through service spokespersons, allowing the product to spread quickly on social networks. Of course, using this method also requires content operation, incentive mechanisms, and task management measures. More content can be found in the next section "Guiding the Water of C-end Users to Irrigate the B-end of Everything".

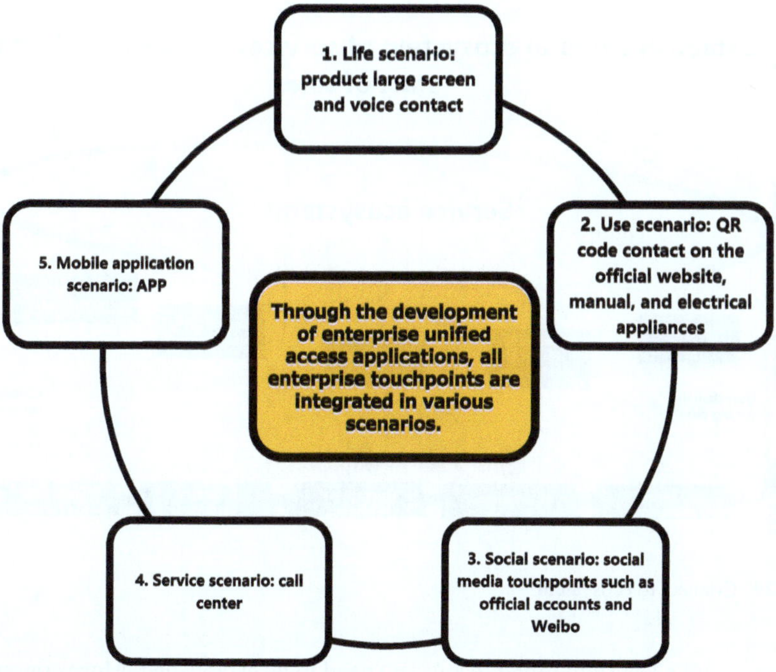

Fig. 3.27 Integrating five types of service touchpoints

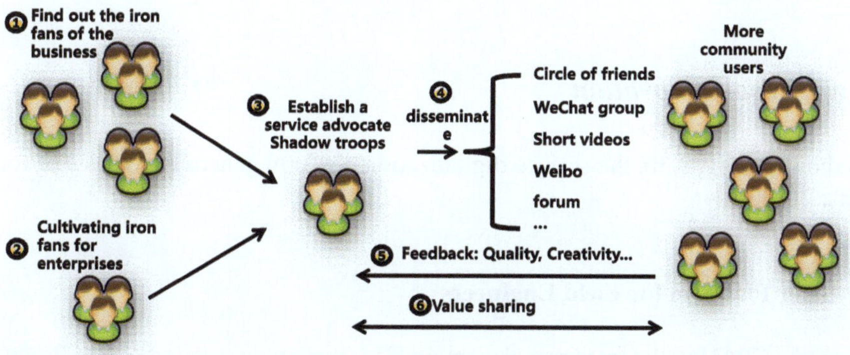

Fig. 3.28 Igniting the community

Connect to Ecosystem

As shown in Fig. 3.29, to connect the service ecosystem, new mechanisms (service mechanisms, third-party resource mechanisms, assessment mechanisms, value-sharing mechanisms, and terminal training mechanisms) and new resources (team resources, information technology resources, operational resources, industrial

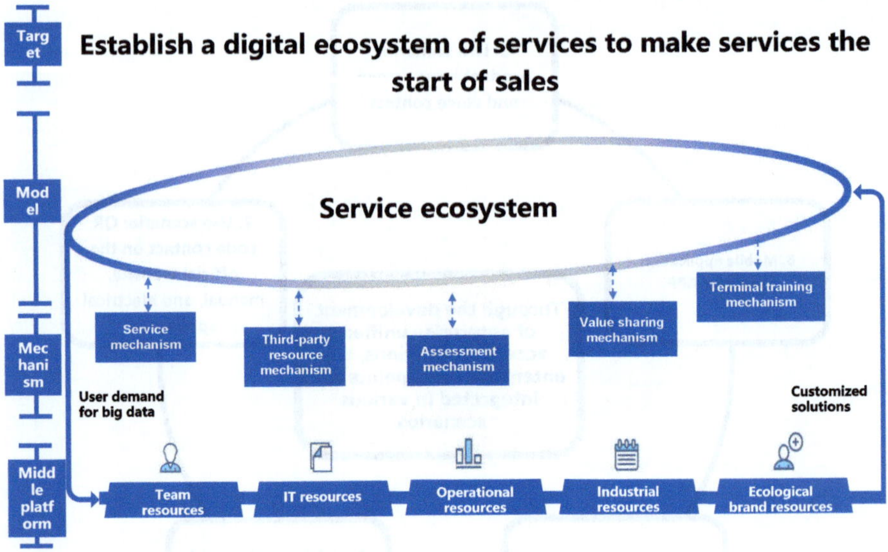

Fig. 3.29 Connect to ecosystem

resources, and ecosystem brand resources) need to be established. More content can be found in the next section "Guiding the Water of C-end Users to Irrigate the B-end of Everything".

Digital Tool Innovation

As shown in Fig. 3.30, the service digitalization platform generally consists of four parts.

A Maker Platform for Field Engineers

This is the CRM intelligent terminal mentioned in the previous section "CRM Product Innovation in the Digital Age". It mainly helps service personnel achieve 3 transformations: 1. Centralization → Decentralization, 2. Passive order taking → Active entrepreneurship, 3. Selling goods for commission → Operating users for commission. This platform is the work, learning, and entrepreneurship platform for on-site engineers.

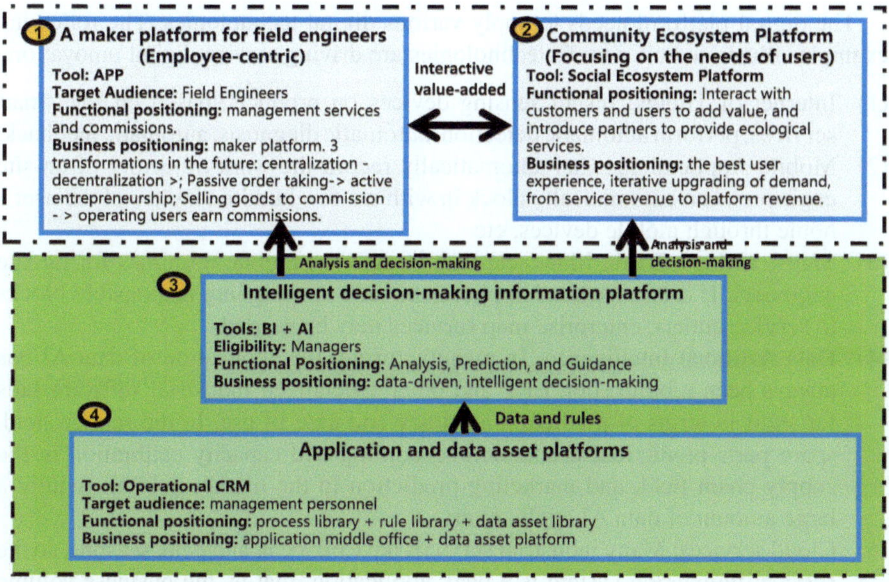

Fig. 3.30 Service digital platform architecture

Community Ecosystem Platform

This is the CRM win–win platform mentioned in the previous section "CRM Product Innovation in the Digital Age". It is a platform for on-site engineers, customers, users, and ecosystem partners to interact and add value. This platform is mainly used to achieve the best user experience, demand iteration upgrade, and interactive value addition.

Intelligent Decision-Making Information Platform

This is the CRM intelligent brain mentioned in the previous section "CRM Product Innovation in the Digital Age". Using the experience gained from machine learning and artificial intelligence, it predicts, decides, and commands all service-related matters through seven command centers.

Application and Data Asset Platform

This is the CRM application platform and CRM data asset platform mentioned in the previous section "CRM Product Innovation in the Digital Age". It completes the output and management of various capabilities in the service process, as well as the accumulation and application of various experiences.

The digital platform needs to apply various digital technologies. The following examples illustrate how new IT technologies are driving service digital innovation:

(1) Internet of Things: Install sensing devices on products, based on IoT smart services, perform automatic detection, automatic diagnosis, automatic feedback.
(2) Mobile Applications: Can automatically record the work trajectory of on-site engineers, can automatically clock in within a few hundred meters of the user's home through mobile devices, etc.
(3) Maps: AMaps, Baidu Maps, etc. can be used as mobile terminals for on-site engineers. If it is a backend application, such as assigning responsible blocks to service outlets, enterprise map services may be needed.
(4) Data Artificial Intelligence: In manufacturing, the application of data AI has always been a blind spot. ERP and other specialized Industrial software falls far short in terms of prediction accuracy and ease of use. In the service field, spare parts prediction, production scheduling and capacity calibration in the supply chain field, and marketing prediction in the market field all require a large amount of data AI applications.
(5) Cloud services: Many industrial services have off-peak and peak seasons, so the service digitization system is a peak application, that is, the business volume during the peak season is several times or even dozens of times the usual, so it needs on-demand cloud services, which can greatly save costs and improve efficiency.
(6) Face recognition: The phenomenon of mismatch between the on-site engineer and the order is quite common, which greatly affects the user experience and service quality. Enterprises can use technologies such as face recognition to ensure that the engineer who provides the on-site service is the engineer who was dispatched.

New era, new services. The new generation is gradually becoming the main force of consumption, they pay more attention to experience and feelings, and their requirements for services and purchases are also different. As times change, services also need to keep up with the times. The digital transformation of services is a hurdle that enterprises will face sooner or later. The digital transformation of services is difficult and not difficult. It mainly depends on the determination and courage of corporate decision-makers. As long as three things are done well, success can be achieved: ① Take the right path; ② Choose the right people; ③ Distribute money well.

Summary > This section introduces six types of innovations that support the digital transformation of services: ① Innovation in service methods; ② Innovation in profit models; ③ Innovation in service support systems; ④ Transformation of service personnel positioning and capabilities; ⑤ Innovation in community and ecosystem operations; ⑥ Innovation in digital tools.

Watering of B-End by C-End Users

This section will introduce an application of service digital transformation. Due to the rise of social software and new retail in recent years, domestic software applications for the C-end have reached the extreme. But for B-end software applications, such as ERP, CRM, PLM, etc., the pace of digital innovation and transformation is not large, and it has never been able to connect with the C-end. Starting from 2018, the market began to focus on B-end applications, and corporate giants such as Alibaba and Tencent, as well as capital giants such as Hillhouse Capital Group, are all laying out the B-end application market. The next ten years will be the "golden decade" for B-end applications.

Countless people are thinking about how to empower B-end applications with the capabilities and traffic of the C-end, so that companies can "overtake on a curve" and quickly gain an advantage in the B-end market. The demand in this area is real and very large. For example, in the manufacturing field, it is necessary to collect a large amount of user demand and orders for large-scale customization; in the R&D field, it is necessary to collect user feedback and suggestions for design; in the sales and supply chain field, it is necessary to formulate production plans based on user future purchase intentions. If a company can control C-end users, it can have an absolute advantage in product design, customization flexibility, and production and sales coordination.

But where to start to "draw water from C-end users to irrigate the B-end of everything" has always been a problem that troubles all companies. In my experience, the breakthrough must be in the service field. Because if you want to use the water of C-end users for B-end, the premise must be that there is a place to store water, forming a large user reservoir. Take the manufacturing industry as an example, in the fields of manufacturing, R&D, supply chain, etc., they rarely interact with users, so it is impossible to form User Reservoir. In the field of marketing, companies basically sell through e-commerce and channels or stores, separated from users by a layer. Even if they have their own specialty stores, it is difficult for salespeople and customers (note that they are customers, not users) to form a trust relationship and establish continuous contact during the sales process. Many products are low-frequency consumption, and customers will not repurchase within a few years, so even if they are attracted by giving membership benefits, they are not attractive. Only in the service link, users need to understand and pay attention to product maintenance information, you and the user may have a period of time alone, this is the best time to establish association and trust, forming a user reservoir.

As shown in Fig. 3.31, the "watering of B-end by C-end users" can be completed through three steps: ① Create an entrance through service, form user stickiness and generate trust; ② Introduce users, form a user reservoir, and generate dependence and activity through continuous content operation; ③ Value output, that is, guide the user demand in the user reservoir to the company's internal R&D department, offline specialty stores, product business department, Industry 4.0 platform, Internet of Things platform, corporate ecological platform, etc.

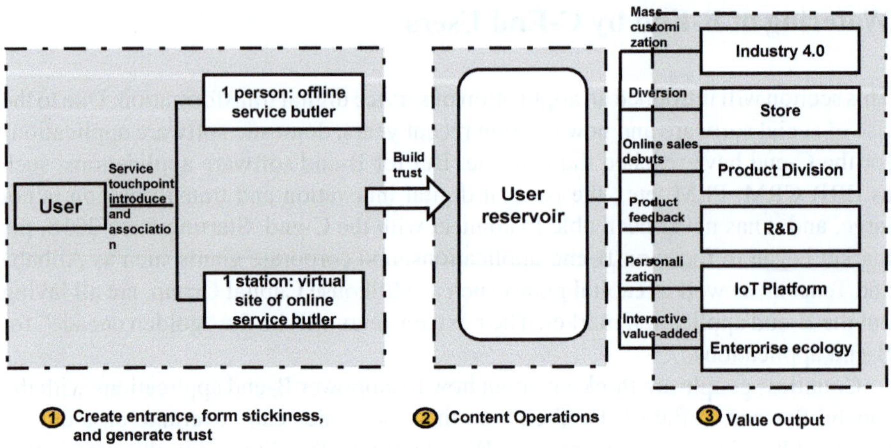

Fig. 3.31 Using the service as the entrance to attract C-end users

The most difficult here are the first and second steps, that is, how to bring users in through service, and how to operate the user reservoir. As for the third step, as long as there is a user reservoir, each department of the company knows best how to output value.

Below, I will introduce how to complete the introduction of users and the operation of the user reservoir in five steps.

Step 1: Decentralization, Operating the Individual Brand of Service Personnel

If you want to attract users, you must rely on service personnel, and service personnel must actively do this, otherwise what is brought in is dead water. If you want service personnel to willingly do this, you have to make service personnel feel that they are doing it for themselves. So this process must be decentralized, from being a company's service brand to the outside world, to being the brand of thousands of service personnel to the outside world. Everything that service personnel do is to operate their own brand. Of course, the individual brand of service personnel is endorsed by the company brand.

As shown in Fig. 3.32, service personnel operate their own brand through service decentralization. But if you want to operate your own brand, you must have the scene of service personnel establishing a steward relationship with users, so that service personnel can operate their own users. Moreover, once a steward relationship is established, service personnel can receive corresponding rewards for any consumption of users, which will greatly stimulate the enthusiasm of service personnel to operate their own brand.

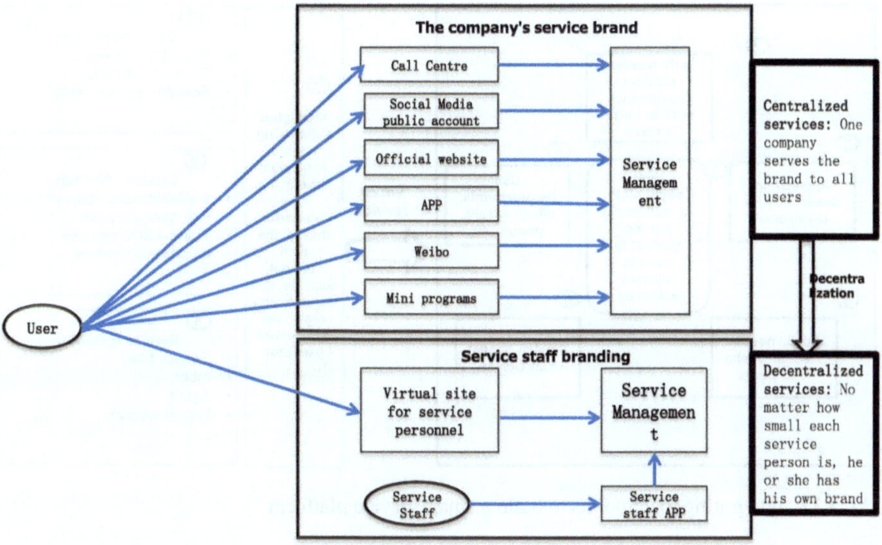

Fig. 3.32 Service decentralization example

Scene Design:

Figure 3.18 is an example of a scene where home service is used to establish a steward relationship. Through this scene, a channel for transforming one-time service into long-term interaction is introduced. When designing service scenes, in order to achieve the expected effect, the points that need to be paid attention to have been introduced in the previous Fig. 3.18, and will not be repeated here.

Step 2: Integrate Touchpoints, Build a Smart Service Platform

As shown in Fig. 3.33, it is far from enough to introduce users only through the scene of service personnel providing services. We need to integrate all touchpoints, build a service middle platform, and develop a smart service engine.

Integrate All Touchpoints

(1) Life needs: Integrate touchpoints on products, such as large screens.
(2) Application needs: Integrate all App touchpoints.
(3) Social needs: Integrate all WeChat, Weibo touchpoints.
(4) Service needs: Integrate voice, SMS, and email touchpoints such as call centers.
(5) Usage requirements: Integrate official website, instruction manual, and other touchpoints.

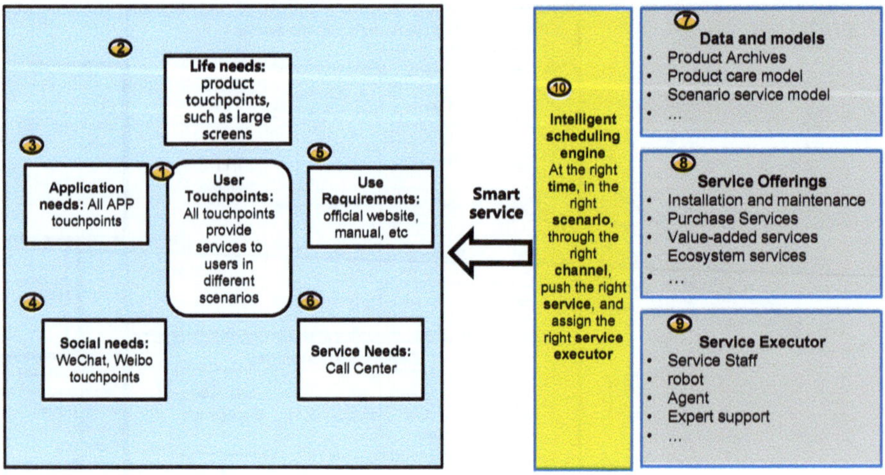

Fig. 3.33 Integrating touchpoints to build a smart service platform

Build a Service Platform

This refers to the CRM application platform and CRM data asset platform mentioned in the previous section "CRM Product Innovation in the Digital Age".

(1) Data and models: Relying solely on the proactive service of service personnel is far from enough. Enterprises need to establish a data-driven mechanism, triggering services automatically by establishing small user data. Small user data includes product archives, product maintenance models, scene service models, etc.
(2) Service offerings: After establishing a stable connection with users, the enterprise provides continuous and stable services for user interaction and value addition, such as installation and maintenance, purchase services, value-added services, ecological services, etc.
(3) Service executors: After establishing a stable connection with users, who will provide the service, such as service personnel, robots, seat members, expert support, etc.

Develop a Smart Service Engine

This refers to the CRM smart brain mentioned in the previous section "CRM Product Innovation in the Digital Age". To provide intelligent services, services must be ubiquitous and provided as needed, that is, at the right time, in the right scene, through the right channel, pushing the right service, and assigning the right service executor. This requires the development of a smart service engine based on small user data.

Step 3: Service Endorsement, Ignite the Community

After integrating all touchpoints and having a smart service platform, the next step for the enterprise is to have its own die-hard fans, that is, service endorsers, to help the enterprise spread and promote in the community, and create momentum for the enterprise.

As shown in Fig. 3.34, this refers to the CRM co-creation and win–win platform and CRM smart terminal mentioned in the previous section "CRM Product Innovation in the Digital Age".

(1) How to find the first batch of service endorsers: It is recommended that enterprises first develop service personnel as the first batch of endorsers.
(2) How to expand service endorsers: Enterprises can develop loyal members of the enterprise as service endorsers, such as gold card, silver card members; the first batch of endorsers can also expand the service endorser group by developing their friends and relatives.
(3) Endorser value sharing platform: Endorser management must have a matching digital platform.
(1) Endorser management. Manage endorser applications, approvals, promotions and demotions, permissions, etc.
(2) Task management. Assign various tasks to endorsers to execute, such as promotion tasks, event notifications, etc.
(3) Value sharing management. Rewards should be given according to the contribution of the endorser.
(4) Points management. Maintain the loyalty and activity of endorsers through points and points redemption.

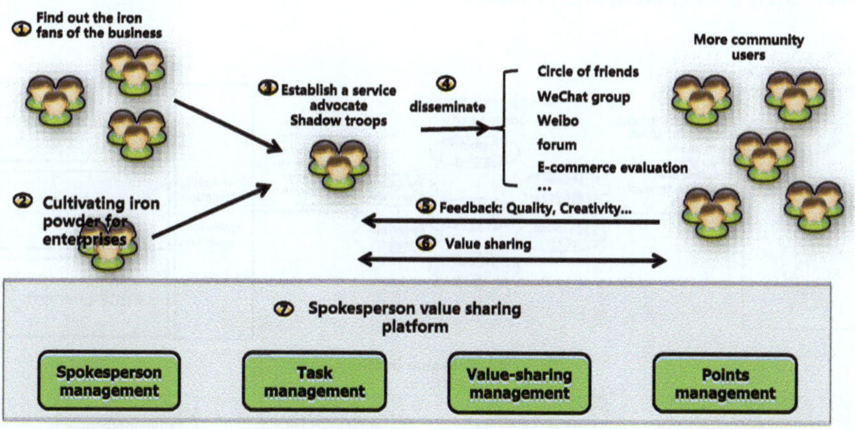

Fig. 3.34 Service endorsement and ignite the community

Step 4: Connected Ecosystems Create a Win–win Situation

As shown in Fig. 3.35, when the number of users reaches a certain level, it is necessary to parallel the ecology to maintain the stickiness and activity of users. This refers to the CRM co-creation and win–win platform mentioned in the previous section "CRM Product Innovation in the Digital Age".

Content Is King

At the beginning of ecological operation, "content is king" is a must. Enterprises need to segment users through content and divert users to different communities.

Diversified and Complementary Partners

Partners need to be diversified, including content providers, product and solution providers, and profit providers. The ecosystem requires diversity and complementarity.

Establishing an Ecological Value Sharing Platform

CRM companies should be the rule makers and regulators of the ecosystem, not the executors. They don't have to do everything themselves. Therefore, we need to establish a digital platform that allows partners to manage their own users and provide their own content and products.

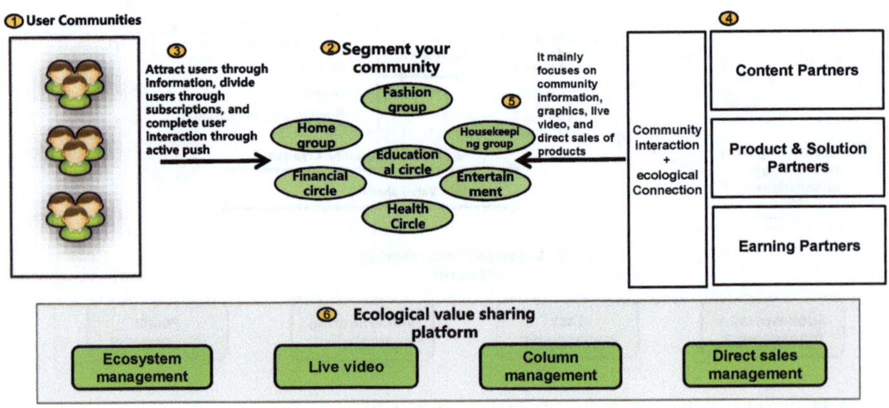

Fig. 3.35 Connected ecosystems create a win–win situation

Step 5: Service Tuning, Focusing on Small Communities

The final step is to consider what a company should do if, after attracting users, the activity level is still too low.

Many companies provide low-frequency services, offering services only once every few months or even years. Due to the nature of the product itself, no matter how the company designs value-added services based on the product, it cannot become a high-frequency demand like catering or socializing. Low-frequency services limit the service staff's deep understanding of user needs and make it difficult for users to develop strong dependence and trust in the service staff.

Therefore, we can change our thinking, and the service target changes from one user to one physical community. China's 1.4 billion population is distributed in 300,000–500,000 communities and about 700,000 villages. Services for individuals are low-frequency, but services for communities are high-frequency.

Suggestions for Mini-Program Functions

Establish a community entity for each of the 300,000–500,000 communities nationwide, displaying service content, service personnel interaction information, and activity information related to the community.

(1) Interaction: Community users can raise any service-related questions, and on-site engineers, customer service, or robots will answer online. Users can also share service-related photos, etc.
(2) Service: Community users can choose various services, or they can choose to dispatch orders to the on-site engineer based on the engineer's evaluation.
(3) On-site Engineers: The mini-program should display relevant information about all on-site engineers in the community. Users can evaluate the on-site engineers. The mini-program can comprehensively rank engineers based on the quality and quantity of services they provide for the community.
(4) Notification: The on-site engineer's service to the community, recent activities, etc., will be notified to each user in the community in the form of a message template.
(5) Discount: Different discounts are given based on the community's rating, business volume, geographical location, etc., with a unique approach for each community.
(6) Assessment: The basic unit of assessment is the community, such as the service volume per thousand households, the number of complaints per thousand households, year-on-year and month-on-month comparisons, etc.

Suggestions for Service Personnel Related Functions

(1) One or more on-site engineers can be responsible for each community.

(2) On-site engineers respond to questions from users in the communities they are responsible for.
(3) On-site engineers are displayed in order of comprehensive points.
(4) When the on-site engineer services the community, the relevant information should be notified to the community users in the form of a message, and users can place orders to continue scheduling.

Suggestions for User-Related Functions

(1) Users can bind multiple communities.
(2) Users can ask questions, review services (with the option to add photos), give thumbs up to on-site engineers (who have provided services), apply for services (with the option to prefer a certain on-site engineer), receive coupons, register for activities, etc., in the communities they have bound.
(3) Users will receive message notifications for home service in the community or discount activities, etc.
(4) Users who actively participate in community activities or review services can receive coupons.

Summary > This section introduces how to use service as a lever, through five steps, to guide the flow of end-users to irrigate everything on the business side. These five steps are: ① Decentralization, operating individual service personnel brands; ② Integrating touchpoints, building a smart service platform; ③ Service endorsement, igniting the community; ④ Ecological parallel, co-creation and win–win; ⑤ Service tuning, focusing on the community.

B2B Service Digital Innovation and Transformation

The previous chapters mainly focused on the service transformation of B2C. How B2B should transform in the digital age has always been a big confusion in the industry. More than a decade ago when I was consulting, I told clients that B2B service transformation is about productizing services, pricing services, and turning cost centers into profit centers, etc. But after saying this for more than ten years, there has not been a particularly good implementation plan or successful case.

I define digital transformation as a change driven by digital technology, and digital innovation as the optimization and efficiency of existing models and processes. Some of the content introduced later belongs to innovation, and some belongs to transformation.

Speaking of B2B services, our basic requirements are: cost reduction, efficiency increase, and customer satisfaction improvement. In the digital age, in addition to these three requirements, we also position service as the beginning of sales: generating trust and dependence through services, generating continuous interaction

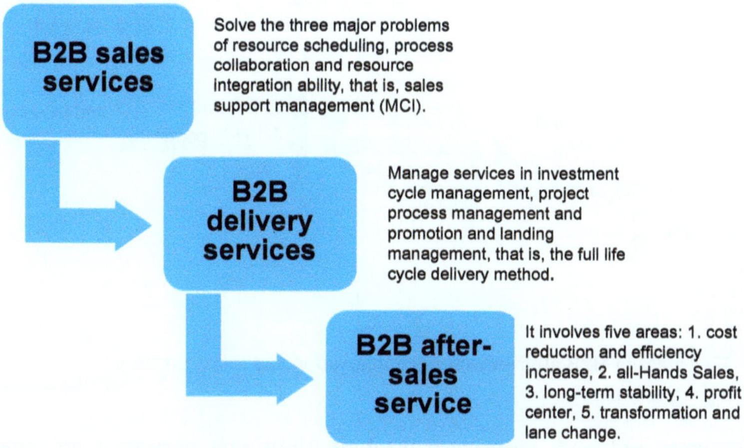

Fig. 3.36 Three areas of B2B service innovation and transformation

through trust and dependence, understanding more customer needs through continuous interaction to generate continuous sales, and iterative innovation of products and solutions. Since the above process will be spread throughout the entire lifecycle, the digital innovation and transformation of services not only occur after sales, but also extend forward to pre-sales and during sales.

As shown in Fig. 3.36, a complete B2B innovation and transformation should include three areas: ① B2B sales process service; ② B2B delivery process service; ③ B2B after-sales process service.

B2B After-Sales Process Service

Because when it comes to B2B service innovation and transformation, we usually think of after-sales service first, so let's start with the after-sales process.

As shown in Fig. 3.37, the five areas of B2B after-sales service innovation and transformation are:

(1) **Service grading support system** is the adaptation of services, that is, providing different service resources and standards according to different customers and different projects, so that the best resources flow to the best customers and projects, that is, good steel should be used on the blade, and the input–output ratio should be maximized.
(2) **Sales and service integration** is when the service department also undertakes sales tasks, discovers new sales opportunities in the service process, leads or participates in the sales process, and receives rewards according to contribution after successful sales.

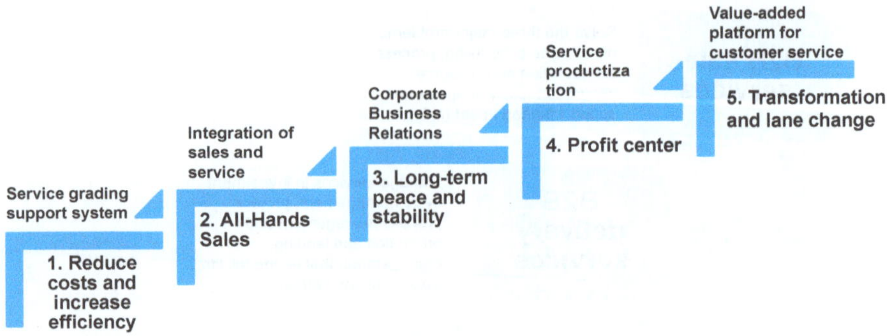

Fig. 3.37 Five areas of B2B after-sales service innovation and transformation

(3) **Corporate network resources** is about digitizing corporate networks and improving and utilizing them.
(4) **Service productization** is about how to customize service products according to customer needs, which can help customers solve pain points and help the company complete the transformation, from one-time product sales revenue to continuous service revenue.
(5) **Customer service value-added platform** is a complete mechanism at the company level to continuously monitor customer needs after the product or project is delivered, and to effectively manage the launch and operation of innovative service products.

Service Grading Support System

Figure 3.38 provides a more complex example. Company A, from a management structure perspective, operates under a matrix management system, with both horizontal regional branches and vertical industry divisions. In terms of products, it offers consultations for large clients, solution-oriented large projects that combine hardware and software, as well as smaller projects primarily focused on installation and delivery for small and medium-sized clients. It also sells products for small businesses and consumer use in stores. From a sales model perspective, it has company-led project sales, partner-led project sales, and product sales primarily through e-commerce or distributors.

For large enterprises with diverse products and solutions, and a customer base that spans various scales of businesses and consumer users, I suggest adopting a tiered support service system. For example:

(1) First-level support: This is for large projects led by the company. It is recommended to adopt a delivery center model, i.e., establish a delivery center where pre-sales, in-sales, and after-sales are provided by one team. This means that resources other than sales are managed and coordinated by the delivery team, including product line resources and regional branch resources. The delivery

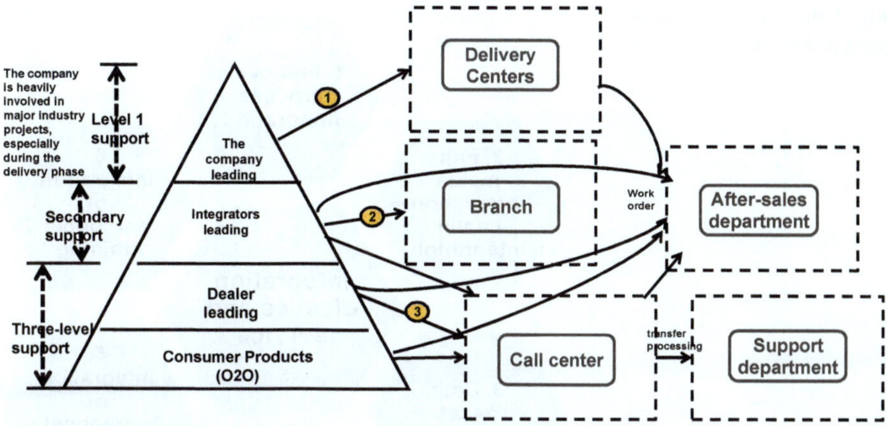

Fig. 3.38 Example of service grading support system

center can be an independent department or belong to an industry division, depending on whether the solutions led by the delivery center serve one or multiple industry divisions. Additionally, the delivery center can adopt a dual accounting mechanism with the industry division, meaning the delivery center also assesses the amount of project delivery, which helps the delivery center transition towards a market-centric approach.

(2) Second-level support: This is for projects led by partners. For larger and more complex projects, support can be provided by the technical team of the project's branch. For smaller and simpler projects, a call center customer service can be used directly.
(3) Third-level support: This is for customers who purchase products directly from the company or from distributors. At this point, a call center customer service can be used directly, with a technical department providing expert support behind the call center, and an after-sales department responsible for installation, maintenance, and return and exchange management.

Sales and Service Integration

As shown in Fig. 3.39, sales and service need to achieve six integrations:

(1) Full-cycle process integration: Good service provided by sales leads to word-of-mouth promotion, which generates more sales, and after-sales service is needed after sales.
(2) Full-media interaction center integration: The interaction center is both the entrance and exit for service and sales. During interaction, companies can make sales in service, such as selling value-added products, other category products, product combinations, etc.; they can also provide service in sales, such as supporting and giving suggestions for problems encountered in product use.

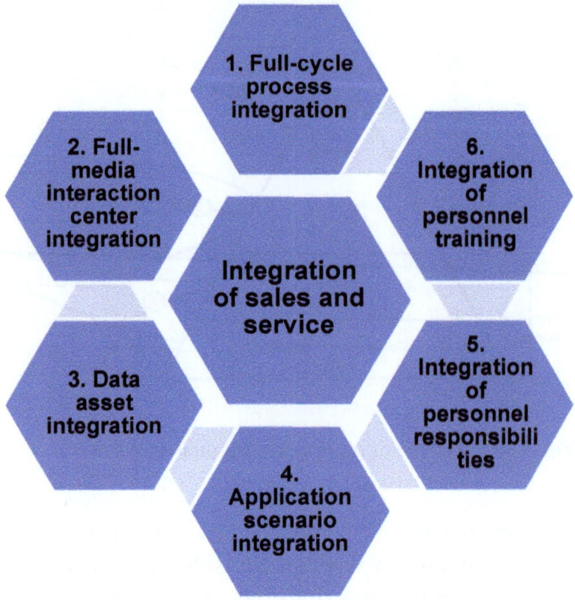

Fig. 3.39 Six integration of sales and service

(3) Data asset integration: Information about customers, products and projects, sales, etc., is managed, modeled, analyzed, and predicted in a unified manner.
(4) Application scenario integration: The scenarios of sales and service are integrated, such as recommending expert services after project launch during the sales process, and discovering new customer needs and new business opportunities during the service process.
(5) Integration of personnel responsibilities: The responsibilities and assessments of sales personnel should include service indicators, and sales personnel need to be responsible for the entire lifecycle; the responsibilities and assessments of service personnel should include sales indicators, with corresponding incentives.
(6) Integration of personnel training: The training of sales personnel should include delivery and service knowledge training, During the training of service personnel, sales techniques, product prices, and sales processes, among other sales-related training, should be conducted.

Every enterprise has its unique genes. How to achieve sales-service integration specifically needs to be analyzed according to the situation of the enterprise and the right remedy should be applied. In this process, some principles can be followed, that is, the five key elements of sales-service integration (PKITT) in Fig. 3.40:

(1) Product: Define simple and easy-to-sell products in the service, such as expert services, hardware, software, etc.
(2) KPI: Quantify and assess the sales indicators of service personnel and service departments.

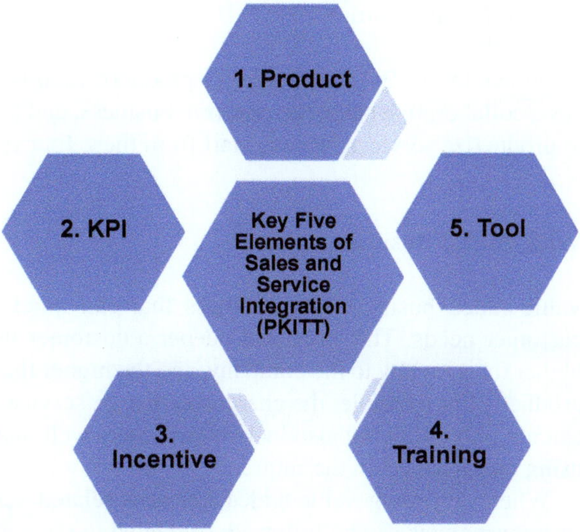

Fig. 3.40 Key five elements of sales and service integration (PKITT)

(3) Incentive: Quantify service and sales incentives, make them visible in real-time, and quickly cash them out.
(4) Training: Conduct a large amount of product sales training for service personnel.
(5) Tool: Use AI and mobile tools to guide service personnel to complete the product sales process.

Corporate Connections

The most important and valuable data in B2B business are corporate connection resource data and project history information data, that is, Business Relationship Management (BRM) data. Most B2B enterprises have not seriously collected and managed these two types of data, resulting in B2B sales mainly relying on the experience and intuition of sales personnel.

The after-sales service stage is the easiest stage to establish a mutually trusting customer relationship and the easiest stage to collect business relationship data. Because at this stage, the roles of both parties are reversed, and the customer has no need to hide some information. Even if it costs more money and time, the enterprise must maintain the customer relationship and collect the corporate connection resource information and project relationship data assets. The related content has been detailed in the chapters on business relationship management, corporate connection resource management, and project behavior management, so it will not be repeated here.

Service Productization

As shown in Fig. 3.41, B2B service productization is divided into value-added business, collaborative business, platform business, and knowledge business. If we want to productize services, we can start from these four types of business.

Value-Added Business

Value-added business is a business that can quickly profit and can fully cover customer needs. The more and deeper a customer uses a company's services, the higher their loyalty to the company, and the higher the cost of leaving the company's products. For example, the chargeable expert service business in after-sales service can not only profit but also lock in customers well, making them willing to continue using our products in the future.

When designing value-added business-related service products, the following seven principles can be followed: ① related to the company's existing products and solutions; ② service capabilities can cover support; ③ customers have general needs; ④ can be quantified and priced; ⑤ can be quickly promoted and replicated; ⑥ can profit and enhance customer loyalty, such as locking in future product purchases; ⑦ no negative impact on other products and solutions of the company.

Collaborative Business

Collaborative business is a service that collaborates with the sales process and delivery process during the service process, assists the enterprise in discovering

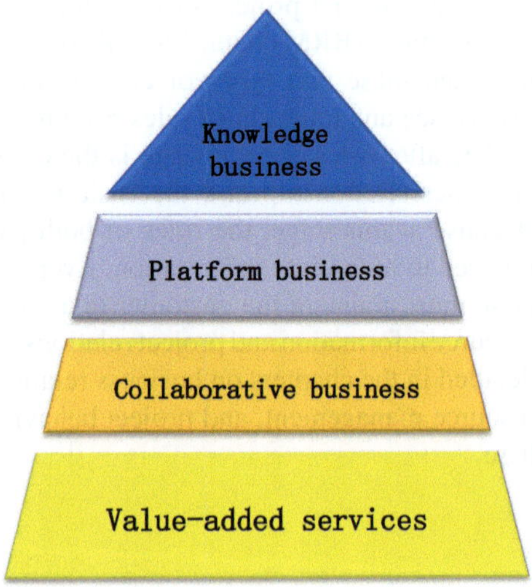

Fig. 3.41 Four types of service productization

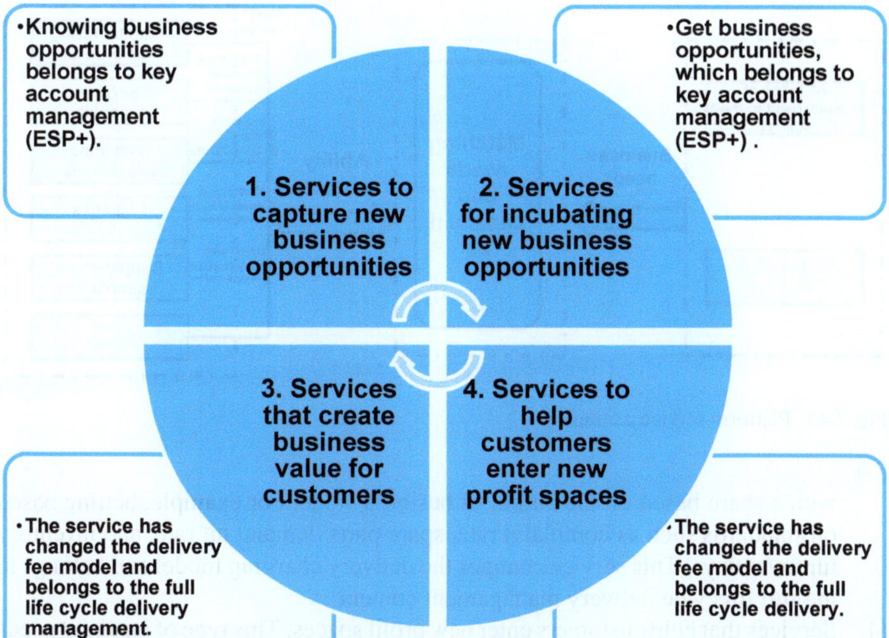

Fig. 3.42 Four aspects of collaborative business

business opportunities and winning orders, or helps customers succeed. This type of service requires a longer time from input to harvest.

As shown in Fig. 3.42, this type of service can be approached from four aspects:

(1) Services that capture new business opportunities These types of services are mainly used to create more opportunities for contact with customers, understand customer needs, and capture new business opportunities. For example, diagnosing existing projects, making annual regular visits to major customers, or holding "brainstorming" sessions to understand customer needs, regularly taking customers to visit successful cases, etc. This is about knowing business opportunities and is part of Key Account Management (ESP+).

(2) Services for incubating new business opportunities. These services require companies to proactively help customers plan, thereby guiding needs, and incubating new business opportunities. For example, through regular guidance from customer success managers to customers, initiating or participating in consulting projects to help customers with long-term, medium-term, and short-term planning. This is about getting business opportunities and is part of Key Account Management (ESP+).

(3) Services that create business value for customers. These services need to assist customers in defining value output indicators and achieving business value through operations. Sometimes this type of business will adopt a betting method,

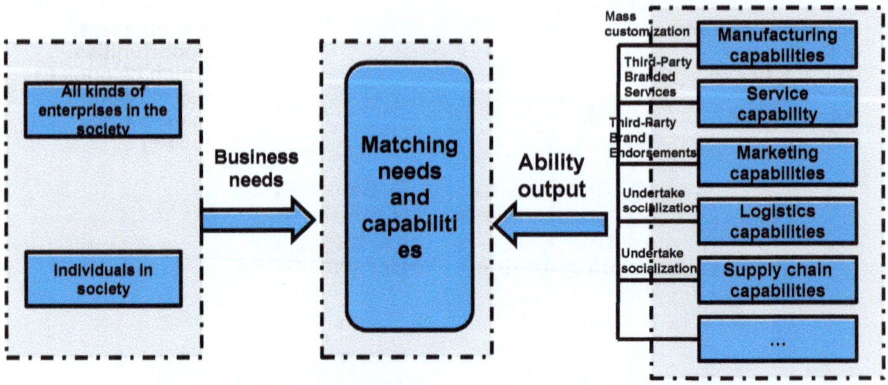

Fig. 3.43 Platform service example

with a share based on the output of business value. For example, betting based on standards such as complaint rate, spare parts demand hit rate, and inventory turnover days. This service changes the delivery charging model and belongs to the full lifecycle delivery management content.

(4) Services that help customers enter new profit spaces. This type of business needs to use the company's own resources to help customers enter new profit spaces. If a company has a massive global enterprise customer resources and ecosystem, it can establish a global strategic partnership with a certain customer and jointly promote the customer's products and solutions worldwide. The company can use its own resources to help customers, bridge between customers and customers, and promote the development of business. This service changes the delivery charging model and belongs to the full lifecycle delivery management content.

Platform Business

As shown in Fig. 3.43, platform business refers to the company's marketing, service, manufacturing, supply chain, logistics, R&D capabilities, while meeting the company's own needs, opening up the remaining capabilities to society. Platform business will cross brands, attract many partners and users, and is a service business that can help companies occupy a dominant market position.

Knowledge Business

In the digital age, with the explosive growth of the quality and quantity of corporate data, knowledge business is also at a new tipping point. Companies need to process the accumulated massive data, complete knowledge accumulation through artificial intelligence means such as machine learning, form knowledge assets, and output to

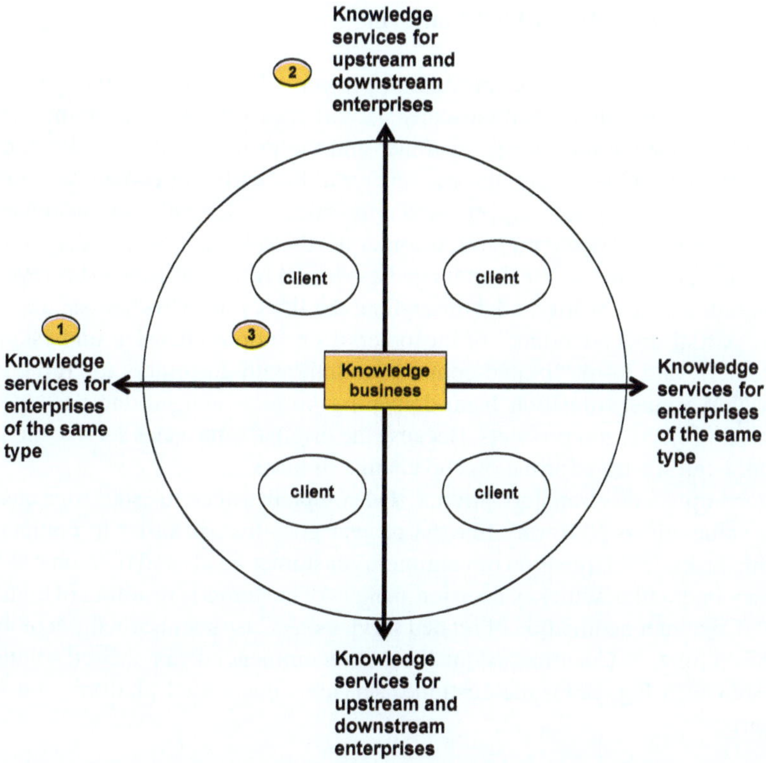

Fig. 3.44 Three types of knowledge services

society, which is knowledge business. Knowledge business has a high threshold and uniqueness, and is a high-profit service business.

As shown in Fig. 3.44, there are three types of knowledge business. Companies can do horizontal knowledge services for the same type of customers, or vertical knowledge services for upstream and downstream companies, or introduce users and various companies to do ecosystem services. For example, a certain company has done spare parts demand forecasting for the mainframe factory. The first step is to provide spare parts forecasting services to all mainframe factories through data and optimized algorithm models; the second step is to provide spare parts demand knowledge services to many upstream spare parts manufacturers of the mainframe factory; The third step is to introduce end users, let them enter the platform, collect their demands for large-scale customization, and also provide various services for these users, and build an ecosystem.

Customer Service Value-Added Platform

Once a B2B project completes product or project delivery, if the other party is not a key customer, resources will basically be withdrawn from the customer, and the company's understanding of the customer and the project will basically end here, unless there is a sudden event, the customer will basically not contact the company again. Therefore, the sales, delivery, and after-sales service links are disjointed, and the CRM company's perception of customer needs and experience is disjointed.

The business model in the digital age has shifted from one-time sales revenue to a continuous service profit model throughout the life cycle. This necessitates a shift from a "partial understanding" of customers to a "comprehensive understanding" of customers, and from "limited communication" with customers to "full communication". We must transition from delivering projects and products to operating customers, projects, and products. Because the original after-sales service model has changed, I call it a transformation and change of lanes.

To accomplish this transformation, CRM companies need to establish a customer service value-added platform after the project goes live, in order to complete the following tasks: ① Acquisition of continuous customer needs and opinions; ② High-frequency interaction with key decision-makers of customers, resulting in high stickiness; ③ Customer acquisition of related services; ④ Customer acquisition of various types of training; ⑤ Customer acquisition of recommended customized solutions.

As shown in Fig. 3.45, the customer service value-added platform consists of three parts:

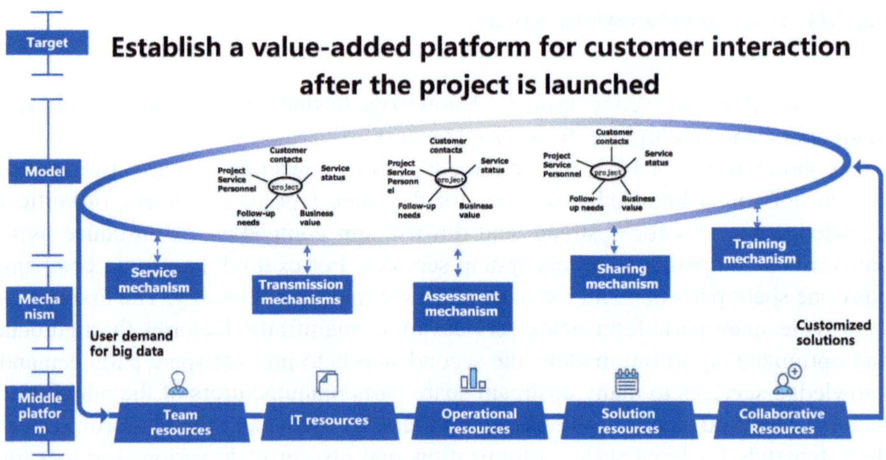

Fig. 3.45 Value-added customer service platform

Model

It is to continuously operate and add value to each project after delivery, no matter how small the project, it has its own brand.

Mechanism

(1) Service mechanism. After the project goes live, the types, standards, processes, and responsible persons of the services, etc.
(2) Communication mechanism. The service interface person communicates and interacts directly with the decision-makers and key users in the customer through multiple channels.
(3) Assessment mechanism. Evaluation, assessment, and rectification of the project status after going live.
(4) Sharing mechanism. Incentives for the direct and indirect value created by service personnel in the service.
(5) Training mechanism. Training and guidance for key customers and key users.

Middle Platform

(1) Team resources. Service team resources.
(2) IT resources. Development resources for the customer service value-added platform.
(3) Operational resources. Resources for the operation of the customer service value-added platform system and content.
(4) Solution resources. New products, new solutions, new trends, and various activity resources from our company and partners.
(5) Cooperation resources. Various partner resources.

B2B Sales Process Service

The sales process also needs service, such as pre-sales experts providing this service. The service support capability of the sales process largely determines the input–output ratio of pre-sales costs. The larger the sales team, the more important the sales service support system. Sales support system management is to solve the three major problems of resource scheduling, process collaboration, and resource integration capabilities. Detailed introductions have been given in previous chapters, so I won't go into detail here.

B2B Delivery Process Service

The delivery process of a project is a service process that connects the previous and the next. On the one hand, it is for the sales stage, it undertakes the process of converting orders to cash, that is, the return of products and projects; on the other hand, it is for the after-sales stage, it sets goals, sets directions, and guides customers to purchase service products in the future. For example, if a company sets business value operation indicators during the delivery stage, it is easy to encourage customers to purchase "services that create business value for customers" in the "collaborative business" during the after-sales service stage.

Delivery service management can adopt the full life cycle delivery method, which includes input cycle management, project process management, promotion and landing management, all of which contain services. The full life cycle delivery method will be detailed in later chapters, so I won't go into detail here.

Summary > This section introduces the B2B service innovation and transformation in the digital age. The three main service stages: the B2B sales process services, B2B delivery process services, and B2B after-sales process services, with a particular emphasis on five areas of after-sales service innovation and transformation: ① cost reduction and efficiency improvement; ② full staff sales; ③ long-term stability; ④ profit center; ⑤ transformation and change of track.

The Contradiction Between Service Business Model and Service Satisfaction

Many times, the management decisions made by companies are driven by pressure and fear. Just like when an accident occurs, people often panic and run around, but ignore the correct direction. In terms of service, companies should strive for zero complaints and 100% user satisfaction, but some companies always focus on improving processes and service standards, but do not carefully consider whether the direction of service management is correct, such as whether the service business model is reasonable, and whether the service standards need to be set so high.

Introduction to the Traditional Service Business Model

Now countless manufacturers complain that service investment is increasing, but user satisfaction is getting lower and lower, and the sense of honor and loyalty of service personnel is also getting worse. And no matter how the company transforms, innovates, and invests, it seems to be no better. In fact, the root of this problem is often that there is a problem with the service business model. That is, the interests of manufacturers, users, service outlets, and service personnel are opposed, which leads

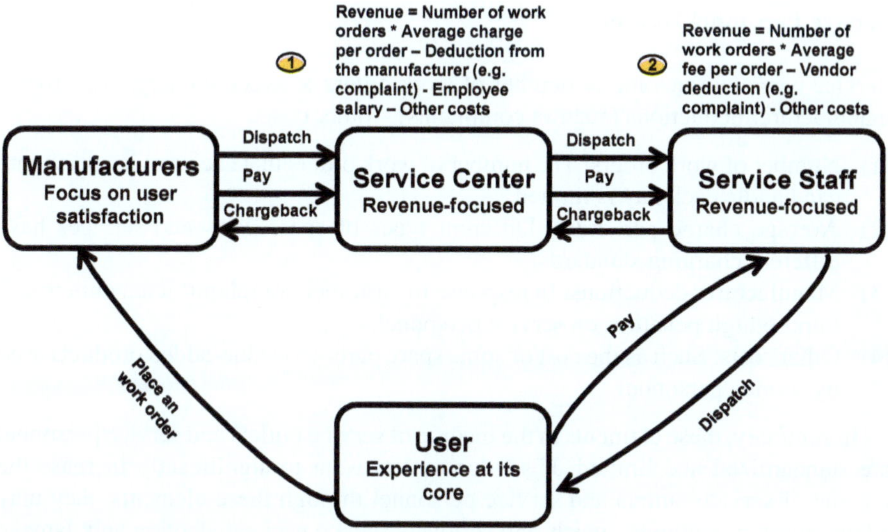

Fig. 3.46 Example of the relationship between four service related parties

to the difficulty of improving service satisfaction no matter how much the company invests.

As shown in Fig. 3.46, the real problem of the company is the profit model of service outlets and service personnel. Many manufacturers' service outlets adopt the form of outsourcing. The demands of service outlets and service personnel are income, but the demands of manufacturers and users are experience and satisfaction. There is a great conflict between the income demands of service outlets and service personnel and the user experience and satisfaction.

Outlet Income Analysis

Outlet income = number of work orders × average charge per order – manufacturer deductions (such as complaints) – employee wages – other costs

(1) Number of work orders: Generally, outlets have coverage areas, so the number of work orders will not have much room for increase.
(2) Average charge per order: Different types of spare parts and services have different charging standards.
(3) Manufacturer deductions: In response to customer complaints, etc., manufacturers will impose high penalties on outlets.
(4) Employee wages: Employee wages and social security are important components of outlet costs.
(5) Other costs: Such as spare parts procurement, warehousing, logistics, property, etc.

Service Personnel Income

Service personnel income = number of work orders × average charge per order – manufacturer deductions (such as complaints) – other costs.

(1) Number of work orders: The number of work orders that each service personnel can handle each day is limited.
(2) Average charge per order: Different types of spare parts and services have different charging standards.
(3) Manufacturer deductions: In response to customer complaints, etc., outlets will impose high penalties on service personnel.
(4) Other costs: Such as the cost of some spare parts and value-added products used by service personnel.

In summary, these elements in the income of service outlets and service personnel are standardized and limited, If service outlets want to significantly increase the income of service outlets and service personnel through these elements, they may adopt incorrect methods, which will seriously reduce user satisfaction and damage the interests of manufacturers. We don't need to blame service outlets and service personnel unilaterally, as profit is their main goal. The first thing manufacturers need to consider is how to find a good mechanism that can make the income of service outlets and service personnel positively correlated with user satisfaction, that is, the more satisfied the user, the higher the income of the outlets and service personnel.

Introduction to the New Service Business Model

As shown in Fig. 3.47, we can build a new service business model in the digital age. As shown in the figure below, we can sort out this new model through the "three transformations": ① service outlet platformization; ② service personnel makerization; ③ income ecologization.

Service Outlet Platformization

Outlets need to be repositioned, and manufacturers can integrate several service outlets in a certain area to form a regional operation center, which changes from merely charging for services to operating the entire regional service support system (such as spare parts, warehouses, vehicles, etc.). The main task of the new service outlets is to improve user and service personnel satisfaction, build an ecological system, plan activities, and operate service businesses. The income of service personnel is no longer mainly determined by the number of work orders, but is comprehensively evaluated based on operational effects, user satisfaction, service personnel satisfaction, and ecological income.

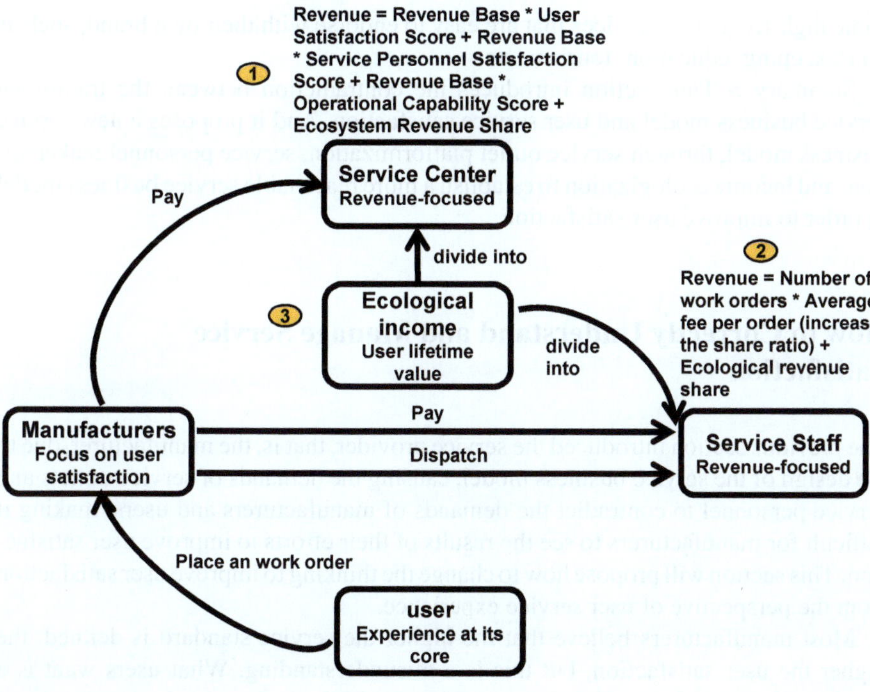

Fig. 3.47 Example of a new service business model

Service Personnel Makerization

Service personnel become independent operators. Manufacturers directly assign orders to service personnel and pay the corresponding fees directly, eliminating the intermediate link of service outlets, thereby greatly enhancing the control over service personnel. Each user is assigned a service steward based on the service relationship. In the future, the service personnel can get a share of any items purchased by the user in the ecological system, thus changing from a simple one-time service to long-term operation. In addition, by increasing the proportion of ecological income in the income of service personnel, and diversifying the income of service personnel, they will pay more attention to user satisfaction in order to obtain continuous user income.

Income Ecologization

Manufacturers need to provide users with more products and services to meet the needs of users' daily lives. Manufacturers can start from products, product maintenance services, related spare parts sales, and trade-ins. Then gradually transition to some high-frequency services that are easy to endorse with their own brand, such as housekeeping, education, tourism, etc.

Summary > This section introduces the contradiction between the traditional service business model and user service satisfaction. And it proposes a new service business model, through service outlet platformization, service personnel makerization, and income ecologization to establish a more reasonable service business model in order to improve user satisfaction.

How to Correctly Understand and Manage Service Satisfaction

The previous section introduced the service provider, that is, the manufacturer, due to the design of the service business model, causing the demands of service outlets and service personnel to contradict the demands of manufacturers and users, making it difficult for manufacturers to see the results of their efforts to improve user satisfaction. This section will propose how to change the thinking to improve user satisfaction from the perspective of user service experience.

Most manufacturers believe that the higher the service standard is defined, the higher the user satisfaction, but this is a misunderstanding. What users want is a good service experience, they want results, not high service standards in text and propaganda. "The hollow is filled, the worn is renewed, the less is gained, the more is confused" speaks to this point. The service standard of the manufacturer Setting lower standards makes it easier to meet requirements and often brings surprises to users; setting fewer service standards makes it easier to focus and improve services.

Let's look at what factors determine service satisfaction.

As shown in Fig. 3.48, the actual satisfaction of users with the service comes from the user gap, which is the gap between the service expected by the user and the service perceived. Most companies set service standards based on the company gap, that is, the gap between the perception of user expectations by senior management and the currently established user-oriented service standards. Because senior executives often have higher service requirements than ordinary users, they often set high service standards. High service standards often raise users' expectations of the service, but the company's service resources determine the actual service perception of users. Therefore, it leads to an increase in user service expectations, but the company's own capabilities and resources cannot keep up, leading to poor user experience and a large number of complaints.

As shown in Fig. 3.49, through five steps, companies can more reasonably and profitably manage user satisfaction. These five steps are ① reasonably setting service standards; ② appropriately lowering user expectations; ③ raising user tolerance thresholds and appropriately creating touching moments for users; ④ rationally resolving complaints; ⑤ comprehensively monitoring emergencies.

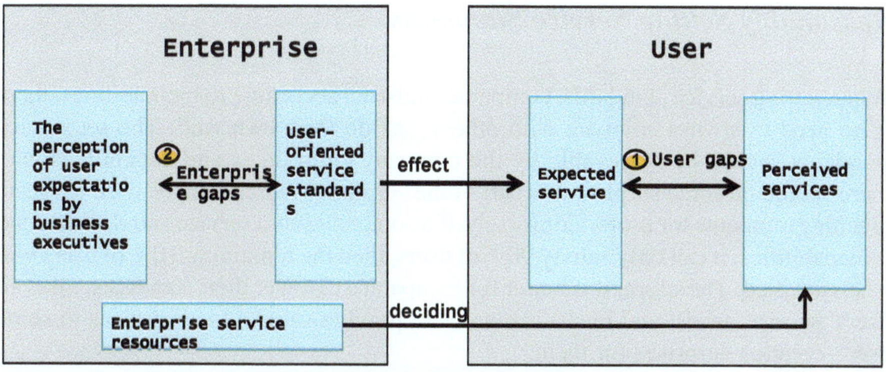

Fig. 3.48 User satisfaction

Fig. 3.49 Five step method for managing user satisfaction

Reasonably Setting Service Standards

When setting service standards, companies must act according to their abilities, there is no need to always compare with others, just do their own well. The set service standards should be achievable by the company's resources and capabilities, and there should be some surplus, this part of the surplus resources can be used to create touching moments for users. Conversely, if a company sets a service standard beyond its capabilities, it can only satisfy 90% of users, then the remaining 10% of users will be dissatisfied. Therefore, it is better for companies to lower their standards, meet all users' service needs, and invest resources to provide value-added services to some users, creating surprises for them.

When setting service standards, companies must act according to their abilities. If the standard is higher than the current resources and capabilities of the company, either continue to invest more resources or lower the standard. Therefore, before setting service standards, companies should conduct systematic and comprehensive service standard and resource matching analysis.

Appropriately Lowering User Expectations

When promoting services externally, it is best not to exaggerate service standards for market effects. If user expectations are raised, but service capabilities cannot be met, the market evaluation will be disastrous. Slogans such as "zero delay" and "100% user satisfaction" should be replaced by specific service standards and user rights propaganda. The service enjoyed by users is proportional to the fees paid by users, which also conforms to business rules.

Raising User Tolerance Thresholds and Appropriately Creating Touching Moments for Users

When encountering unsatisfactory services, users' tolerance thresholds for acquaintances are much higher than for strangers. Therefore, companies must find ways to establish close relationships between service personnel and users, such as steward relationships. Once users encounter unsatisfactory services, the first thing they think of is to find the steward to solve it, rather than complain through other channels.

The company's service standards should leave some room, these resources can be directly given to frontline service personnel for independent deployment, can be used to create touching moments for users, and can also be used to handle user complaints. If service personnel have on-site disposal rights, then the effect that can be achieved on-site with 1 dollar may not be achieved with 100 dollars afterwards. Good things should be provided as soon as possible, and bad things should be resolved as soon as possible.

Rationally Resolving Complaints

Complaints must be handled rationally. They are not a catastrophic event, but a normal occurrence. When dealing with complaints, two points should be considered: first, whether the number of complaints is within a reasonable proportion. Do not deny the overall service quality because of one or two complaints, but focus on the overall service quality; second, it is necessary to distinguish whether the complaint is malicious. There should be standards and principles, and different treatments should be applied. When it is time to stick to principles, stick to them. The handling should also be as complete as possible in one go, otherwise, it indirectly encourages more people to participate in complaints.

Comprehensive Monitoring of Emergencies

Emergencies are very likely to occur during the service process, and businesses are often easily disrupted by the negative impact of one or two events, disrupting the entire service transformation and improvement layout. Especially in today's mobile internet era, any small spark can quickly cause a major disaster in the media. Larger enterprises should establish a public opinion management team, invest funds in this area, detect emergencies, and respond and handle them quickly.

Summary > This section introduces how businesses can more reasonably and profitably manage customer satisfaction. These five steps are: ① Reasonably establish service standards; ② Appropriately lower customer expectations; ③ Raise customer tolerance threshold and appropriately create touching moments for customers; ④ Rationally resolve complaints; ⑤ Comprehensive monitoring of emergencies.

Evaluation of Customer Satisfaction Value Output

Evaluating customer satisfaction is not difficult, a simple survey can do the job. However, how to evaluate the value brought by satisfaction has always been a big problem, which in some ways limits the company's investment in service. Therefore, here we briefly discuss two methods of evaluating the value of customer satisfaction: 2C customer satisfaction value evaluation method and 2B customer satisfaction value evaluation method. The value of 2C customer satisfaction is evaluated based on the community as the basic unit, and the value is reflected in the increase in sales; the value of 2B customer satisfaction is evaluated based on individual customers, and the value is reflected in the closeness of customer relationships.

Evaluation of Individual Customer Satisfaction Value

I have previously been in charge of 2C customer after-sales service, and I deeply feel that there are three major difficulties in evaluating the value of individual customer after-sales service satisfaction.

Unable to Evaluate Value Output

Many 2C products are not high-frequency consumption products, such as home appliances and cars, which are usually purchased only once every few years, so it is impossible to evaluate the relationship between satisfaction and new purchases or repurchases. Even for high-frequency consumption products, it is difficult to judge whether the increase in sales is due to market promotion, channel layout, product design, product promotion, or an increase in customer satisfaction.

Unable to Confirm the Credibility of Satisfaction

No matter what customer satisfaction model is used; whether it is self-evaluated or third-party evaluated, even if the company has done a lot of work and invested a lot of resources, it is difficult to prove the credibility of whether the satisfaction is reasonable and whether there is human intervention.

Any Problem Can Be Blamed on Service

Because satisfaction and value output are implicitly related and difficult to evaluate, once there are problems in sales and other links, everyone can blame it on the service, blaming it on low customer satisfaction.

In view of this, I believe that a more comprehensive evaluation method needs to meet three conditions:

(1) Obvious causal relationship

That is, the sample can clearly show the relationship between satisfaction and new purchases or repurchases. As an individual C-end customer, this causal relationship is not very obvious, but we can take the community as a sample. China's 1.4 billion population is distributed in 300,000–500,000 communities and about 700,000 villages. The service is low-frequency for individuals, but high-frequency for communities. Therefore, at the community level, the causal relationship is very obvious, that is, whether high service satisfaction brings new purchases and repurchases.

(2) Noise reduction

Because many other factors can also cause changes in sales performance, it is necessary to delete the changes caused by other factors as much as possible. It is recommended to take two circles that are close and geographically adjacent communities as references to eliminate the influence of other factors. The effects brought by market promotion, channel layout, product design, and product promotion should be similar to the impact on similar circles and adjacent community groups, so the different sales performance is more likely to be caused by customer satisfaction.

(3) Large enough sample

That is, the number of reference communities selected is sufficient. For example, 1,000 or 10,000 communities.

Next, let me introduce the "CRM3.0 Community Reference Value Evaluation Method". This is just a simple example, and more parameters and more complex models will definitely be needed in the future to improve and optimize this method.

The CRM3.0 Community Reference Value Evaluation Method is shown in Fig. 3.50.

Step one: Find enough control communities, and each pair of communities in the control group must meet the conditions of being close in circle and geographically adjacent.

Step two: Calculate the monthly satisfaction growth rate and sales growth rate in each pair of control communities. Assume that the community with low satisfaction growth is community A, and the one with high growth is community B. Subtract the satisfaction growth of community A from that of community B to get C, and subtract the sales growth of community A from that of community

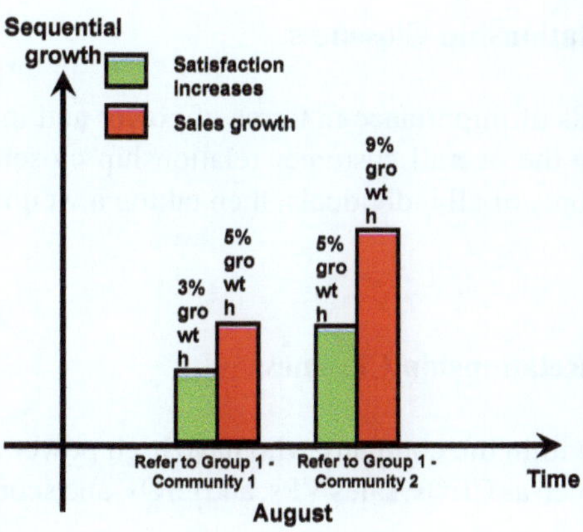

Example:
Reference Group 1:
Relative improvement in customer satisfaction:
5%-3%= 2%.
Relative increase in sales: 9%-5% = 4%.
That's 2% satisfaction, which leads to 4% growth in Community 2. That is, the increase in satisfaction of each 1% of the reference group 1 leads to 2% of sales.
Note: In addition to the 3% increase in satisfaction in the 5% growth of community 1, it also takes into account the effects of marketing, channel layout, product design, product promotion, etc.

Average percentage increase in sales due to a 1% increase in satisfaction A = ∑ increase in sales from reference group 1-n / ∑ improvement in satisfaction from reference group 1-n

Business Value Output from Satisfaction Growth TV = A * Average Satisfaction Growth B * Sales in the previous month C
Assumption C: 10 Billion A: 2% B: 3%
10 billion * (2 * 3%) = 600 million

Fig. 3.50 CRM3.0 community-referenced value assessment

B to get D. We assume that sales growth D is brought about by satisfaction growth C. This premise assumes that the effects brought by market promotion, channel layout, product design, and product promotion on the sales increase of communities A and B are the same.

Step three: Calculate the average value of the sales increase brought by every 1% increase in customer satisfaction in all control groups.

Step four: Calculate the sales increase brought by this month's customer satisfaction according to the formula: this month's sales × this month's customer satisfaction increase ratio × the average value of the sales increase brought by this month's customer satisfaction increase × 100.

The above evaluation method is just a prototype, and we need to iterate and update it based on data and evaluation results.

The Value Evaluation of Enterprise Customer Satisfaction

It is difficult to evaluate the satisfaction of enterprise customers and the increase in sales revenue brought by customer satisfaction. Because: ① Enterprises have a small number of large customers, the sample size is too small, and they may belong to different industries. Business, so it's hard to make a comparison and find the corresponding relationship between satisfaction and sales revenue. ② The purchasing behavior of corporate customers is very complex and cannot be achieved by satisfaction alone.

Therefore, the value assessment of corporate customer satisfaction can be evaluated not by business income, but by the closeness of customer relationships. That is, the value of corporate customer satisfaction is reflected in the overall relationship closeness of customers and the individual relationship closeness of key decision-makers, as follows:

Evaluation of Overall Customer Relationship Closeness

This involves identifying all individuals of importance in terms of power and influence within the company, and scoring the overall customer relationship closeness based on the relationship closeness scores of all individuals, then taking a weighted average.

Evaluation of Key Decision-Maker Relationship Closeness

This involves identifying individuals within the company who have high power and significant influence on our company, such as CEOs, sales VPs, and CIOs, and scoring their relationship closeness.

Evaluation of High-Influence Individual Relationship Closeness

This involves identifying individuals within the customer who have a significant influence on key decision-makers. After identifying the center of influence, score its relationship closeness.

Summary > This section introduces the evaluation methods of satisfaction value for individual customers and corporate customers. For individual customers, we can use the "CRM3.0 Community Reference Value Evaluation Method", using two circles of similar layers and neighboring communities as the basic reference units for evaluation, with the value reflected in the increase in sales; corporate customers use the Enterprise Contact Management (ECM) method for evaluation, with the value reflected in the increase in customer relationship closeness.

Chapter 4
Building the CRM3.0 Support System

CRM3.0 Full Lifecycle Delivery Method

Currently, the delivery methods of various CRM companies are similar to the delivery methods I used when I worked at Siebel Canada twenty years ago. At that time, we saw CRM as a software, and as long as we could share data and complete process automation after going online, it was enough; but today, twenty years later in the digital age, companies generally link CRM with customer management, marketing, product sales, customer service, channel management and other areas of digital transformation, model change and process innovation, and companies generally require the output of business value. Therefore, in the digital age, CRM delivery methods also need to keep up with the times. In the CRM3.0 era, there are three aspects of project delivery changes: ① from focusing on software selection to focusing on digital innovation; ② from focusing on software functions to focusing on business output; ③ from focusing on project launch to focusing on continuous input and output over a longer period.

The biggest flaw in the current CRM delivery method is: only care about birth, not about nurturing. Just like taking care of a child, we need to provide prenatal education before birth, and we need to continue to invest after birth. Having a child is expensive, but raising a child is even more expensive. Now, the vast majority of funds and resources for CRM projects are invested in the development and launch phase of CRM, but after going online, resources are basically withdrawn. That is, at the stage where we should invest well and reflect business output, we give up investment, and the probability that the child can become an excellent student is also very small. For example, If the budget for CRM is 10 million yuan (excluding licenses and computer hardware), many companies will spend seven to eight million yuan on the project development and launch phase (including licensing and hardware costs), and then only pay a small amount of maintenance fees in the following years. In fact, such a project is doomed to be difficult to succeed from the beginning, because the remaining two to three million yuan is not enough to fix problems and improve

© China Science and Technology Press Co., Ltd. 2025

J. Yang, *Sales and Service Digital Transformation*,
https://doi.org/10.1007/978-981-96-5961-6_4

performance in the years after the project goes live, let alone continue to invest in digital innovation and business value output.

For CRM projects, I suggest a cycle of about 6 years, with a complete budget. Spend 30% of the cost on the development and launch phase, and the remaining cost on system operation, optimization, and business value output after the system goes live; in addition, to achieve greater business output, companies can introduce business operation services. A portion of the investment in business operations can be paid through a betting method, according to the proportion of business value output.

In the digital age, I propose a full lifecycle CRM delivery method for your reference.

As shown in Fig. 4.1, the full lifecycle CRM delivery method is based on two basic points, supported by three pillars, to achieve three transformations.

(1) Two basic points

   (1) From the perspective of delivery purpose, CRM not only focuses on software functions, but also equally emphasizes software functions, digital innovation, and quantifiable business value.
   (2) From the perspective of the delivery process, CRM is not only development-oriented, but also equally emphasizes planning, development, and operation.

(2) Three pillars

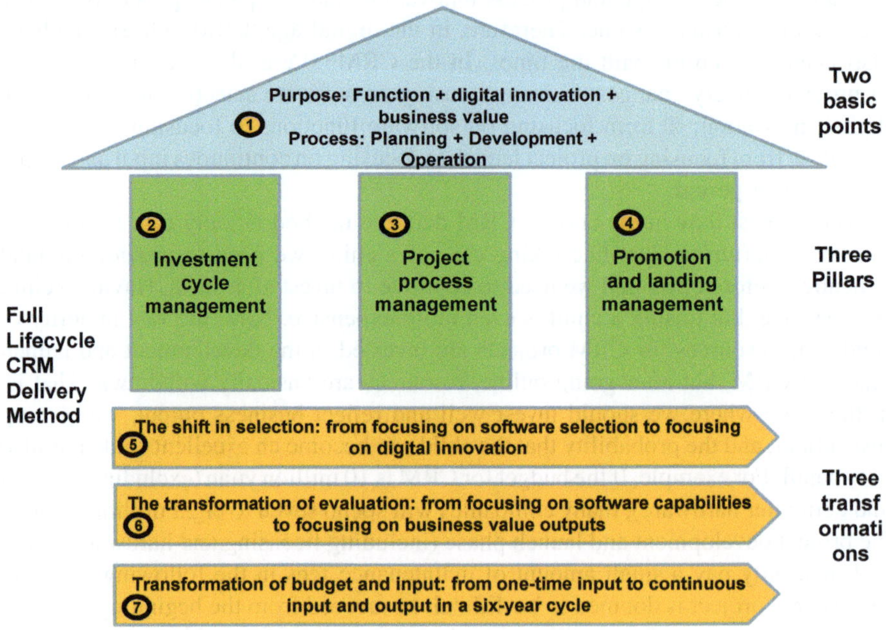

Fig. 4.1 Full lifecycle CRM delivery method

The three pillars are the focus of the following discussion.

(1) Investment cycle management: It introduces how the CRM project should be divided into several stages from project planning to project delivery, and then to 1 to 5 years after going live, as well as the budget suggestions for each stage.
(2) Project process management: It introduces the management methods, processes, and deliverables of CRM in the planning phase, delivery phase, and operation phase.
(3) Promotion and implementation management: It introduces how we adapt to the requirements of the full lifecycle CRM delivery method through transformation based on the traditional CRM project management framework.

(3) Three transformations

(1) The transformation of selection. From focusing on software selection to focusing on digital innovation. Ten years ago, CRM was only used by internal employees of the company, mainly for data sharing and effective management of sales. But in recent years, with the popularity of a series of digital technologies such as mobile applications, big data, artificial intelligence, social software, cloud computing, the Internet of Things, blockchain, maps, etc., it has become possible to realize intelligent management, scenario-based operation, and digital business on a technical level, and digital innovation and transformation in business has become a must.
(2) The transformation of evaluation. From focusing on software functions to focusing on business value output. A big problem with CRM delivery is that CRM companies often focus on the functions of the SOW (Scope of Work), using the functions in the SOW as the acceptance and payment standards. But the realization of software functions and the output of business value are two different things, and the business operations of the company change rapidly, and the requirements set half a year ago may have already changed. So we should first provide the core functions and functions that can produce business value in the short term to the buyer, mainly focusing on whether the current period has achieved the business value output required by the project, and not overly concerned about a few function points. Additional functions can be iteratively developed every year.
(3) The transformation of budget and investment. From one-time investment to focusing on continuous investment in a six-year cycle. Out. In the management of the investment cycle, I will elaborate on this issue. CRM is a marathon, not a 50-m sprint. What we need is continuous investment and continuous output of business value. CRM projects should have a full budget for a six-year cycle, rather than investing some money in a project first, and then deciding on the next step based on the project's effectiveness.

Next, I will introduce the three main supports in the full lifecycle CRM delivery method: ① Investment cycle management; ② Project process management; ③ Promotion and implementation management.

Investment Cycle Management

As shown in Fig. 4.2, a complete full lifecycle CRM delivery method is divided into seven stages, lasting about six years. The budget mentioned below refers to the project implementation cost, excluding hardware purchases, user license purchases, cloud service rentals, etc.

Planning Stage

It is best to separate planning and delivery. Because once project planning and delivery are done together, the project manager's main consideration is to control the project scope and ensure that the project is launched on time, rather than considering business value. If you are worried that the content of the plan cannot be implemented in the delivery phase, you can require the core members of the planning phase to participate in the early stage of delivery, and the final payment of the planning phase will be paid after the functional requirements design of the delivery phase comes out. It is recommended that the budget investment in the planning stage accounts for

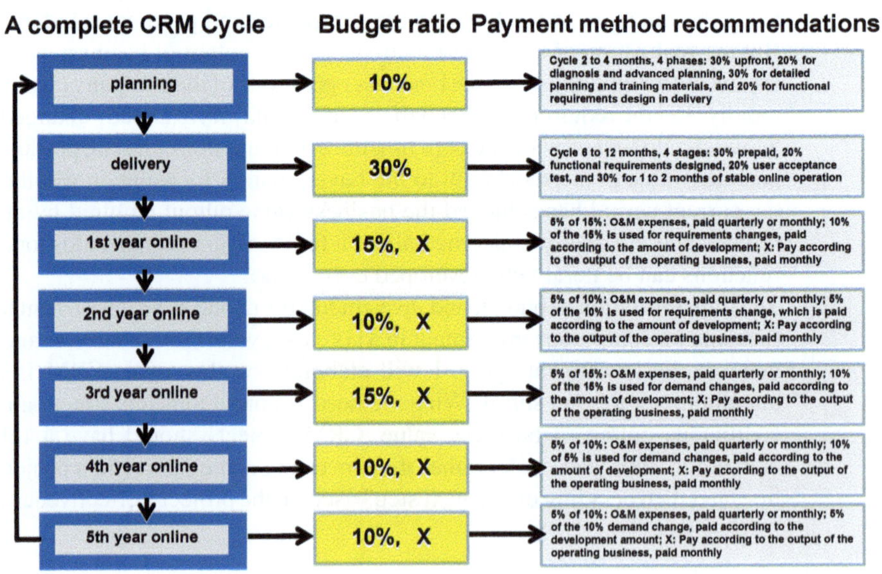

Fig. 4.2 Investment cycle management

10% of the total CRM cycle investment, generally takes 2 to 4 months, and can be paid in 4 stages: prepayment accounts for 30%, diagnosis and high-level planning account for 20%, detailed planning and training materials account for 30%, and the functional requirements design of the delivery phase accounts for 20%.

Delivery Stage

The delivery stage is the part that CRM implementation companies are best at, and basically every implementation company's methods and steps are similar. It is recommended to develop and launch core functions and functions that can enhance business value in the short term in this stage, and other functions will be continuously improved in the later stages. It is recommended that the budget investment in the planning stage accounts for 30% of the total CRM cycle investment, generally 6 to 12 months, the specific length of time can vary according to the difficulty of the project, and can be paid in 4 stages: prepayment accounts for 30%, functional requirements design accounts for 20%, user acceptance testing accounts for 20%, and the remaining 30% is paid 1 to 2 months after stable operation.

First Year After Launch

Basically, all CRM projects pay very little in the first year after launch, and some even maintain for free in the first year. Many customers may think that CRM should be stable in the first year after launch and should not pay more. Often in the first year after CRM goes online, the party A really starts to understand CRM and starts to think about how to improve it to generate business value. If we don't invest at this time, the effect will be very poor. This stage is the real output stage of CRM, we must invest more. It is recommended that the budget investment in the first year after launch accounts for 15% of the total CRM cycle investment, that is, if you spend 4 million yuan on CRM delivery, then please prepare 2 million yuan for the first year after launch. Among them, 5% of the cost is used for this year's operation and maintenance costs, paid quarterly or monthly; another 10% of the cost is used for demand changes, paid according to the development volume. After CRM goes online, in addition to system operation and maintenance, we also need to have business operations, that is, a professional team is responsible for the continuous output of business value by CRM. This part of the cost is difficult to estimate. I suggest using a gambling form, that is, everyone quantifies the business value and shares it according to the output ratio. Therefore, X is shown in the above figure. X represents the share of business operations output, paid monthly.

Second Year After Launch

I suggest that the budget investment in the second year after launch accounts for 10% of the total CRM cycle investment, of which 5% of the cost is used for monthly operation and maintenance costs, paid quarterly or monthly; another 5% of the cost is used for demand changes, paid according to the development volume. Payment. After the CRM goes live, in addition to system maintenance, we also need to have business operations, that is, a professional team is responsible for the continuous output of business value from the CRM. This part of the cost is difficult to estimate, so I suggest adopting a betting form, that is, everyone quantifies the business value and shares it according to the output ratio. Therefore, X is represented in the above figure. X represents the share of business output from operations, paid monthly.

Third Year After Going Live

The third year after going live is considered a mid-term revision, and we need to invest more funds. It is recommended that the budget input accounts for 15% of the total CRM cycle input, of which 5% is used for monthly maintenance costs, paid quarterly or monthly; another 10% of the cost is used for demand changes, paid according to the development volume. After the CRM goes live, in addition to system maintenance, we also need to have business operations, that is, a professional team is responsible for the continuous output of business value from the CRM. This part of the cost is difficult to estimate, so I suggest adopting a betting form, that is, everyone quantifies the business value and shares it according to the output ratio. Therefore, X is represented in the above figure. X represents the share of business output from operations, paid monthly.

Fourth and Fifth Years After Going Live

I suggest that the budget input for the fourth and fifth years after going live accounts for 10% of the total CRM cycle input, of which 5% is used for monthly maintenance costs, paid quarterly or monthly; another 5% of the cost is used for demand changes, paid according to the development volume. After the CRM goes live, in addition to system maintenance, we also need to have business operations, that is, a professional team is responsible for the continuous output of business value from the CRM. This part of the cost is difficult to estimate, so I suggest adopting a betting form, that is, everyone quantifies the business value and shares it according to the output ratio. Therefore, X is represented in the above figure. X represents the share of business output from operations, paid monthly.

In the digital age, the iteration speed of sales and service in business and technology is very fast. The CRM project needs to be re-planned and designed after five or six years to cope with the new business environment and business needs. So after the five or six year lifecycle of the CRM, we need to start a new CRM delivery cycle.

Project Process Management

As shown in Fig. 4.3, the project management process of the full lifecycle CRM delivery method consists of three stages: ① planning; ② delivery; ③ online system maintenance, function iteration and online business operations. I have marked several key points in the figure.

(1) Quantifiable business value indicators should be set in the planning stage: such as sales increase, sales cycle shortening, success rate increase, etc.
(2) In order to ensure that the plan can be implemented in the delivery stage, it can be required that the core members in the planning stage participate in the early stage of delivery, and the last payment of the plan is made after the function requirement design document comes out in the delivery stage.
(3) After the CRM goes live, it is necessary to always monitor system operation indicators and business operation indicators, and correct them immediately if they deviate.
(4) The payment method for business operations is recommended to adopt a betting method, and payment is made according to the quantified value of business output improvement.

The following introduces the three stages of project management:

Planning Stage

As suggested earlier, planning and delivery are best divided into two separate projects. Because as long as planning and delivery are combined, the project manager will take controlling scope and timely launch as the basic principle, and will not carefully consider methods to improve business value.

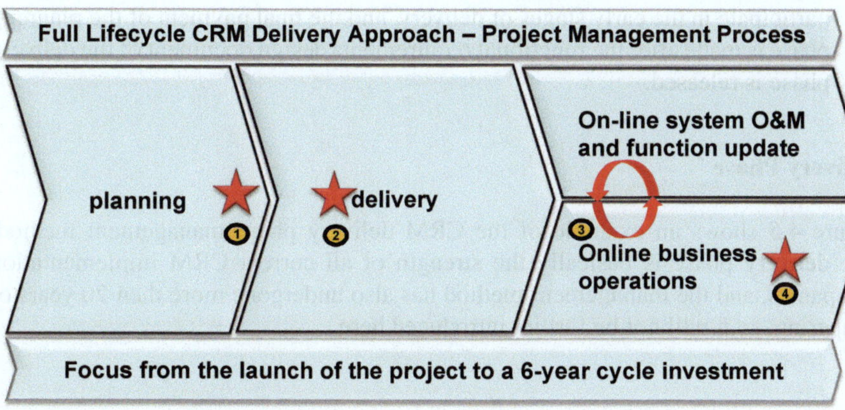

Fig. 4.3 Project management process

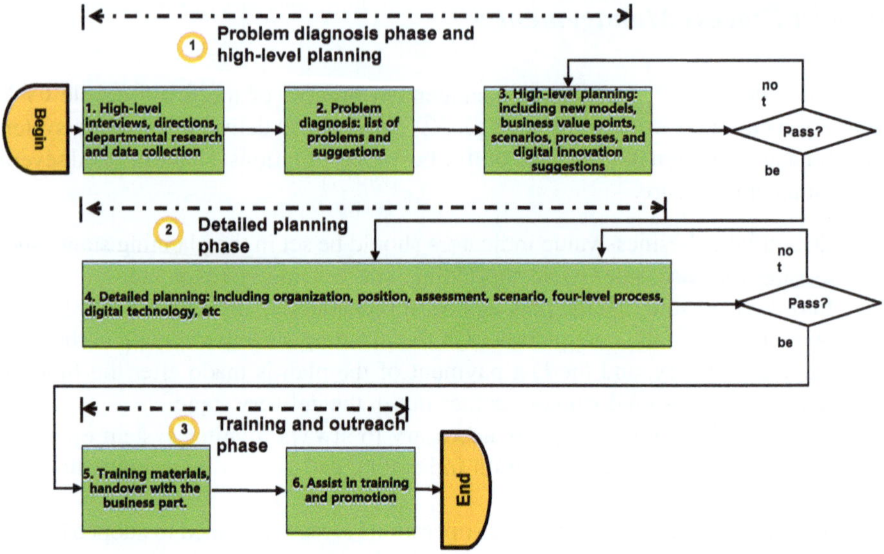

Fig. 4.4 Example of Planning Stage

Figure 4.4 is an introduction to the planning stage, with the following key points:

(1) The planning stage is important to divide into three small stages: ① problem diagnosis and high-level planning stage; ② detailed planning stage; ③ training and promotion stage.
(2) The main deliverables of the planning phase include: problem diagnostic reports, high-level planning reports, detailed planning reports, training manuals, and management forms, etc.
(3) Implementation of planning content: To ensure that the planning content can be implemented, it is recommended that the core members of the planning phase participate in the early stages of delivery, and the final payment of the planning phase is made after the functional requirements design document of the delivery phase is released.

Delivery Phase

Figure 4.5 shows an example of the CRM delivery phase management method. The delivery phase is basically the strength of all current CRM implementation companies, and the management method has also undergone more than 20 years of tempering, so it will not be further introduced here.

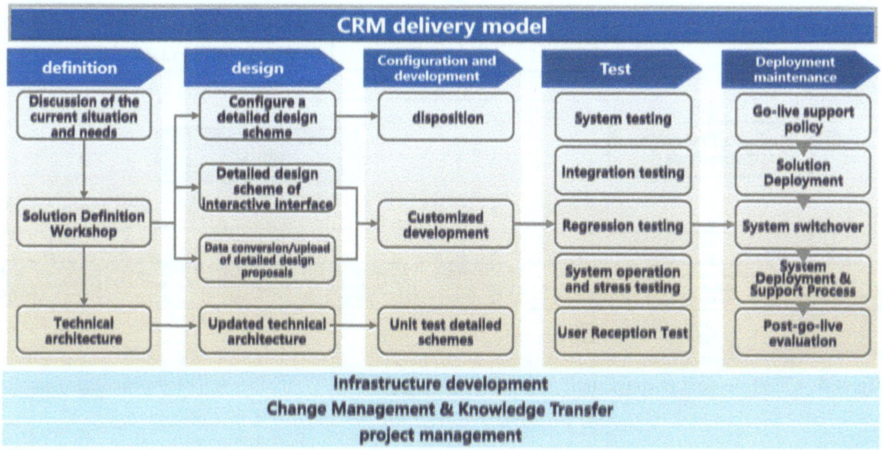

Fig. 4.5 Example of Delivery Stage

System Operation and Maintenance and Functional Iteration and Business Operation Phase

(1) System operation and maintenance and functional iteration: How to do system operation and maintenance after CRM goes online, how to provide first-line and second-line support, how to carry out functional optimization iteration, these processes are very mature, so no more introduction is made here.
(2) Business operation: After CRM goes online, how to do business operation, how to bet, this part mainly depends on the trust level and courage of Party A and Party B, and a customized plan must be made according to the specific project and specific situation. However, I have two suggestions here:
    (1) Generally speaking, it is difficult for large companies of Party B to do business operations according to the betting agreement. Because the return in the betting agreement is difficult to evaluate, there is a great risk for Party B, so the legal department of Party B may not approve it during the contract review process.
    (2) To do business operations and betting, it can be undertaken by personnel of Party A who are willing to take risks, or by senior independent consultants in the market.

Promotion and Implementation Management

Traditional CRM project management is mainly undertaken by the Project Management Office (PMO). If the customer's demand is system go-live, it is no problem for the PMO to be responsible; if the customer's demand is to generate business value

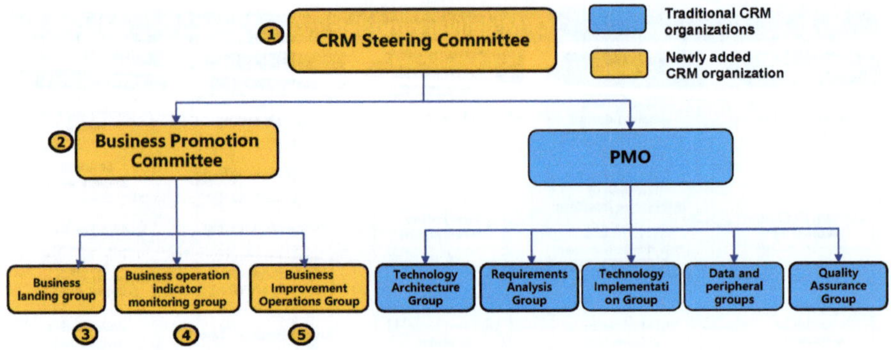

Fig. 4.6 CRM project management organization suggestions

and improve business operation capabilities, the project management structure of the PMO alone seems to be insufficient.

As shown in Fig. 4.6, for the CRM delivery method of the full lifecycle in the digital age, in order to generate business value and improve business operation capabilities, I suggest adding the following organizations:

(1) CRM Steering Committee: If you want to generate a lot of business value, it is impossible to succeed without the participation and promotion of the top management. Therefore, it is recommended that this steering committee be composed of the company's general manager, the head of the business covered by the CRM project (such as the head of sales or service), and the chief information officer. The purpose of this steering committee is to understand the expectations and feedback of the top management, need to get the approval of the top management, and reach a consensus within the group. It is recommended to have a meeting about every two weeks during the planning phase, and once every one to two months during the delivery and operation phase.
(2) Business Promotion Committee: The Business Promotion Committee is composed of the head of the business covered by the CRM project (such as the head of sales or service), responsible for coordinating various resources to promote and implement various changes and innovations involved in CRM.
(3) Business Implementation Group: The Business Implementation Group is responsible for the specific execution of business changes and innovative measures.
(4) Business Operation Indicator Monitoring Group: The Business Operation Indicator Monitoring Group is responsible for the evaluation and monitoring of all business indicators after CRM goes online.
(5) Business Operations Improvement Group: The Business Operations Improvement Group is the team mentioned earlier that is responsible for continuous operations after the CRM goes live, generating business value through wagering.

Summary > The traditional CRM delivery method has not changed much in over twenty years. In the digital age, we should keep up with the times and innovate and transform our delivery methods. This section provides a detailed introduction to the important components of the full lifecycle CRM delivery method in the digital age: two basic points, three transitions, and three supports.

CRM3.0 Building a Self-Evolving Organization Driving Digital Transformation

In the preface, I introduced the three cornerstones of digital transformation: body, use, and momentum. Digital strategy and digital organization are the body, and the digital organization is the internal driving force of digital transformation. In this section, I will introduce the organization construction and position setting in digital transformation.

Traditional IT Departments Cannot Drive Corporate Digital Transformation

As shown in Fig. 4.7, the traditional IT department aims to make software and hardware functions usable. It has poor integration with business and often speaks different languages from the business department. The two sides only intersect on some business-related IT projects.

This kind of IT department was fine ten years ago. At that time, digital technology did not have a significant impact on customer experience and purchasing behavior;

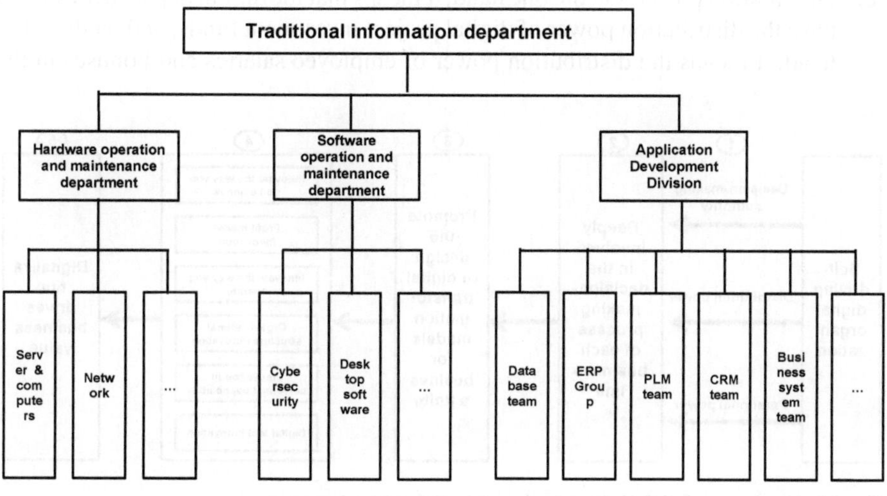

Fig. 4.7 Example of a traditional information department

moreover, due to the lack of widespread use of technologies such as the Internet of Things, artificial intelligence, mobile internet, social media, and big data, the impact on manufacturing, R&D, and supply chain was not significant. But today, when digital technology has penetrated every corner of life, if the traditional IT department structure is still used, the core competitiveness of the enterprise will gradually be lost in the digital age.

Five Steps of Digital-Driven Sales and Service Transformation

As shown in Fig. 4.8, the five main steps of digital-driven sales and service transformation are as follows:

Three Rights: Necessary Resources and Powers Must Be Given to the Digital Organization to Promote Digital Transformation

(1) Decision-making authority: This does not mean simply giving the Chief Data Officer or Chief Information Officer the decision-making power within the digital department. It means that the digital department should participate in the decision-making of the business department and drive the business department to reconstruct the business model and business process through digital technology. This requires the company to ensure it in the organizational structure and power decision-making mechanism. The following will specifically introduce how to build an organization that drives sales and service digital transformation.
(2) Distribution power: On the one hand, it means that the digital department should have the distribution power of digital project investment funds, and on the other hand, it means the distribution power of employee salaries and bonuses in the

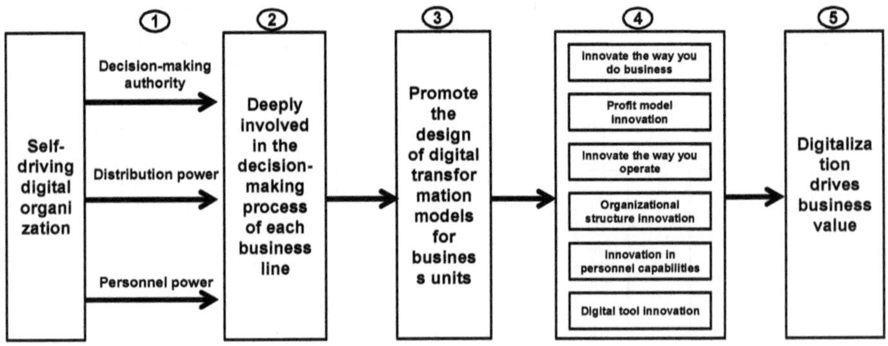

Fig. 4.8 Five steps of digital-driven sales and service transformation

digital department. Especially the latter, to establish a self-evolving digital organization, the premise is to let the digital department have the desire to drive digital transformation. The high output after transformation will bring high returns to itself, thereby generating the desire to promote transformation.

(3) Personnel power: In addition to the personnel power of the digital department, it also needs to have personnel power in the business department related to digital positions. Many companies have digital or information positions in their business departments, which will conflict with the digital department, causing many digital strategies to be difficult to promote, so these positions need personnel rights.

Deeply Participate in the Decision-Making Process of Each Business Line

If the digital department is just sending people to support the business department, that is digital empowerment. The digital department should formulate a digital strategy together with each business line, and have the corresponding organizational structure and mechanism to implement it, and supervise and assess the business line. This is digital driving.

Promoting the Design of Digital Transformation Models in Business Departments

To drive business transformation, it is necessary to remodel and innovate traditional business models based on the latest digital thinking and digital technology. Chapter 3 "Digital Transformation of Service Management" discusses how companies can plan for the digital transformation of their business using the RMB-PT method, using the service digital transformation as an example. This will not be elaborated here.

Implementing Six Types of Innovation for Digital Transformation

To achieve the digital transformation of sales and service business models, six types of innovation can be considered: ① Business method innovation; ② Profit model innovation; ③ Personnel capability innovation; ④ Organizational structure innovation; ⑤ Operational method innovation; ⑥ Digital tool innovation. Chapter 3 "Digital Transformation of Service Management" discusses how to carry out these six types of innovation, using the service digital transformation as an example. This will not be elaborated here.

Realizing the Business Value Output of Digital Transformation

In order for the digital transformation of the enterprise to gain the support of the business department, continuous investment, and continuous iterative upgrades, we need to design the short-term detonation point and business value enhancement measurement method for digital transformation during the third step of model design. Everything must be agreed upon in advance, everything must be quantifiable, and everything must be data-driven. Otherwise, due to some negative events, the digital transformation may be abandoned halfway.

Building an Organization to Drive the Digital Transformation of Sales and Services

Next, let's talk about how to build an organization to drive the digital transformation of sales and services.

As shown in Fig. 4.9, this organizational structure is not just about changing the internal structure of the digital department, but also about making adjustments at the group level.

Digital Strategy Committee

Without the participation and support of the highest level of the enterprise, many things cannot be promoted. Therefore, I suggest establishing a Digital Strategy Committee, composed of the company's top managers, the heads of each business line, and the Chief Data Officer (or Chief Information Officer). The purpose of establishing this committee is to set short-term and long-term digital strategies, and under the supervision of the highest management level, the heads of each business line will promote them.

Digital Assessment Department

A Digital Assessment Department is set up under the Operations Management Department to set digital transformation assessment indicators for each business line and supervise and regulate them. The reason for placing the Digital Assessment Department under the Operations Management Department, rather than establishing a new department, is because the Operations Management Department is the most capable, experienced, and efficient department in managing each business line.

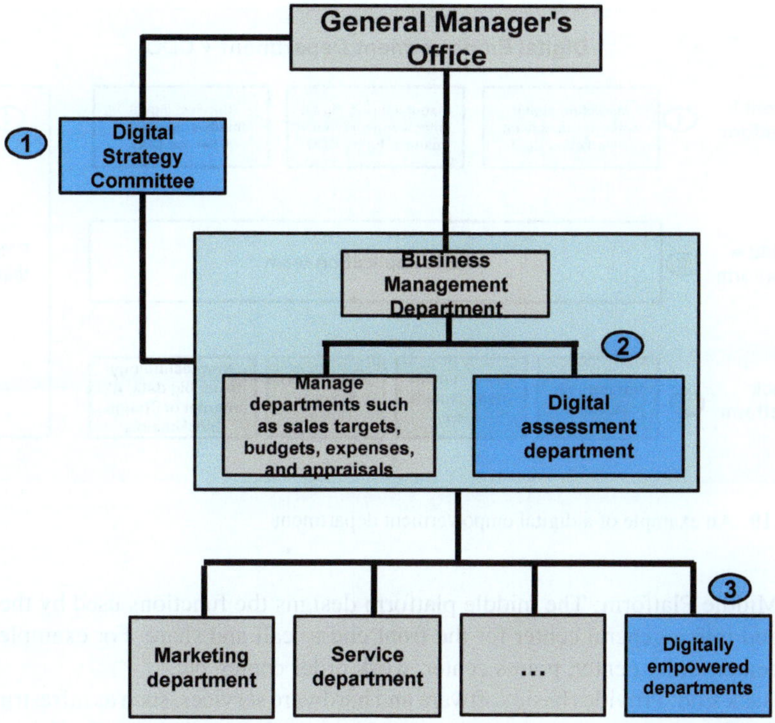

Fig. 4.9 Self-evolving organization driving digital transformation

Digitally Empowered Department

In addition to the Digital Strategy Committee and Digital Assessment Department mentioned above, we also need to restructure the Information Department and transform it into a "Digitally Empowered Department".

As shown in Fig. 4.10, the Digitally Empowered Department is built according to the front-middle, middle-back, and back-end. The biggest advantage of this is that it can directly integrate with the business department and empower the business department through digital technology. The main difference between the Digitally Empowered Department and the traditional Information Department is reflected in the front-end and middle-end teams.

(1) Front-end: The front-end is generally a digitally empowered team equipped according to the business line, directly connected to the business platform, such as the marketing digital empowerment team, the manufacturing R&D digital empowerment team, the service digital empowerment team. The role of these teams is to deeply participate in the decision-making and execution process of each business line, to promote and complete various business Digital innovation and transformation of the service line.

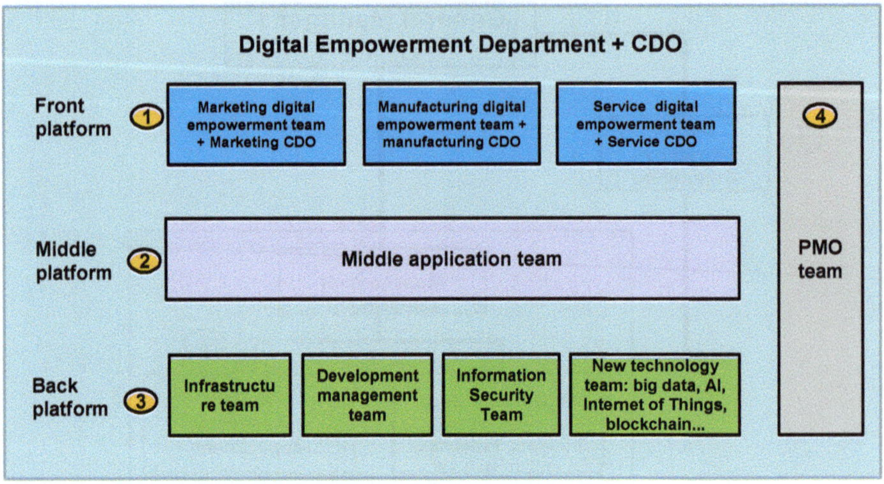

Fig. 4.10 An example of a digital empowerment department

(2) Middle Platform: The middle platform designs the functions used by the front end into a general center for the front end to call and share. For example, user center, order center, points center, work order center, etc.
(3) Back End: Provides basic software and hardware services, such as infrastructure, development resource pool, information security, and new technologies (big data, artificial intelligence, Internet of Things, blockchain, etc.) services.
(4) Project Management Team: The project management team provides project management, project auditing, evaluation, and sprint services for front-end, middle platform, and back-end projects.

Setting Up Positions for Driving Digital Transformation

The previous section discussed the organizational construction for driving digital transformation. Here we will introduce the position setting for driving digital transformation, as shown in Fig. 4.11.

Chief Data Officer

(1) Has decision-making power, distribution power, and personnel power in the digital field.
(2) Has significant say in the digital strategy committee composed of the company's top management, the heads of various business lines, and the chief data officer.
(3) Quantifies and measures the process and results of the digital transformation of each business line through the digital assessment department.

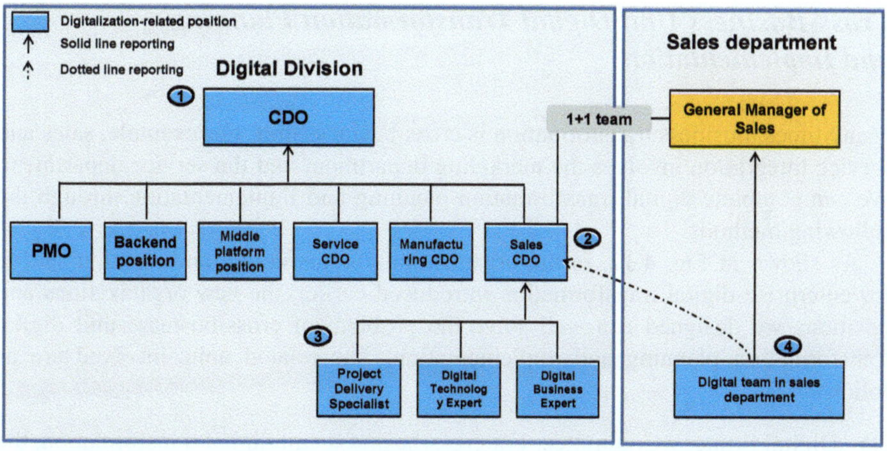

Fig. 4.11 Example of position placement to drive digital transformation

Chief Data Officer for Sales

The sales field also needs its own chief data officer, who teams up one-on-one with the general manager of sales to jointly complete the digital transformation of sales. Therefore, the chief data officer in the sales field must have enough business knowledge and digital knowledge to be a friend and mentor to the general manager of sales, and to plan the overall digital transformation of the sales field.

Sales Digital Team

The Chief Data Officer for Sales needs to have his own digital team. They can do digital projects, enable digital processes, and promote the most cutting-edge digital technologies.

Business Department Digital Team

The sales business departments generally also have their own digital teams. This team is advised to report to the Chief Data Officer for Sales in a dotted line manner, so that the Chief Data Officer for Sales can better understand the current situation of sales business, and better promote the implementation of digital transformation of sales.

Cross-Business Unit Digital Transformation Planning and Implementation

Many times, business transformation is cross-business unit. For example, sales and service integration involves the marketing department and the service department. We can complete digital transformation planning and implementation through the following methods.

As shown in Fig. 4.12, in the organizational construction and position setting for enterprise digital transformation introduced earlier, the new organizations and positions we designed can well solve the problem of cross-business unit digital transformation planning and implementation. The related units involved are as follows.

(1) Digital Strategy Committee: For cross-business unit digital transformation, the top management reaches consensus and sets direction.
(2) Digital Assessment Department: Monitors the process and results of cross-business unit digital transformation.
(3) Chief Data Officers in Various Fields: For cross-business unit digital transformation, they formulate specific implementation plans, complete implementation through process, scenario and position design, and digital projects.

Summary > This section introduces the four important aspects of "Organizational Construction and Position Setting in Digital Transformation". These are: ① The five steps of digital transformation; ② The organizational construction driving digital transformation; ③ The position setting driving digital transformation; ④ The planning and implementation of digital transformation across business units.

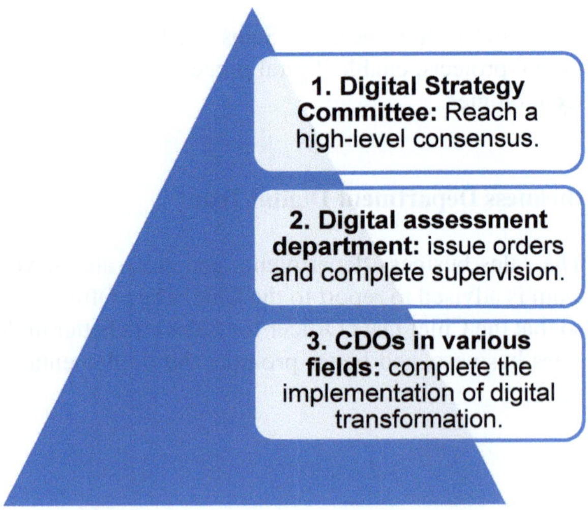

Fig. 4.12 Digital transformation planning and implementation across business units

The Value Assessment System of CRM 3.0

There has always been a lack of a standard value assessment system in the CRM field, that is, how to assess whether CRM is successful, and how to operate CRM to ensure continuous output of business value. In the past, we always explained to customers that use is useful, that is, once the CRM system is online and users are using it, it means that the CRM system has value.

In the digital age, as mentioned in the previous chapters: To be successful in the CRM 3.0 era, five key capabilities must be possessed, one of which is the need to establish a CRM value assessment system.

The CRM value assessment system is closely related to the CRM function areas to be used, the industries involved, and customer attributes. Below, I will take B2B sales in CRM as an example, extract the commonality of the industry and customers, and define a value assessment system.

For B2B sales of CRM, many customers have always wanted to use sales volume or sales cycle as a measurement standard. But many B2B orders depend on the customer's budget and the customer's project cycle, and the role that the second party can play is not significant, so it is difficult to shorten the sales cycle and increase sales through CRM. Even if individual orders can, they do not have universality. Some customers use win rate or opportunity conversion rate for assessment, but it is difficult to analyze which effects are caused by CRM and which effects are caused by market sales input, product solutions, pre-sales team capabilities, and relationship improvement. Therefore, it is difficult to comprehensively evaluate the role of CRM in B2B sales based on one or two indicators. We need a more systematic, comprehensive, and scientific evaluation system.

The reason why we have difficulty in building a value assessment system is that we lack a complete B2B sales theory system. In the past, there was only the methodology from market to lead, lead to opportunity, opportunity to order, order to cash, that is, mainly focusing on LTC management. LTC management only focuses on one opportunity mainline, and is mainly process-oriented, lacking many management and evaluation methods, so it is difficult to establish a complete CRM evaluation indicator system.

As I introduced in Chapter 2 "CRM 3.0's B2B Sales Digital Transformation", B2B sales consist of five main lines: namely, the customer line, opportunity line (TAS+), support line, relationship line (ECM), and project line (PBM). Based on this CRM 3.0 theory, the following introduces the B2B sales evaluation system of CRM 3.0.

As shown in Fig. 4.13, the B2B sales evaluation system of CRM 3.0 consists of five dimensions.

(1) Customer management capability is also the management capability of the customer line, as well as the data accumulation capability of the relationship line (ECM) and project line (PBM).
(2) The control capability of the order process is also the management capability of the opportunity line (TAS+).

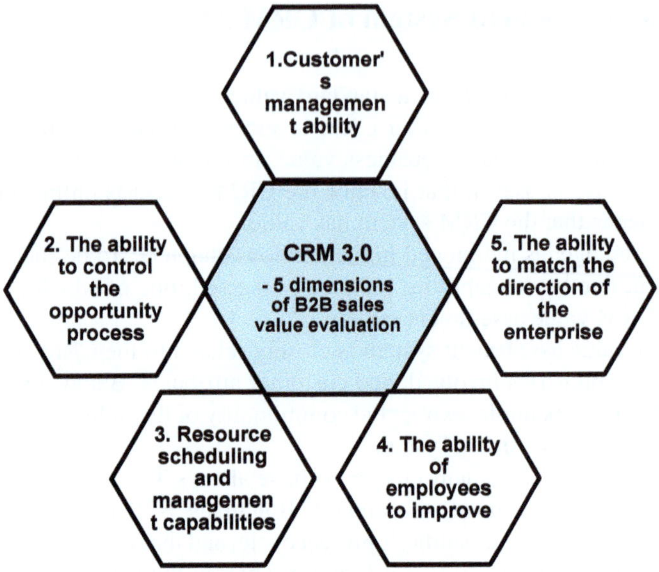

Fig. 4.13 CRM 3.0 5 dimensions of B2B sales evaluation

(3) Resource scheduling and management capability is also the management capability of the support line.
(4) Employee improvement capability is also the application capability of employee resources.
(5) The ability to match the direction of the enterprise, which is the ability to execute strategy.

As shown in Fig. 4.14, I will now provide a detailed introduction to the level 2 KPI of the five dimensions of the B2B sales evaluation system.

Customer Management Ability

The purpose of managing major customers is to establish advantages in relationships and solutions, suppress competitors, and incubate more high-quality business opportunities. In addition, effective coverage of customers, as well as the accumulation and operation of relationship capabilities and project relationship information, are also crucial in managing major customers. Therefore, the assessment indicators of customer management ability are as follows:

(1) Relationship Intimacy: Used to assess our company's overall relationship ability and the relationship ability of individual employees. I have detailed this in the previous section "B2B Sales: Enterprise Networking Resource Management (ECM) Ability", so I will not elaborate here.

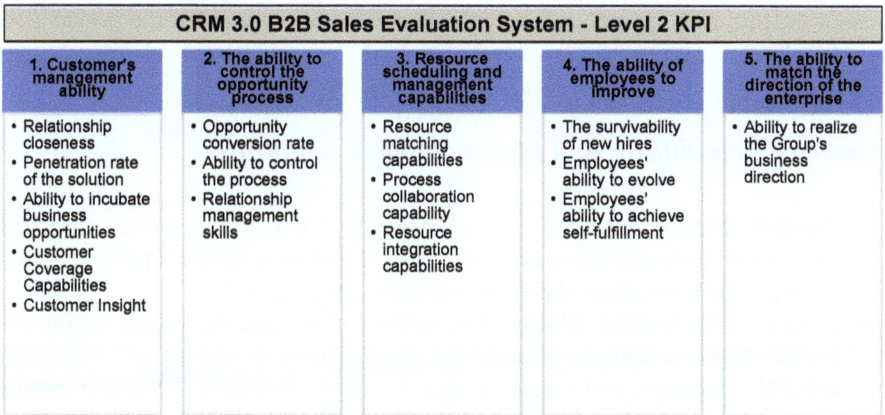

Fig. 4.14 B2B sales evaluation system—Level 2 KPI

(2) Solution Penetration: The categories and quantity of our company's solutions and products used by customers; the winning rate of our company's solutions and products in customer choices.
(3) Business Opportunity Incubation Ability: The number and amount of incubated business opportunities entering the project initiation stage.
(4) Customer Coverage Ability: The number of large, medium, and small customers responsible for the addition of purchased products and solutions; the number of lost customers among customers who have purchased products and solutions.
(5) Customer Insight Ability: Insight into the customer's networking ability, that is, the customer relationship map and the data completeness and accuracy of the customer's key person perspective in the networking line (ECM). For details, please see the previous section "B2B Sales: Enterprise Networking Resource Management (ECM) Ability". Insight into customer project data, that is, the completeness and accuracy of customer project data. For details, please see the previous section "B2B Sales: Project Behavior Management (PBM)".

The Ability to Control the Opportunity Process

It is actually the control ability of the business opportunity line (TAS+).

(1) Conversion Rate: The conversion rate between project initiation and winning business opportunities.
(2) Process Control Ability: The proportion of business opportunities that occupy the most customer time and the proportion of business opportunities involved in customer budget and tender document preparation.
(3) Relationship Control Ability: The completeness and accuracy of the data filled in the project decision chain; the degree of projection of the value proposition

of the project's key person; the completeness and accuracy of the project data filled in.

Resource Scheduling and Management Capabilities

(1) Resource Matching Ability: The efficiency and ability of resource placement for large projects; the efficiency and ability of general resource support for small projects; the proportion of pre-sales costs in the project.
(2) Process Collaboration Ability: The ability to manage uniformly during the project process, that is, whether the main person in charge can efficiently schedule resources, and whether each participant can clearly define job responsibilities; collaborative assessment ability, that is, whether the main person in charge can fairly and transparently score each project participant.
(3) Resource Integration Ability: Whether large projects can efficiently integrate each participant in the order taking process, such as pre-sales, testing, delivery, after-sales, secondary development, and other team members.
(4) Resource Return Ability: The improvement of pre-sales resource ROI and the overall sales increase.

Employee Improvement Ability

It is about how to help sales employees succeed. This has been detailed in the previous section "CRM Application: Three-Wheel Drive System".

(1) Survival Ability of New Employees: The retention rate of employees in the subsistence stage.
(2) Employee's ability to advance: The advancement rate of employees in the subsistence and moderately prosperous stages.
(3) Employee's self-realization ability: The self-realization rate of employees in the affluent stage.

The Ability to Match the Direction of the Enterprise

This mainly refers to the ability to implement the group's business direction, that is, whether CRM can help the group's strategy to be successfully implemented. You can take out the performance indicators of the group's key areas and compare them with before using CRM. For example, the market share of Plan A in key first-tier cities, contract amounts, etc.

Summary > This section introduces the value assessment system of CRM3.0, and takes the value assessment system of B2B sales as an example, introducing five dimensions and the secondary indicators of each dimension. The five dimensions are:

① Customer management ability; ② Control ability in the order process; ③ Resource scheduling and management ability; ④ Employee's ability to improve; ⑤ The ability to match the direction of the enterprise.

How to Implement CRM3.0 Enterprise Digital Strategy

In this section, I will introduce how each business unit can be implemented after the enterprise has a digital strategy, as well as the order and relationship between value flow, business flow and data flow, or organization, position, process and assessment.

As shown in Fig. 4.15, the digital strategy and implementation are divided into three main parts, namely digital planning, digital design, and digital empowerment. Digital implementation mainly occurs in digital design and digital empowerment, specifically divided into five steps:

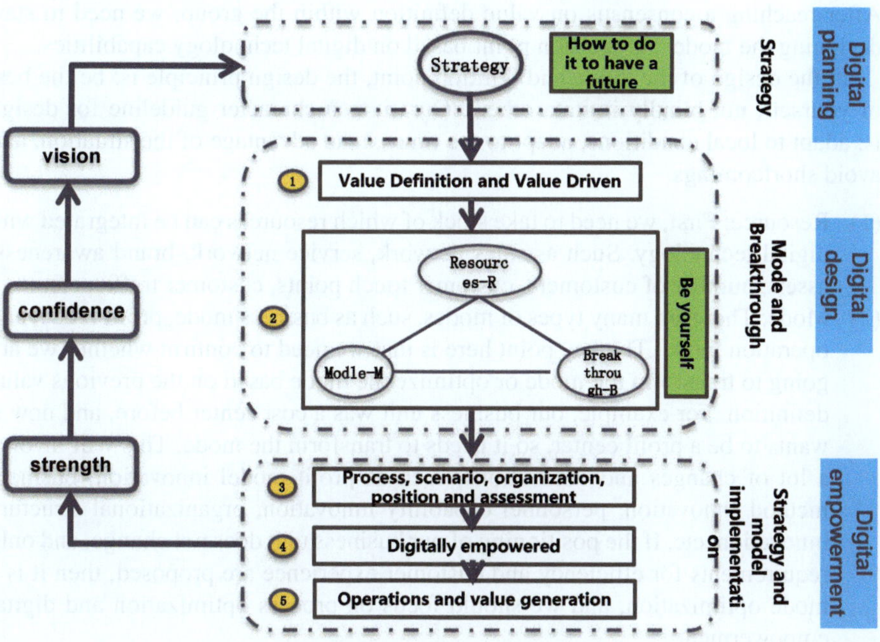

Fig. 4.15 Five steps to implement the digital strategy

Value Definition and Value-Driven

After the digital strategy is formulated, each business unit must clearly define the value positioning and value assessment methods of this business unit in the group strategy with the top management of the group. And drive the design of the business model based on the value definition and assessment method recognized by the group after discussion.

This step must be done, and you must not be self-righteous in this matter. For example, if the group defines our business unit as a cost center, we only need to do our job well, but if we define ourselves as a profit center, all subsequent designs will have a huge deviation.

Define the Mode and Ignition Point Through the RMB Method

After reaching a consensus on value definition within the group, we need to start designing the mode and ignition point based on digital technology capabilities.

In the design of the mode and ignition point, the design principle is: be the best of yourself, not blindly imitate others. Our sixteen-character guideline for design is: adapt to local conditions, adapt to the times, take advantage of the situation, and avoid shortcomings.

(1) Resource: First, we need to take stock of which resources can be integrated with digital technology. Such as sales network, service network, brand awareness, assets, number of customers, customer touch points, customer traffic, etc.
(2) Mode: There are many types of modes, such as business mode, profit mode, and operation mode. The key point here is that we need to confirm whether we are going to transform the mode or optimize the mode based on the previous value definition. For example, our business unit was a cost center before, and now it wants to be a profit center, so it needs to transform the mode. This will involve a lot of changes and innovations, such as profit model innovation, business method Innovation, personnel capability innovation, organizational structure innovation, etc. If the positioning of our business unit does not change, and only requirements for efficiency and customer experience are proposed, then it is a mode optimization, and we should focus on process optimization and digital empowerment.
(3) Breakthrough: A breakthrough is a quantifiable improvement indicator that can be brought about in the short term (for example, within 1 year), and these measurement indicators are recognized by the highest level of the group. Because doing so can ensure that your transformation or optimization can continue. The most feared thing in the transformation or optimization of business units is that some sudden events disrupt your process, or the success standards defined by the business unit are inconsistent with the evaluation standards of the group leaders. In this case, even if the transformation or optimization has

achieved great results, the group leaders may not recognize it from their sources of information or perspectives, causing the transformation or optimization to be abandoned halfway. Therefore, we need to achieve and exceed the evaluation standards recognized by the group leaders in the short term, constantly ignite, and constantly give the group confidence. In this way, we can get more support and help and eliminate unnecessary noise.

The RMB-PT method is introduced in Chapter 3 "CRM3.0 Service Digital Transformation", so I won't go into details here.

Establishment of Processes, Organizations, Positions, and Assessments

After the mode and breakthrough points are established, it is necessary to start designing processes, scenarios, organizations, positions, and assessments, sometimes we call it Business Process Reengineering (BPR).

Digital Empowerment

It is to choose digital tools to support the transformation or optimization of the previous modes, processes, scenarios, organizations, positions, and assessments. Which digital technologies to use, which related products to apply, need to be determined by the industry, by the application, and by the customer, there is a huge difference. But the delivery method is common, you can use the previously introduced CRM3.0 full lifecycle delivery method to complete the three changes in delivery: (1) Selection change: from focusing on software selection to focusing on digital innovation; (2) Evaluation change: from focusing on software functions to focusing on business value output; (3) Budget and input change: from one-time investment to continuous investment output over several years.

Continuous Operation and Business Value Output

In traditional methods, the launch and operation of digital systems are considered separately, and generally focus more on delivery and less on operation. But this method of only caring about birth and not nurturing will result in the system being launched, but no business value is generated. I introduced the investment cycle management in the CRM3.0 full lifecycle delivery method, which explains how to invest each year after the system is launched to carry out system maintenance and business operations.

When the above five steps are effectively executed, the strength of the enterprise will continue to increase; as the strength increases, the enterprise will naturally have more confidence; with confidence, the vision will be longer, and it will naturally be reflected in the enterprise strategy, thus forming a virtuous cycle.

After introducing the "Five Steps of Strategy Landing", I will answer a few common questions in the process of strategy landing:

Question 1: What are the major risk points in the process of strategy landing?

(1) The business unit and the group are not on the same channel for value definition. The strategy is easily disrupted by sudden events, so it is necessary to reach a consensus with the group on value definition and value driving direction in the first step, and reach a consensus with the group on breakthrough points and evaluation standards in the second step.
(2) When people leave, the tea gets cold. When the main leader changes, all the previous transformations and optimizations gradually stop. tem, and the original transformation and optimization are still operating in the system.
(3) Only giving birth, not raising. Transformation and optimization are certainly not perfect at the beginning, they need continuous operation, constant correction and optimization. Transformation and optimization need to be given time, space and resources to protect their growth.

Question 2: How can a cost center be transformed into a profit center?

If a cost center wants to become a profit center, it generally needs to go through a transformation of the model, that is, the transformation of the business model, profit model, and operation model. At the same time, major adjustments need to be made to the organizational structure of the business unit, and the power of operation, personnel, and distribution must be given to the profit center in order to achieve self-driving, self-organizing, self-evolving, and self-profit.

Question 3: What is the assessment model for the front, middle, and back office after organizational transformation?

(1) Front office: By bringing high experience and high value to customers, you can get high income. The front office assessment comes from customers and the market, and you need to find the most reasonable and quantifiable indicators.
(2) Middle and back office: It changes from a management function to an operation and support function. The front office calls on the resources of the middle and back office, and the middle and back office are assessed through the overall operation effect.

Question 4: What is the order of organization, process, scene, position, and assessment? Is it organization first and then process, or process first and then organization?

(1) If you are making a major business model transformation, you may need to consider organizational change first, and then look at other elements such as processes and scenes. That is, first see if the group can meet the requirements for organizational change, such as upgrading the business unit level, granting personnel rights, operating rights, and distribution rights, etc.

(2) If the business model does not change, and only process and scene optimization are done, you can prioritize the process and scene, design the best process and scene, and then see how the organization, position, and assessment can cooperate with the optimized process and scene.

Question 5: What is the order of value stream, business flow, and data flow?

(1) In the design, planning, and landing stage, you can first design the value stream, then the business flow, and finally the data flow.
(2) In the operation stage, the value stream, business flow, and data flow should complement each other and cycle upwards.

Summary > This section introduces the five steps of corporate strategic planning and implementation: ① Value definition and value driving; ② Define the mode and ignition point through the RMB method; ③ Establishment of process, scene, organization, position, and assessment; ④ Digital empowerment; ⑤ Continuous operation and business value output.

CRM3.0 Four-Dimensional Planning Method (MSTT)

The previous section introduced how to implement digital strategy. After we have defined the mode and ignition point in the digital design, we can use the four-dimensional digital planning method to design digital empowerment.

At present, a large number of digital technologies have emerged, such as artificial intelligence, blockchain, big data, edge computing, AIoT, mixed reality, as well as many mobile and social applications. But these technologies are mainly reflected in the system. On the implementation level, the field of business consulting and planning is still using traditional consulting and planning methodologies. This leads to a situation where digital capabilities are not well integrated with business operations, and the effectiveness of digitalization is not well reflected. If a company does not plan at the level of models, scenarios, and processes, and is merely digitalizing for the sake of digitalization, it is like "walking the old path in new shoes", which may lead the company further down the wrong path.

When carrying out digital innovation and transformation in sales and services in the digital age, the MSTT planning method of CRM3.0 can be adopted, i.e., planning in four dimensions: Model, Space, Time, and Technology. That is, business model digital innovation, business scenario digital innovation, business process digital innovation, and technology digital innovation should be perfectly integrated in the planning process.

As shown in Fig. 4.16, when planning for digital transformation in sales and services, in addition to traditional consulting and planning methods, we can plan from four dimensions: digitalization of business models, digitalization of space, digitalization of time, and digitalization of technology.

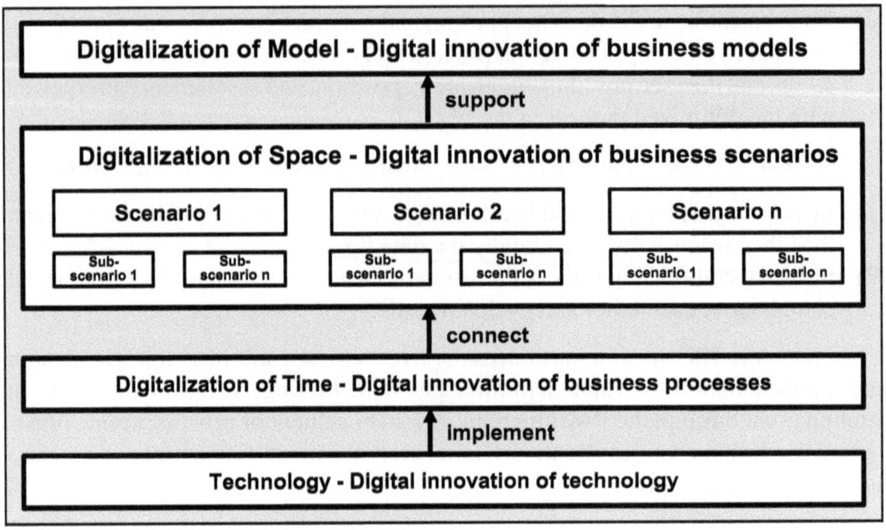

Fig. 4.16 Four-dimensional digital planning (MSTT)

Digitalization of Model—Digital Innovation of Business Model

Innovative companies often need to change lanes. Changing lanes refers to leading competitors by a large margin, such as digital innovation; changing lanes refers to competing from different fields and dimensions, such as digital transformation. Digital innovation of the business model belongs to changing lanes, i.e., digital transformation, which is to obtain huge competitive advantages by changing business models, profit models, and operation models, etc., supported by digital technology.

Digital innovation of the model can be considered from the following two aspects:

(1) Can digital technology create new business models? This is due to the development of digital technology, making previously non-existent models possible. For example, e-commerce, new retail, social media, short videos, etc. are all such cases. As mentioned later in the "Preliminary Analysis of Digital Transformation in the Home Appliance, Automobile, and Real Estate Industries", services need to transform from work order-driven transactional services to demand-driven steward services, which requires the transformation of service stewardship, personnel creation, network platformization, and income ecology. If we use digital technology to undertake this transformation and plan in this regard, it belongs to digital innovation of the business model.
(2) Can digital technology support the new business model under the new strategy of the group? For example, if the group's future positioning is a "provider of a better life" or a "builder and service provider of urban and rural areas", it will inevitably have to make major adjustments in business models, operation

models, and profit models, etc. Can our digital technology strongly support this major adjustment?

Digitalization of Space—Digital Innovation of Scenarios

The execution of sales and services will definitely occur in certain scenarios, so digitalization of space is necessary. Of course, an activity that occurs in a certain scenario may also involve one or more business processes. Scenarios are often customer and user-centric, designed around customer and user experience. And processes are often centered around the internal management loop of the enterprise. Therefore, in today's emphasis on customer and user experience, personalized service as the core competitiveness, if we do not plan and design for important scenarios, it will greatly weaken the effect of digitalization. And traditional consulting and planning methods still have some shortcomings in the digital planning and design of scenarios.

Because there are too many different scenarios in the process of sales and services, we can focus on some key scenarios, break down the key scenarios into sub-scenarios, and carry out digital design separately.

As shown in Fig. 4.17, one of the most important scenarios for major appliance services is on-site repair. We divide the appliance repair scenario into four sub-scenarios: home visits, appliance repair, housekeeping services, and settlement completion. Each sub-scenario involves many points that can be digitally empowered.

(1) Sub-scenario 1: Home visits

- How to arrive on time?
- How to standardize dress, behavior, and language?

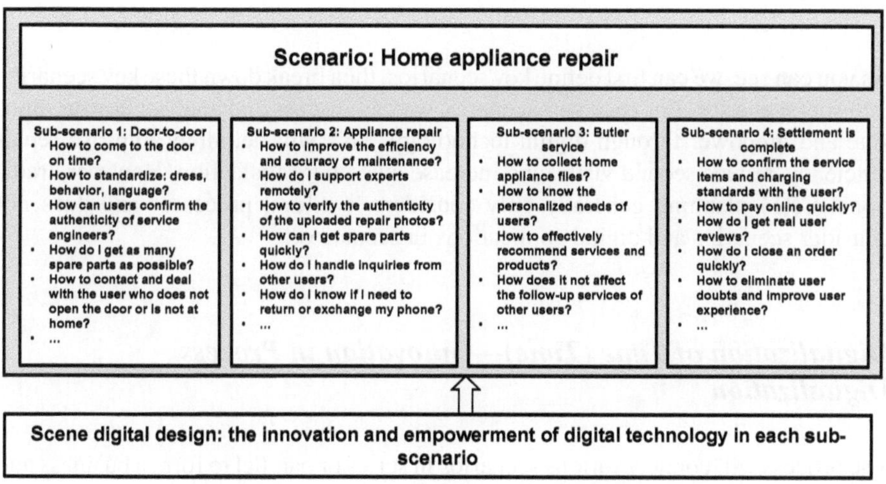

Fig. 4.17 Example of digital design in a home appliance maintenance scenario

- How can users verify the authenticity of the service engineer?
- How to bring all necessary spare parts?
- How to contact and handle situations when the user does not open the door or is not at home?
- ……

(2) Sub-scenario 2: Appliance repair

- How to improve repair efficiency and accuracy?
- How to implement remote expert support?
- How to verify the authenticity of uploaded repair photos?
- How to quickly obtain spare parts?
- How to handle inquiries from other users simultaneously?
- How to determine whether a replacement is needed?
- ……

(3) Sub-scenario 3: Housekeeping services

- How to collect appliance records?
- How to understand user's personalized needs?
- How to effectively recommend services and products?
- How to not affect subsequent services for other users?
- ……

(4) Sub-scenario 4: Settlement completion

- How to confirm service items and charging standards with users?
- How to quickly pay online?
- How to obtain genuine user reviews?
- How to quickly close the order?
- How to eliminate user doubts and enhance user experience?
- ……

As you can see, we can first define key scenarios, then break down these key scenarios into sub-scenarios. For each sub-scenario, we can discuss and analyze how to innovate and empower through digital technology. This will definitely improve repair efficiency, reduce second visits, and increase customer satisfaction. However, traditional CRM planning generally only considers five-level processes and does not consider scenarios and digital applications in scenarios.

Digitalization of Time (Time)—Innovation in Process Digitalization

The process will connect various scenarios in series or parallel to form a business and information closed loop. The节 Points often have a chronological order, so they are also a digitization of time. For example, the entire process of home appliance repair involves multiple scenarios such as demand access, dispatching orders, on-site repair, evaluation, closing orders, returning old parts, checking for counterfeits, and settlement. Since each scenario has been designed in the digitization of the scenario, all process digitization will string these scenarios together, putting execution efficiency and management efficiency first through digital technology.

The digitization of scenarios often focuses on user experience and business efficiency; the digitization of processes often focuses on management efficiency and execution efficiency.

Digitization of Technology (Technology)—Innovation of Technology

The digitization of technology is the strength of every product company, and related products and introductions are very easy to obtain. In "Digital Age CRM Product Innovation," I also introduced how to use digital technology to reconstruct CRM and the application of various digital technologies in CRM.

Summary > This section introduces a new digital planning method in the sales and service field, namely CRM3.0 four-dimensional planning method (MSTT): Digitization of Model, Digitization of Space, Digitization of Time, and Digitization of Technology.

CRM3.0 Application: Three-Wheel Drive System

Since its inception, CRM products have faced a huge dilemma. The company's management may be eager for CRM, thinking it is a good solution to sales problems, but frontline sales staff are very resistant, either unwilling to use it or entering a lot of invalid information. I started in the CRM field in 1999, and basically every customer is asking how to get frontline sales staff to use CRM. To this day, this problem is still one of the biggest challenges customers face.

When customers ask similar questions, we used to tell customers to strengthen assessments, ensure usage rates, and have existing reasons. As long as employees are using it, it means that CRM has value. We often encourage customers to include employee CRM usage rates in assessments, and deduct performance if usage rates are low. But in fact, this is a negative incentive method, using punishment as management. Even if the CRM usage rate is high, it does not necessarily mean there is business value.

The reason for this problem is related to CRM design thinking. Since the birth of CRM, we have adopted a two-wheel drive model for sales functions, namely, a

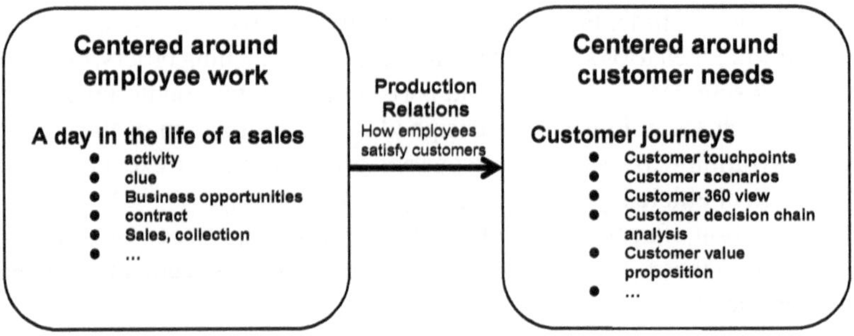

Fig. 4.18 The traditional two wheel drive mode of CRM

design method centered on daily sales work and customer needs. But we have never seriously considered the real needs of sales staff, especially frontline sales staff.

As shown in Fig. 4.18, our current CRM focuses on:

(1) Centered on employee work, that is, how the sales completes his own work around customer needs, with common functions such as activities, leads, opportunities, contracts, quotes, and payments.
(2) Centered on customer needs, that is, to understand customer needs, provide the best experience for customers through various scenarios and touchpoints, thereby increasing the win rate.

The problem with this model is that it focuses on how sales staff meet customers, that is, it establishes a production relationship between employees and customers. That is, centered on the customer, how the sales staff meet the customer's needs through daily work to achieve sales tasks.

But it overlooks the issue of productivity. Employees are the source of productivity. The development and changes in productivity determine With the development and transformation of production relations. Only by improving productivity can we truly improve production relations and thus enhance the overall sales capability of the company. Unhappy salespeople find it hard to bring high satisfaction to customers, so we cannot only focus on customer needs and ignore the needs of salespeople.

Establish a Three-Wheel Drive Model to Improve Production Relations Through Enhancing Productivity

As shown in Fig. 4.19, I believe that a third wheel (centered on employee needs) needs to be established for CRM to balance the CRM sales system, thereby making salespeople love and rely on CRM.

Many CRM products provide employees with knowledge bases, online training, etc. Does this count as being centered on employee needs? Yes, but it's far from enough.

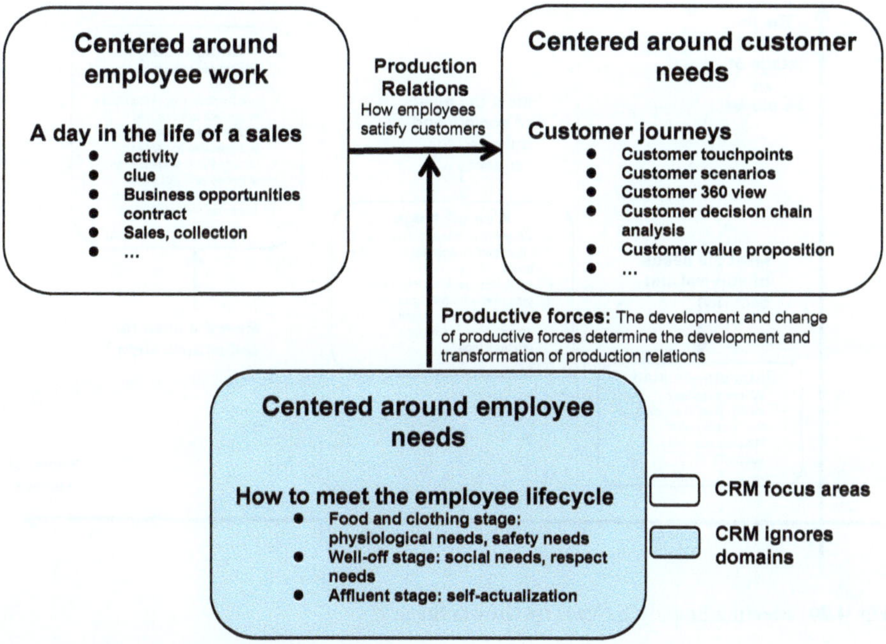

Fig. 4.19 CRM three-wheel drive mode

Just like in "centered on customer needs", we manage customers through the customer lifecycle; in "centered on employee needs", we manage through the employee lifecycle.

How CRM Realizes "Centered on Employee Needs"

As shown in Fig. 4.20, the lifecycle of an employee does not refer to the years a salesperson has worked in the company, nor does it refer to his career advancement path, but his survival and need status in the company. Some people may stay in one stage for a long time, while others may pass through quickly. Salespeople generally fall into one of the following three stages:

(1) Subsistence stage: This is often the state of salespeople who have just joined the company, lacking orders, understanding of the case, and related support resources.
(2) Well-off stage: This is often when salespeople have stable customers, with continuous orders coming in each year, the pressure to meet numbers is not great, and they have entered a virtuous cycle.
(3) Affluent stage: This is a stage that most salespeople cannot reach. Salespeople at this stage often find it relatively easy to meet performance indicators. They

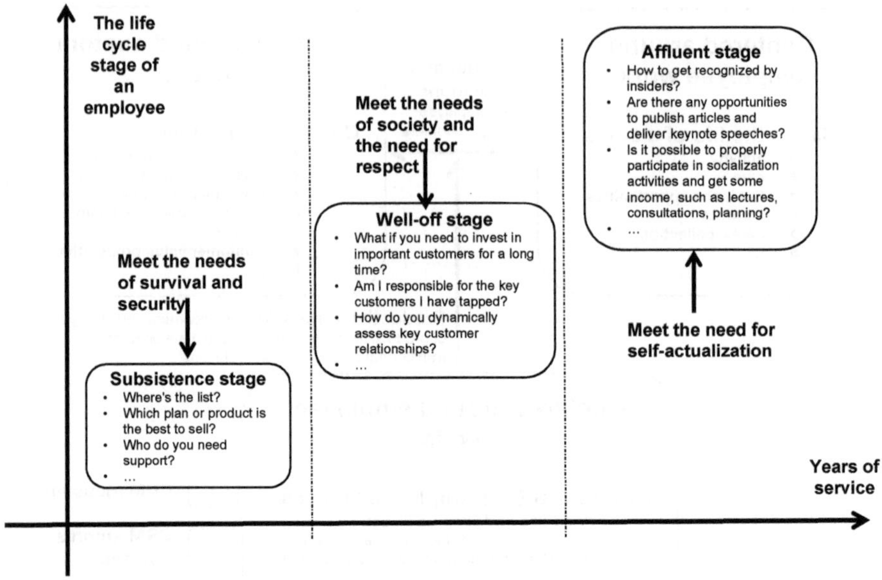

Fig. 4.20 Meeting Employee Needs by Growth Stage

have accumulated a lot in the industry and are more concerned about their reputation in the industry and everyone's affirmation of them, hoping to become an influential center in the industry.

When salespeople are at these stages, how do we design CRM to meet their different needs? In the subsistence stage, we need to help salespeople survive, i.e., help them find business opportunities through CRM, recommend the most suitable solutions, and provide the best pre-sales support during the order process; in the comfortable stage, CRM needs to provide various resources to help salespeople maintain some important customers, gain advantages in relationships and solutions, and accelerate the incubation of business opportunities; in the wealthy stage, CRM needs to help salespeople connect with various resources within the group and society to reflect their own value and become an industry big shot and influence center.

As shown in Fig. 4.21, we center on employee needs, build a creative platform, and add more employee-centered features in sales process management, sales support system management, key customer management, and enterprise resource sharing platform.

(1) Subsistence stage: We can more reasonably allocate business opportunities to new employees at the node of sales process management, and recommend the best-selling and matching solutions for them through the CRM system; we can also tilt resources towards new sales through sales support system management.

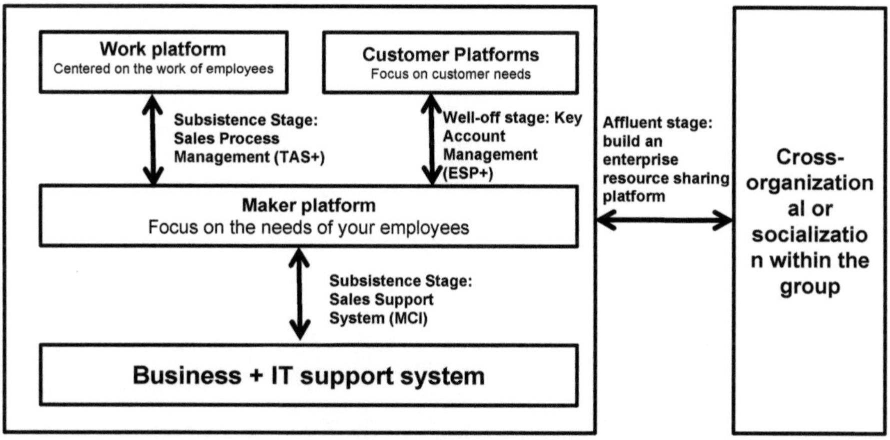

Fig. 4.21 Implementing a CRM function centered on employee needs

(2) Well-off stage: We can layout in advance in key customer management, provide various resources for sales, establish relationship and solution advantages, suppress competitors, and thus accelerate the incubation of business opportunities.
(3) Affluent stage: For salespeople at this stage, we should integrate the sales resources and relationships in the group The organization can share internally and also open to the society, giving him the opportunity to become an industry expert and influence center. The sales network resources, project resources, and expert resources at this stage can be fully utilized through the methods introduced in the "Enterprise Resource Sharing Platform" in the previous chapters.

Summary > This section introduces the three-wheel drive model of CRM (centered on customer needs, centered on employee work and centered on employee needs), and how to achieve the employee-centered function of CRM according to the sales growth stage, through sales process management, sales support system management, key account management, and enterprise resource sharing platform.

Chapter 5
Best Practices and Case Analysis

How to Do CRM Planning from a Business Value Perspective

Before starting to read this chapter, let me state: writing case analysis is not to judge whether past projects were good or bad, because each project has time limitations, and it might have been the best choice at that time. I write these cases to introduce a way of thinking about analyzing and planning CRM in the digital age.

Below is an introduction to a classic overall planning case of CRM.

Figure 5.1 shows the classic CRM planning method, that is, the horizontal CRM planning method. According to strategic planning, operation management, and system implementation, CRM planning is carried out from the four main lines of customers, marketing, service, and business.

The advantage of the horizontal CRM planning method is that it is very comprehensive, covering all aspects of CRM, and can be used anywhere. It can be used to do CRM planning for various customers. But this method also has prominent problems:

(1) It is not driven by business value, there is no guidance of business value, and many times it is done for the sake of doing, and many functions cannot generate business value.
(2) Because from the beginning, I don't know what I want, so I can't judge whether the CRM plan is useful, and often leads to the result of one consultation after another.

So let's change our perspective and consider how to do CRM planning from a business value perspective.

First, abandon the traditional method of starting from the function, and plan CRM from the perspective of business value, divided into four steps: exploration, positioning, mode, and action.

© China Science and Technology Press Co., Ltd. 2025
J. Yang, *Sales and Service Digital Transformation*,
https://doi.org/10.1007/978-981-96-5961-6_5

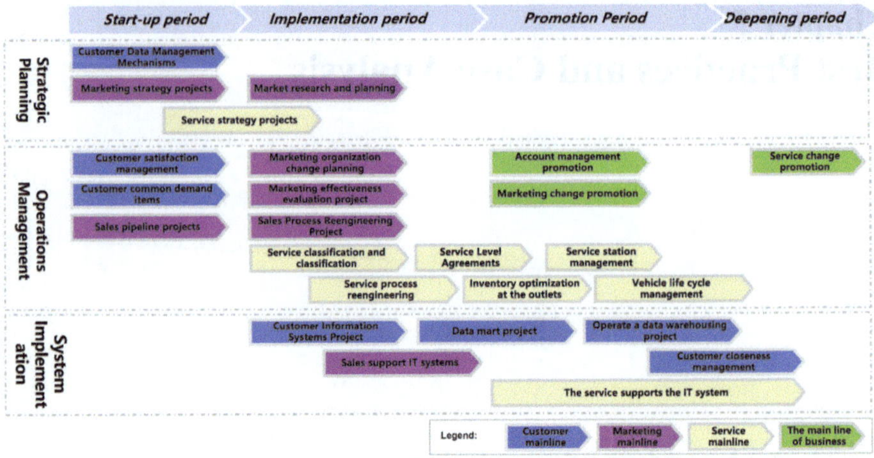

Fig. 5.1 Example of traditional CRM planning

Exploration: Start with Business Analysis and Dig for Core Business Value Improvement Points

In CRM projects, many BAs (Business Analysts) will avoid discussing business, and guide customers from the perspective of CRM functions, such as asking what the customer management process is, what the customer purchase process is, and pain points, etc. This is also understandable, one is that BA is worried that the customer will find out that they are not familiar with the business, and the second is afraid of expanding the scope and unable to close the project. But the problem is if we don't even understand the business direction, how can we judge whether the detailed CRM functions we have are useful?

As shown in Fig. 5.2, in the CRM planning guided by business value, we first need to understand the customer of business distribution, identify the core business and the business with the greatest future potential of the customer. From these businesses, find out which regions, fields, industries, products, and solutions have problems. In the example shown in the figure below, the company is facing huge challenges in its core business in first- and second-tier cities.

Positioning: Analyze the Reasons and Find the Direction

The positioning process is a personalized process, and the reasons are generally known only after discussions with the senior management of the company's business. Suppose in the case, Company A is doing B2B business, and the problems encountered in first- and second-tier cities are due to the large amount and long cycle

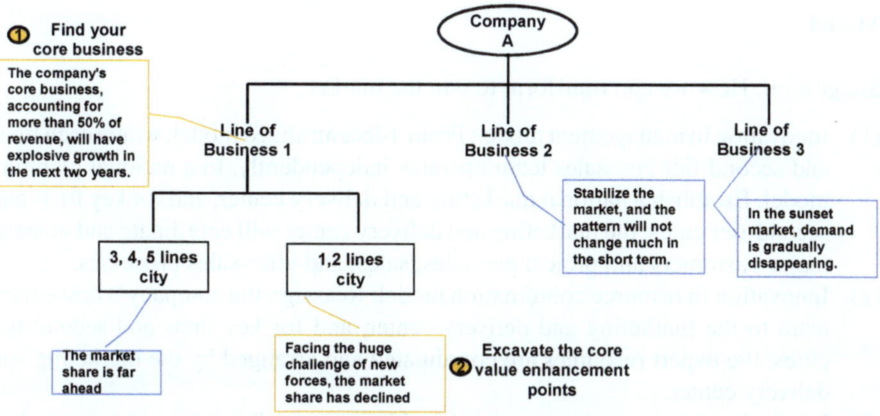

Fig. 5.2 Example of identifying core business enhancement points

of such projects. In many first- and second-tier cities, competitors usually layout a few years in advance, make large-scale investments, and have a great advantage by the time of bidding, making it difficult for Company A to win big orders in these cities.

Model: Use the RMB-PT Model to Find a Solution

We can plan how to realize business value according to the RMB-PT introduced in Chapter 3 "CRM3.0 Service Digital Transformation".

Insight and Resources

Analysis: Our capabilities and the gap with competitors.

Existing resources: Company A's "core business line 1" is responsible for an independent business unit, and there are independent sales teams and pre-sales teams in first-tier cities.

Insight gap: The main competitors have strategic agreements with key first- and second-tier cities, have commitments for fixed asset investment, have well-known expert teams, and participate in planning in advance.

Model

Suggestion: How we can transform to win the market.

(1) Innovation in management model: From a decentralized model, where each first- and second-tier city sales team operates independently, to a national planning model. Establish a national marketing and delivery center, and for key first- and second-tier cities, the marketing and delivery center will coordinate and manage major customers and project pre-sales, sales, and after-sales processes.
(2) Innovation in resource coordination model: Reassign the company's best expert team to the marketing and delivery center, and for key first- and second-tier cities, the expert resources are coordinated and arranged by the marketing and delivery center.
(3) Innovation in cooperation model: In addition to traditional partners, establish cooperative relationships with major research institutes, standard organizations, etc., and participate in their standard setting and pre-research planning projects.
(4) Innovation in investment model: The investment in the marketing and delivery center is not linked to the project amount, does not require short-term returns, but is proportional to the market size of key first- and second-tier cities.
5) Innovation in personnel capability: In addition to the company's own expert team, establish an external team, hire well-known experts at home and abroad, and form a strong external support team.
(6) Innovation in assessment model: The assessment of the marketing and delivery center is not based on short-term sales, but on the advantages and closeness in terms of solutions and relationships compared with competitors, and the size and number of business opportunities incubated in the next two years for key first- and second-tier cities.

Tipping Point

In the next 2–3 years, take 3–5 key first- and second-tier cities from competitors, while ensuring that the key first- and second-tier city projects owned by themselves are not lost.

Action: Implement Through the CRM3.0 Management Model

(1) Process, scenario, organization, and assessment: Traditional CRM planning generally recommends sales process management Function. But if we analyze from the perspective of business value, we can find that what customers urgently need now is the ability to manage large customers. Therefore, we should design processes, scenarios, organizations, and assessments around large customer management. Chapter 2 "CRM3.0 B2B Sales Digital Transformation" has

a detailed introduction to large customer management (ESP+), so I won't elaborate here.

(2) Digital tools After we have a clear understanding of business value exploration, problem positioning, model innovation and transformation, business improvement and focus, we enter the stage of digital platform selection, which is the stage of software selection.

Therefore, if we do not analyze the value of the previous business, we cannot guide the software selection. When enterprises choose CRM software, they often don't know how to realize the value of the enterprise, that is, they don't know what they really need. At this time, they usually compare the functions, technology and architecture of the software, but the functions of the top CRM products will not differ too much, so the enterprise will be very entangled. But in this section, if we analyze and evaluate from the perspective of business value, and plan CRM, it is easy to get the result. The CRM large customer management function is the top priority. The required function is to support six types of model innovation: management model innovation, resource coordination model innovation, cooperation model innovation, input model innovation, personnel ability innovation, and assessment model innovation.

Summary > This section introduces the method of CRM planning based on business value and the difference from traditional CRM planning. And through an example, it introduces how to do CRM planning based on the method of business value from the four steps of exploration, positioning, model and action.

B2B Sales Diagnosis and Planning

This section will introduce through a case how to analyze the problems of enterprises in the B2B sales process, how to find the root causes behind the problems, and how to help enterprises solve problems and enhance core competitiveness through sales process management and sales support system management in terms of model, organization, process, scenario, assessment, digital tools, etc.

Problem Diagnosis and High-Level Suggestions

Current Situation Analysis and Problem Diagnosis

The customer in this case is a large listed company with a scale of about 10,000 people. The sales team is about 3,000 people. There are branches in various regions of the country, and customers are distributed in many fields such as power, finance, and government.

As shown in Fig. 5.3, in the stage of problem diagnosis and high-level suggestions, we sort out the current situation from seven aspects and analyze the current situation

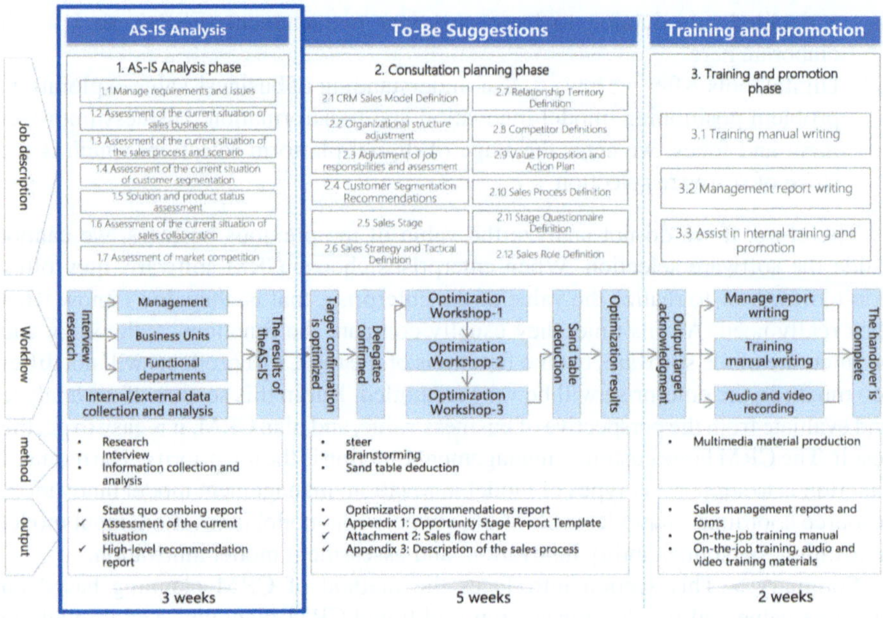

Fig. 5.3 AS-IS analysis and diagnosis phases

from five dimensions. These five dimensions are: ① Large customer management; ② Sales process management; ③ Sales support system management; ④ Delivery management; ⑤ Information technology system. The seven aspects of the current situation are as follows:

(1) Management needs and problems Interview with the customer's senior management on the macro needs and problems of large customer management, sales process management, sales support system management, delivery management, and IT system.
(2) Sales business current situation assessment Evaluate the overall issues and current situation of the market, sales, and solutions with the person in charge of sales, and evaluate issues such as value, resources, and models.
(3) Assessment of the current state of sales processes and scenarios: Interviews are conducted with sales-related personnel regarding the management of sales processes and scenarios (TAS+).
(4) Assessment of the current state of customer segmentation: Interviews are conducted with sales-related personnel regarding the management of major customers.
(5) Assessment of the current state of solutions and products: Interviews are conducted with sales and delivery personnel regarding product competitiveness and management of the delivery process.

(6) Assessment of the current state of sales collaboration: Interviews are conducted with sales, pre-sales, service, and delivery-related personnel regarding the management of the sales support system.
(7) Assessment of the current state of market competition: High-level, sales, and pre-sales related personnel are consulted to understand the market competition landscape and the situation of competitors.

Regarding the IT system, all of the above interviews can provide insight into the current state and support capabilities of the information technology system. Below, we will evaluate the current state analysis from five dimensions.

Major Customer Management

Current State and Problem 1: Customer Segmentation

(1) The definition standards for key major customers in each industry and region are different, and each team and each management level considers it from different perspectives. Some consider influence, level of financial investment, and continuity of demand; some believe that old customers, wealthy customers, customers with clear demands, and customers with strong continuity are Class A customers, while customers with weak continuity, insufficient funds, and weak demand are Class B customers; customers who have not been deeply contacted, have a low level of informatization but have room for improvement in the future, and customers who have never been contacted are Class C customers; some evaluate customer levels based on last year's sales revenue; some evaluate customer levels based on this year's sales expectations.
(2) When assigning customers to sales, different branches and industry departments have different standards. Some are first-come-first-served, some look at who the customer belonged to before, or sales go to the resource pool to claim customers.
(3) There is currently no unified customer management channel, making it difficult to form a comprehensive analysis of target customers, so it is not possible to systematically determine which customers are strategic customers, which are key customers, and which are potential customers.

Analysis

Customer segmentation has different dimensions: one is based on the rights and interests of customers buying products, that is, according to the Service Level Agreement (SLA), which is what customers should get after paying, we call this rights grading; one is based on contribution, potential, ability to win and do, demonstration role and other dimensions to calculate scores and divide, this is often to define the responsible relationship, that is, who in which team is responsible for this customer, we call this management grading; the third is divided according to the nine-grid, often to define customer maintenance tactics, such as which type of customers to focus on improving, which type of customers to maintain, etc., we call this tactical grading.

Therefore, customer segmentation must first determine what dimension to divide by, and then define clear division standards.

Current State and Problem 2: Customer Coverage and Market Development

(1) There are a large number of unexplored markets in regional coverage. Due to the current team composition, cost mechanism, and resources, there are not more manpower and funds invested in this part, and there is no good business model to cover.
(2) Competitors' differentiated market layout and price competition for key projects pose a great challenge to the company's corresponding business.
(3) The business relying on channels is currently at the project level, with most projects involving channels still primarily led by the manufacturer's sales team. The construction of a channel system initiated at the company level has just begun.
(4) Some salespeople focus mainly on old customers and existing projects, lacking the drive to develop the market.
(5) No unified market attack strategy was collected during the interviews.

Analysis

The company's overall sales strategy is unclear, customer coverage and KPI guidance division are vague, causing frontline sales to be at a loss.

Sales Process Management

Current Situation and Problem 3: Management of Sales Stages and Related Actions

(1) Different teams have different understandings of their market customer needs, and have unique insights and methods in sales activities, with individuality outweighing commonality.
(2) Most interviewees (different teams and salespeople) are good at mobilizing resources to support sales activities, but they do not clearly distinguish when, what kind of resources to invest, and what kind of customers to serve.
(3) Different interviewees have some understanding of the procurement process of large customers, but in the corresponding sales process, they have different perceptions of their progress, position, direction, and win rate.

Analysis

We support experienced sales experts mastering some personalized methods. But we must achieve some key management points' unity and best practices' solidification at the company level: such as sales stages, key actions, order-winning strategies and tactics, value propositions, etc.

Current Situation and Problem 4: Sales Management Methods

(1) The operation management platform mainly focuses on financial performance from different dimensions.
(2) The operation management platform's management cycle for business units is transitioning from quarterly to weekly, but there are some issues with the timeliness, standardization, and accuracy of data collection.
(3) Each interview unit uses its own management logic and tools, and there are differences in the rhythm of sales management, including weekly reviews, irregular reviews, etc., and the content of the reviews also varies.

Analysis

There needs to be unity and optimization in the standardization of sales terminology, as well as the interaction and review mechanisms of sales.

Sales Support System Management

Current Situation and Problem 5: Service Resource Skills Assessment, Input and Scheduling Methods

(1) Different teams and personnel use different resource allocation and scheduling mechanisms in the resource scheduling process, and some teams do not have a resource scheduling mechanism, with no followable and standardized documents and process descriptions.
(2) The resources and teams that each project can call upon sometimes depend on the project sales person in charge or the sales manager's understanding of the company and the personal connections they have.
(3) The main methods of communication are telephone, email, and WeChat.
(4) The existing mechanism makes it difficult to coordinate resources from various teams, form a joint force, and the support force has not been fully utilized.

Analysis

In B2B sales, the competition for solution capabilities is becoming increasingly important, and the reasonable and effective scheduling of resources is crucial to improving the win rate.

Current Situation and Problem 6: Support from Product to Market

(1) The industry department, as the midfield from product to market, has a plan for the overall business function, but due to the reality, it is too much involved in specific projects and is stretched thin.
(2) The accumulation of knowledge is more reflected in each person in each business unit, and a mechanism for integrating and sharing knowledge has not yet been formed.

(3) Some products iterate slowly, delivering two versions a year, which is difficult to fully meet market demand.
(4) For large-scale demands, there is currently no unified channel to transfer them from the front stage to the back stage, but only provide fragmented demands to the back stage based on project situations.
(5) Emerging technologies and business support capabilities are weak. For emerging technologies and businesses, such as big data, cloud computing, virtualization, situational awareness, etc., the company does not yet have mature products and solutions to support, and there is a certain disadvantage compared to competitors. The company is a follower in the market.
(6) The product department is relatively independent, and the collaboration is relatively limited, which makes it difficult to quickly respond and meet the comprehensive needs of the industry.

Analysis

The essence of this problem is how to connect the information from the front, middle, and back stages and how the resources of the middle and back stages can support the front stage sales process.

Current Situation and Problem 7: About the Positioning and Responsibilities of Some Business Units/Positions

(1) The collaboration effect of the matrix industry and region varies greatly in different regions and industries, and the industry and regional collaboration within the scope of the large area leader usually has good results.
(2) In the daily collaboration between the headquarters and the subordinate platforms, there are phenomena of some being over-controlled, some being under-controlled, some being strictly controlled, and some being loosely controlled.
(3) The distribution and division of technical resources in different regions and industries have different distribution and division methods, which need standardized training.
(4) The ratio of industry and regional pre-sales technical personnel to sales personnel is usually determined by the unit managers, and some industries and regions are under-staffed. For the division of technical personnel, some business units have a fine division, some have a rough division, and there are cases of personnel reuse.
(5) Different teams in pre-sales, after-sales, implementation, and production lines have different understandings of the market, industry, customers, and projects.

Analysis

The definition of job responsibilities and rights refers to how various positions coordinate during the sales process and how resources are called.

Current Situation and Problem 8: Transparency and Effective Evaluation of the Technical Team's Capabilities and Efficiency

(1) The performance of pre-sales technical personnel is matched according to the team's sales performance. The results of performance distribution currently cannot directly reflect the business performance of pre-sales personnel and cannot reflect the actual contribution of each pre-sales personnel.
(2) Most of the feedback results from the interviewees are for the reference of the scheduling and management of pre-sales personnel, mainly qualitative, based on the evaluation of leaders or cooperative departments.
(3) Different technical teams have different methods for assigning work tasks. For example, it is determined based on the leader's experience, the personnel's capabilities, the corresponding relationship of the sales team, the technical direction, etc.

Analysis

The essence of the problem is still about how to use resources effectively.

Delivery Management

Current Situation and Problem 9: Project Management and Cycle in the Delivery Link, as Well as Effective Control of Quality, Cost, and Satisfaction

(1) The front field assesses profits, while the delivery link mainly adopts a collaborative mechanism based on working hours, as well as an assessment method based on workload. This approach may increase project costs and affect the achievement of profit targets.
(2) If the baseline product department participates in the formulation of the plan before the project is launched, it may reduce the number of customized implementation projects and alleviate the difficulties in the delivery link.
(3) Word of mouth is very important for customer repurchase. If the delivery link is not smooth, sales often have to play the role of firefighters.
(4) The delivery link of complex projects often involves multiple delivery teams. The role of overall coordination is mostly undertaken by the sales or pre-sales of the business unit, but the responsibility for the overall efficiency and quality of project delivery has not been implemented.
(5) After the service project is completed, the work handover does not go out, and there is a process blank in the upstream and downstream collaboration.

Analysis

The problems in the delivery stage often stem from the hidden dangers buried in the pre-sales stage, but failed delivery will cause the loss of future sales opportunities. The essence of the problem is still a sales collaboration issue.

IT System

Current Situation and Problem 10: Technical Support for Business Processes and Scenarios

(1) The existing business system starts from the second half of the sales process and has not achieved full coverage.
(2) There are parallel online and offline situations in the process, and the online automatic flow has not been fully realized.
(3) The system is isolated and has not effectively docked with other systems. In some cases, manual operation is required for system docking, and there are mismatches in data docking.
(4) The process is long, involves many people, and there is room for optimization in the business-level collaboration mechanism.

Analysis

We need to achieve a full process closed loop, mainly reflected in sales process management and sales support management.

Focus and Positioning

In this project, we will focus on sales process management and sales support system management for the following reasons:

Current Situation and Problem Inference

Among the 10 main problems above, the 3rd to 8th problems are related to sales process management and sales support system management. The first problem and the second problem are related to key account management, but key account management involves customer coverage and market expansion. If adjustments are to be made, it will be time-consuming and laborious. Therefore, we can first focus on the transformation of sales process management and sales support system management.

Industry Experience Inference

As introduced in the second chapter "Different Market Choices Different Sales Strategies for B2B Sales", in a rapidly growing market, we should focus more on sales process management and sales support system management. This customer is in a rapidly growing market.

Vertical Penetration Analysis

The previous analysis of the 10 main problems is horizontal. If we are to focus on sales process management and sales support system management, for the sake of prudence, we need to conduct a vertical penetration analysis, that is, a detailed analysis of the process and scenarios of sales process management and sales support management, to see if there are any problems.

Because the client currently adopts a matrix management style, there are headquarters-initiated project proposals, regional project proposals, and standard small-scale product projects, which are quite complex. I will only use the headquarters-initiated project proposals as an example.

As shown in Fig. 5.4, the headquarters-initiated project proposals have exposed many problems in their management process. In summary, the responsibilities and rights are unclear, everyone is responsible, yet no one is responsible. Each member of the team only cares about completing their own tasks and does not pay attention to the overall results of the project, thus many hidden dangers are buried.

As shown in Fig. 5.5, the main problems in the sales support process of the headquarters-initiated project proposals are complexity, unreasonableness, lack of transparency, and favoritism. Those with good relationships and high positions can get good resources; it is not about which project is good, but who can get good resources. Therefore, there is a mismatch between resources and projects. Also, because pre-sales resources do not assess working hours and costs, it leads to a waste of pre-sales resources.

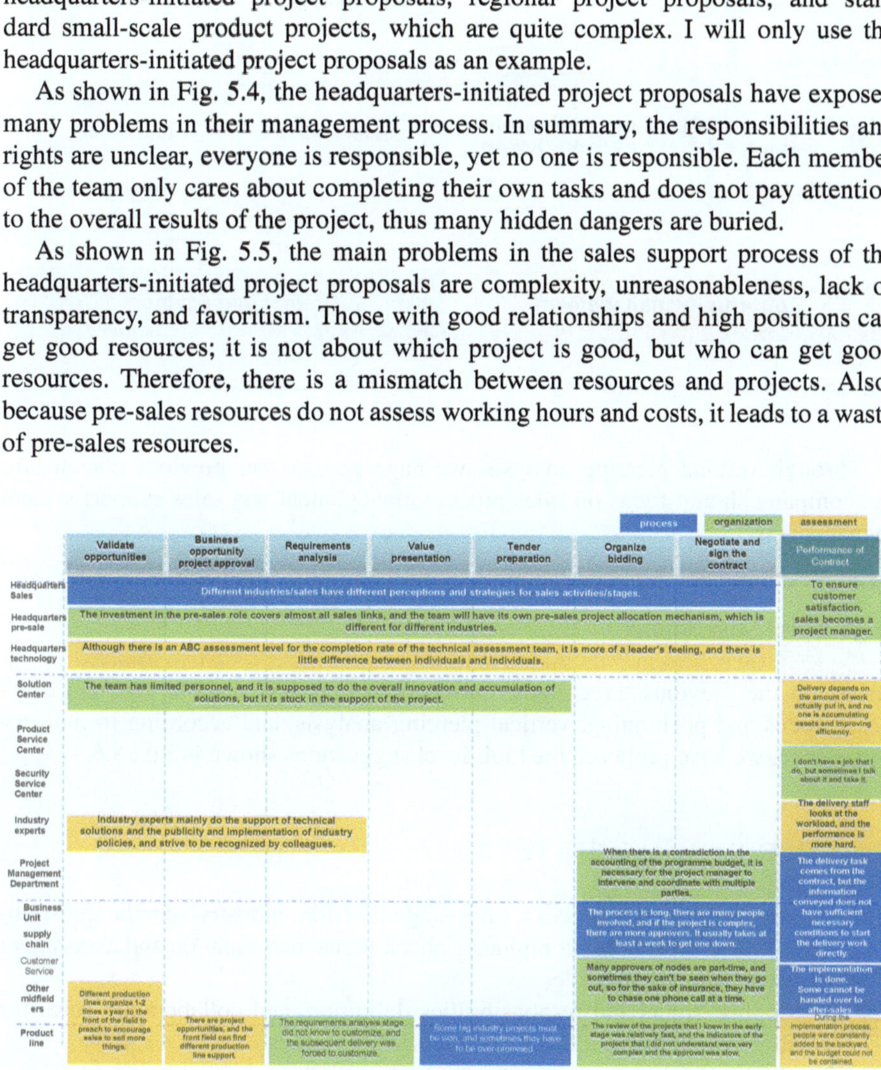

Fig. 5.4 Solution based projects initiated by the headquarter

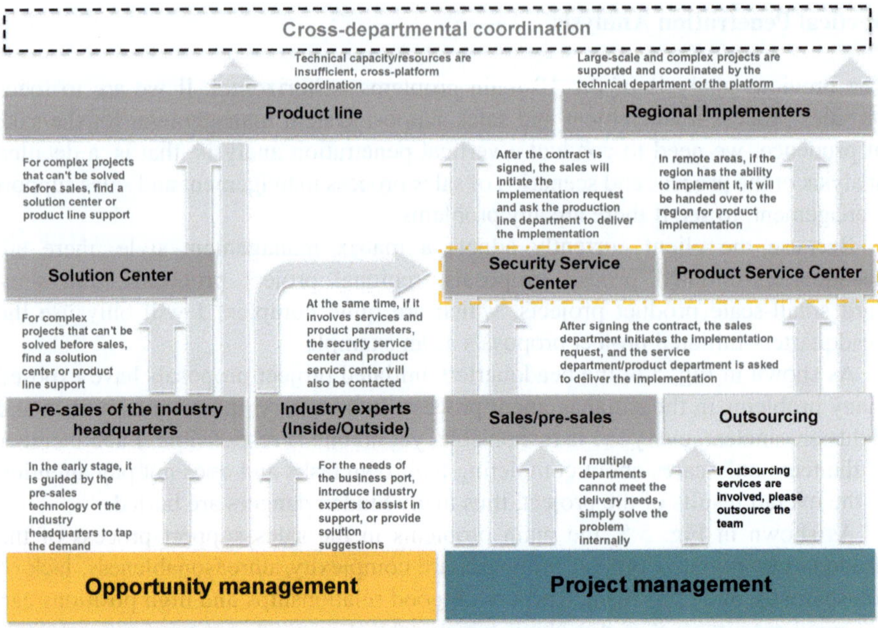

Fig. 5.5 Resource scheduling during sales and delivery at the headquarter

Through vertical piercing analysis, we have verified our previous conclusion: the company should focus on sales process management and sales support system management.

High-Level Suggestions

Based on the previous three steps: current situation analysis and problem diagnosis, focus and positioning, vertical piercing analysis, and according to industry experience, we have proposed the high-level suggestions shown in Fig. 5.6.

Topics for Optimization in This Period

(1) Standardize the sales process: sales stage division, industry-specific questionnaires, standard actions, compliance check items, participation and assessment points of collaborative roles.
(2) Positioning, rights and responsibilities definition, and collaboration rules for collaborative units/positions related to sales activities.
(3) Standardized sales management rules and methods.
(4) Evaluation method for pre-sales resource input.
(5) Transparent assessment mechanism for pre-sales resources.

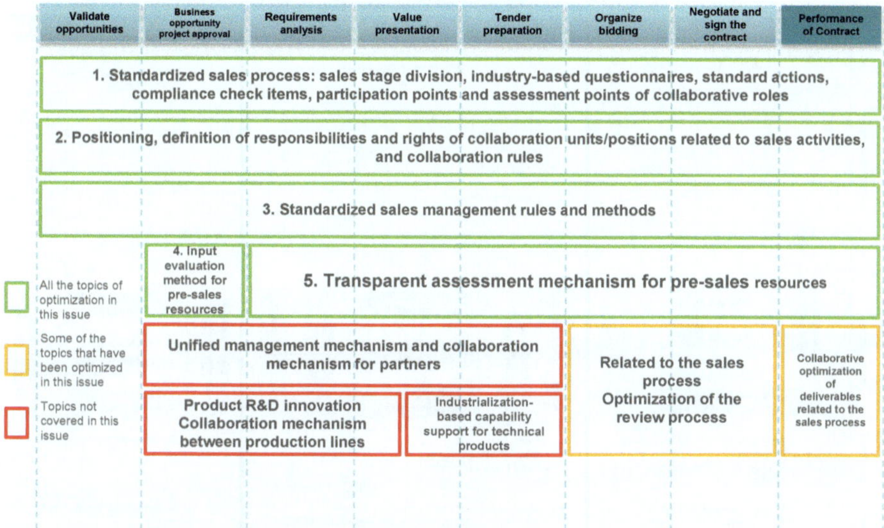

Fig. 5.6 High-level suggestion

Partial Optimization in This Period:

(1) Optimization of processes and scenarios related to the sales process.
(2) Collaborative optimization of delivery links related to the sales process.

Optimization Suggestions and Detailed Planning

After the problem diagnosis and high-level suggestions were accepted by the client, we entered the optimization suggestions and detailed planning stage. The following introduces how to optimize the business through sales process management and sales support system management models.

As shown in Fig. 5.7, we have entered the second stage, the optimization suggestions and detailed planning stage. This case will provide detailed planning suggestions from three aspects: optimization of sales process management and sales support system management, optimization of organization, position and assessment, and optimization of management and business processes.

(1) Optimization of sales process management and sales support system management:
    - Definition of CRM sales model.
    - Customer segmentation suggestions.
    - Sales stage division.

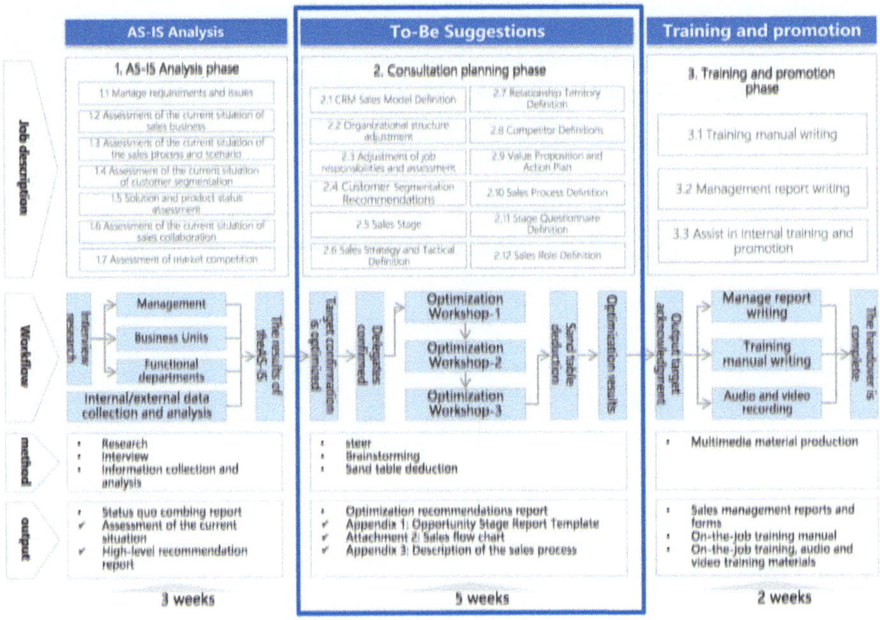

Fig. 5.7 Optimization proposal and detailed planning

- Definition of sales strategy and tactics.
- Definition of relationship map.
- Definition of competitors.
- Value proposition and action plan.
- Definition of stage questionnaire.

(2) Optimization of management and business processes: Definition of sales processes.

- Optimization of organization, position, and assessment:
- Definition of sales roles.
- Organizational structure adjustment.
- Adjustment of job responsibilities and assessments.

(3) Optimization of management and business processes: Definition of sales processes.

Through the optimization of the above three aspects, we help customers achieve the following five tasks and business goals.

(1) Establish a unified, replicable sales management mechanism: Establish the best structure and process for sales management of marketing units, making management unified and replicable. The company can operate effectively in front-line sales activities by following the management mechanism, without relying on individuals. (Sales process management)

(2) Optimize the collaboration model of matrix industries and regions, and optimize the method of industry resource scheduling: Matrix industry projects in the region, based on different business opportunity levels, adopt different resource scheduling strategies, and strengthen the collaboration of matrix industries and regions. (Sales support system management)
(3) Clarify the responsibilities and rights of related roles in the sales activity process: Based on different business opportunity levels and collaboration models, define the phased work activities, collaboration methods, and necessary new assessment indicators of related roles in different sales activity scenarios. (Sales process management)
(4) Pre-sales resource transparency: Establish a pre-sales resource scheduling mechanism, introduce necessary pre-sales management indicators, make the allocation and use of pre-sales resources visible, and quantify pre-sales costs. (Sales support system management)
(5) With the help of auxiliary management tools, achieve sales forecasting and process monitoring: Establish an operation management feedback mechanism, visualize sales opportunities through sales management report templates, achieve sales forecasting in different dimensions, and periodically monitor key activities in the sales process. (Digital tool support)

To complete the above tasks and generate detailed plans, the following five steps need to be completed: ① Optimization of sales process management; ② Optimization of sales support system management; ③ Optimization of organization and positions; ④ Optimization of assessment indicators; ⑤ Optimization of management and business processes.

Optimization of Sales Process Management

We optimize the sales process according to the sales process management model, starting from the static part.

Personalized Customization of the Static Part of Sales Process Management

As shown in Fig. 5.8, based on the sales process management methodology, combined with the typical sales activities of the customer, I defined 5 types of business opportunities, 8 sales stages, and 4 cross-team collaboration scenarios with the main dimension of business opportunity amount, forming a unified sales activity mechanism, solving the problem of reasonable and effective matching of business opportunities and resources. The model in the figure refers to the sales process management model, but the definition of the model was relatively simple at that time.

(1) 5 types of business opportunities: Business opportunities are divided into 5 types according to the size of the amount, strategic significance, and who leads. The

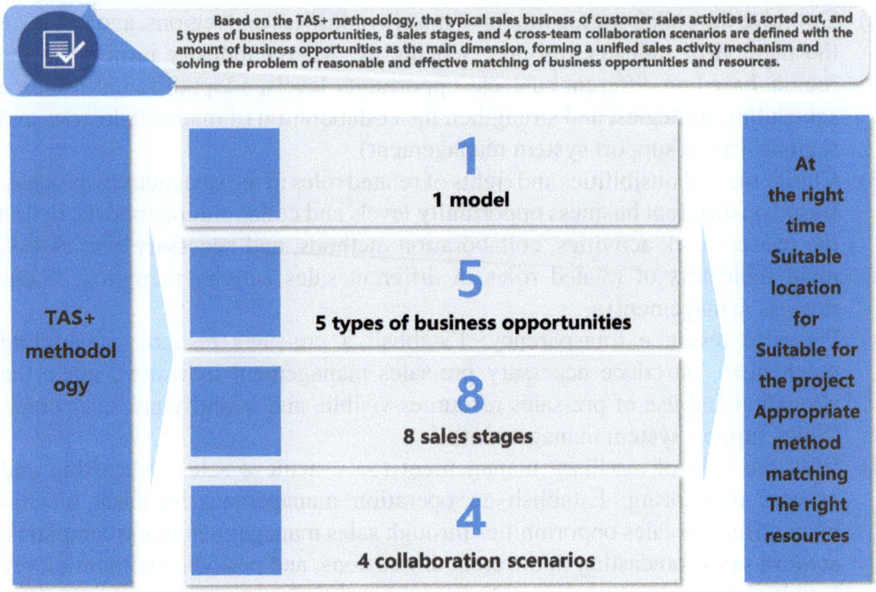

Fig. 5.8 Example of personalized design for static part of sales process

Table 5.1 Example of opportunity classification

Opportunity level	Forecast project amount (RMB)	Strategic significance	Condition
A	More than 2 million	Items that usually do not meet the monetary criteria, but are significant, can be manually upgraded	The company dominates the sales process
B	1 million—2 million		
C	50–1 million		
D	Less than 500,000		
E	Report business opportunities, fast track		Partners lead the sales process

threshold amount of each type of business opportunity can be adjusted according to industry changes, but there are only these 5 types. As shown in Table 5.1.

(2) 8 sales stages: This case divides the project into: ① Business opportunity verification; ② Business opportunity initiation; ③ Requirement analysis; ④ Value presentation; ⑤ Tender preparation; ⑥ Organize bidding; ⑦ Negotiation and signing; ⑧ Contract performance.

At the same time, through the process and control points to improve the win rate, shorten the sales cycle, and control project risks. As shown in Fig. 5.9.

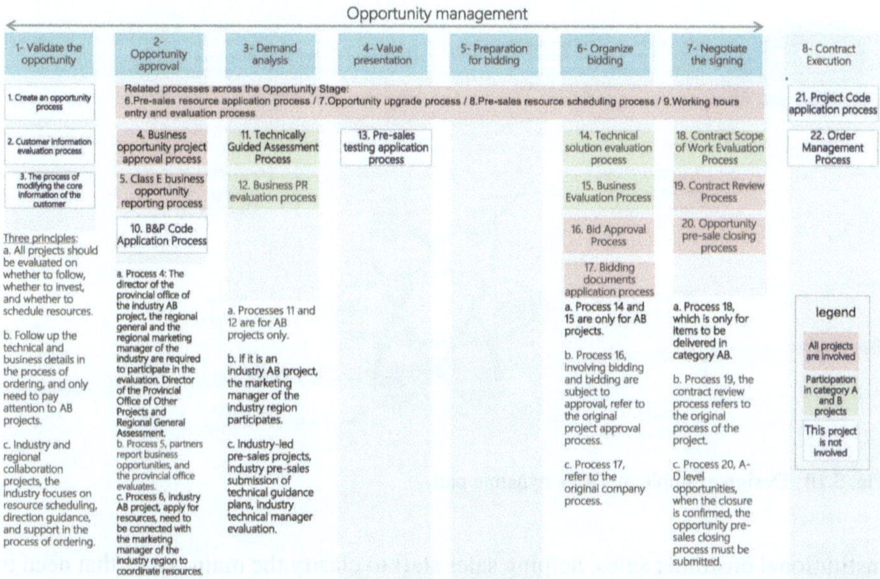

Fig. 5.9 Examples of 8 opportunity stages

If you look closely, you will find that many of the processes and control points belong to sales support system management, which is used to achieve: ① Layered pre-sales resource scheduling mechanism; ② Pre-sales resource cost accounting system; ③ Unique pre-sales stage responsible system; ④ Pre-sales stage everyone assessment system.

Therefore, sales process management and sales support system management often complement each other and integrate into one.

(3) 4 types of cross-team collaboration scenarios. The 4 types of cross-team collaboration scenarios are ① Industry AB project collaboration scenarios; ② Non-industry AB project collaboration scenarios; ③ CD project collaboration scenarios; ④ E project collaboration scenarios.

Chapter 2 introduces the related content, and the "Pre-sales stage sole responsibility system example" shows the industry A Class and B class project collaboration scenarios. In the 8 stages of the project, through different roles, different work content, and The work undertaken by each role in each content defines the entire work collaboration scenario.

Personalized Customization of Part of TAS+ movement

As shown in Fig. 5.10, the method of personalized design for the part of TAS+ movement in the case is: The TAS + methodology provides a variety of tools suitable for

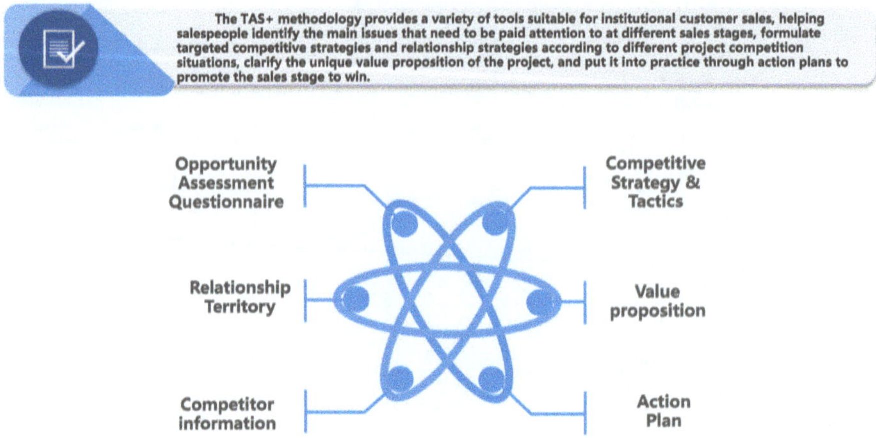

Fig. 5.10 Design example of TAS+ dynamic part

institutional customer sales, helping sales staff to clarify the main issues that need to be focused on at different sales stages, formulate targeted competition strategies and relationship strategies according to different project competition situations, clarify the unique value proposition of the project, and put it into practice through action plans, promoting the sales stage to winning the bid.

Now reviewing this case, I think that the competitor information, competition strategy and tactics, value proposition and The action plan didn't have much problem, but for the business opportunity assessment questionnaire and relationship map, I feel that the design at that time was not Quite accurate, and some important projects are missing.

(1) Business opportunity assessment questionnaire: too idealized. The design idea of the business opportunity assessment questionnaire is: The business opportunity assessment questionnaire is used to describe the key points and key information that the enterprise needs to pay attention to at this stage, and generate a business opportunity stage report. Each key information in the report corresponds to one or more business opportunity assessment questionnaire questions, and is refined based on the characteristics of this stage, serving as a sales weekly report template, helping sales staff to clarify the work that needs to be promoted in the sales process. In addition, the sales management personnel's evaluation of the report can serve as the evaluation basis for the business opportunity stage, achieving unified sales management.

However, it is very difficult to evaluate business opportunities through standardized question models, and it is difficult to achieve this through a single project. When designing the plan before, too much resources and energy were consumed on this issue, but other more important aspects were ignored.

Less is more, more is confusing. I suggest using fewer, more personalized questions to define the business opportunity assessment questionnaire.

For example, whether the content of the tender includes technical parameters that are beneficial to our products, etc. These questions are all in the minds of old salespeople, and after summarizing, they can generate personalized questionnaires for the enterprise, and even different industries and regions can be different.

(2). Relationship Map: Design flaws. The traditional CRM standard relationship map was used at that time. But thinking about it now, this is actually problematic: we did not carefully consider the difference between the internal relationship of the customer and the internal relationship of the project. There are reporting relationships and influence maps inside the customer; there are only decision-making relationships in the business opportunity, and we mixed these three relationships into one, and we put the reporting relationship and influence map that should belong to large customer management on the business opportunity, and mixed the reporting relationship and decision-making relationship together for management.

There are three types of relationships and four types of individual portrait dimensions shared by customers and business opportunities. For specific content, please refer to the content about large customer management and sales process management in Chapter 2.

(3) Necessary conditions: missing. Necessary conditions refer to the original that can confirm that the customer definitely wants to do this project. Because. This is the most basic criterion for judging whether sales are advancing business opportunities. This step was not designed at the time.

(4) Win rate: The design was flawed. At that time, we adopted the general method of gradually increasing the win rate as the business opportunity stage progressed, but this method is actually detached from the actual situation. Many projects start off optimistically, but later more competitors will enter. In addition, after understanding the project situation better, we find that the opportunity is slim, and there is no situation where the win rate increases as the stage progresses. The illusion of an increasing win rate prevents us from adopting different strategies and actions based on its dynamic changes.

We can use the competitor comparison method to calculate the win rate. The detailed method is introduced in the sales process management in Chapter 2.

(5) Supervision and promotion: Missing. Sales process management is not a one-man show of sales. At that time, we did not design well how to make the sales process more effective through the supervision and interaction mechanism of supervisors and sales staff.

Optimization of Sales Support System Management

In the introduction of the 8 sales stages in the optimization of sales process management, we can see that many processes and control points belong to the content of sales support system management optimization. Below, I will give examples to show our optimization methods.

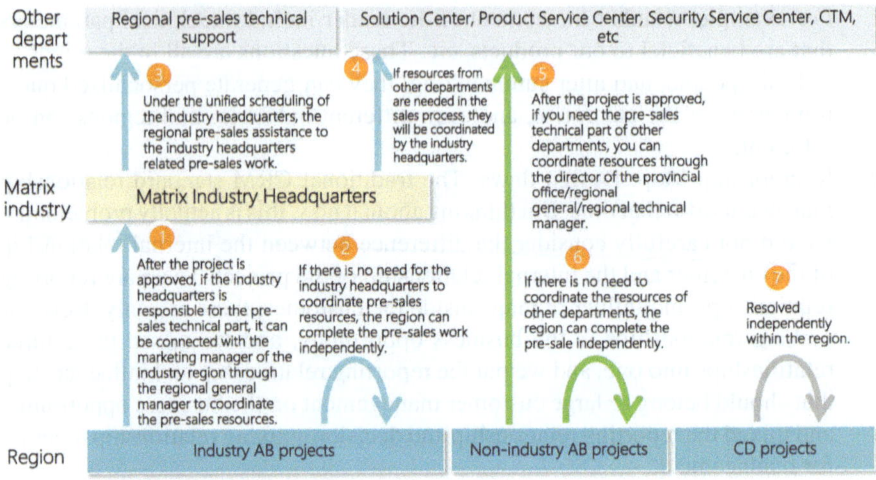

Fig. 5.13 Optimized resource scheduling method

Hierarchical Pre-Sales Resource Scheduling Mechanism

In "Problem Diagnosis and High-Level Suggestions", the customer's original resource scheduling process was extremely complex, and it mainly relied on relationships, familiarity with internal situations, and positions. Now they have transformed into a unified coordination by the matrix industry headquarters according to the project level (as shown in Fig. 5.13), which greatly reduces the complexity of resource scheduling and allows frontline sales to focus more on customers.

Key Industry Solution Delivery Center System

No matter how effectively resources are called, as long as they are distributed everywhere and not centrally managed, it is difficult to produce a swarm effect due to their different interests, that is, the organizational effect of self-organization, self-driving, self-evolution, and self-profit. For the company's key industries and key solutions, I suggest integrating all relevant resources together to establish a multi-in-one delivery center. For example, I once established a five-in-one delivery center for a security customer, that is, pre-sales, testing, delivery, after-sales, and secondary development, providing one-stop service for large projects, forming an overall advantage, that is, potential. And provide the following features in management:

(1) Project manager system: fully activate subjective initiative.
(2) Project scope control.
(3) Project cost management.
(4) All-employee sales, promote sales with service.

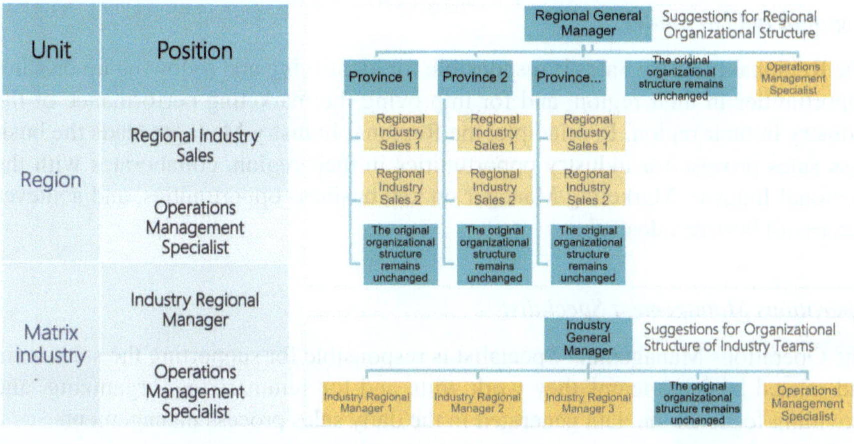

Fig. 5.14 Example of organizational and position optimization

(5) Establish a PMO (Project Management Office) system for the solution department.
(6) Visual management.

Optimization of Organization and Positions

In order to effectively use sales process management and sales support system management, we also helped customers optimize the organizational structure and added four types of positions: ① Region—Regional Industry Manager; ② Region—Operations Management Specialist; ③ Matrix Industry—Industry Regional Marketing Manager; ④ Matrix Industry—Operations Management Specialist.

As shown in Fig. 5.14, by setting up related positions, strengthening the cooperation between regions and industries, improving the marketing performance of the matrix industry, and also improving the visualization of the sales funnel and pre-sales resources. The job definitions are as follows:

Industry Regional Manager

The Industry Regional Manager is responsible for the promotion, advancement, and management of industry business in certain regions, and for improving the marketing performance of the industry in the regions they oversee. The Regional Industry Director collaborates with the Regional Industry Manager, and in principle, does not directly manage customers. Their main role is to provide knowledge input to the Regional Industry Manager, coordinate resources with the consulting delivery center, and provide support at different stages of business opportunities.

Regional Industry Sales

The Regional Industry Sales is responsible for identifying and following up on sales opportunities in their region, and for improving the marketing performance of the industry in their region. In principle, the Regional Industry Manager leads the business sales process for industry opportunities in their region, collaborates with the Regional Industry Marketing Manager on key business opportunities, and achieves successful business deals.

Operations Management Specialist

The Operations Management Specialist is responsible for supporting the sales team and related business teams they work with, and for summarizing, organizing, and providing feedback on data generated in the daily sales process management.

Optimization of Assessment Indicators

In order to guide sales process management and sales support systems through assessments, we have added three new assessment dimensions for sales and pre-sales positions: ① New contract amount for regional industry projects (marketing performance); ② Pre-sales cost (significant difference indicator); ③ Pre-sales UT (significant difference indicator). The new contract amount for regional industry projects is to encourage breakthroughs in key industries; pre-sales cost and pre-sales UT are to form a layered pre-sales resource scheduling mechanism and pre-sales resource cost accounting system. Figure 5.15 shows the new assessment indicators for the positions.

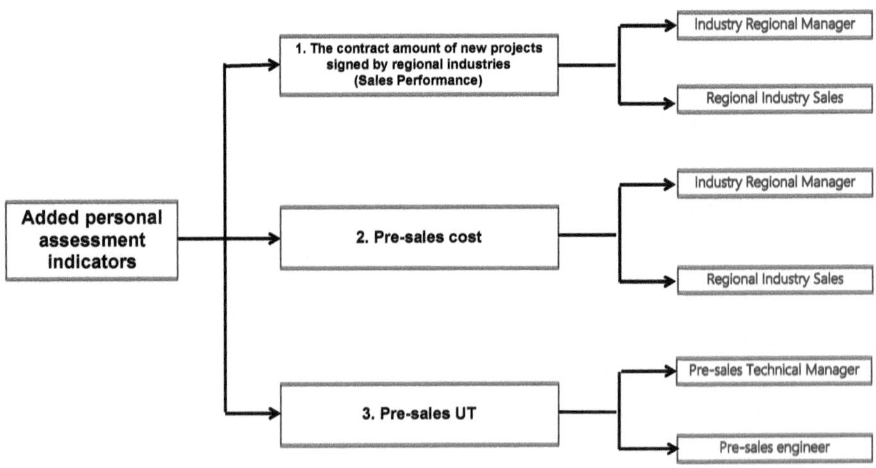

Fig. 5.15 Example of optimization of assessment metrics

Optimization of Business Processes

As shown in Fig. 5.16, according to the optimized sales process management and sales support system management, the optimized organization and positions, and the optimized assessment indicators, we have made corresponding optimizations to the process.

Summary > The planning consulting project introduced in this section took about eight weeks (excluding subsequent training and promotion). The key to the success of this project is to seamlessly integrate sales process management and sales resource scheduling to maximize input–output, thereby transforming frontline sales from management to support and operation. This section introduces how to conduct B2B sales diagnosis and planning through a case study: ① Current situation analysis and problem diagnosis; ② Focus and positioning; ③ Vertical penetration analysis; ④ High-level suggestions; ⑤ Optimization of B2B sales through sales process management and sales support system management models; ⑥ Organization and position optimization; ⑦ Assessment indicator optimization; ⑧ Management and business process optimization.

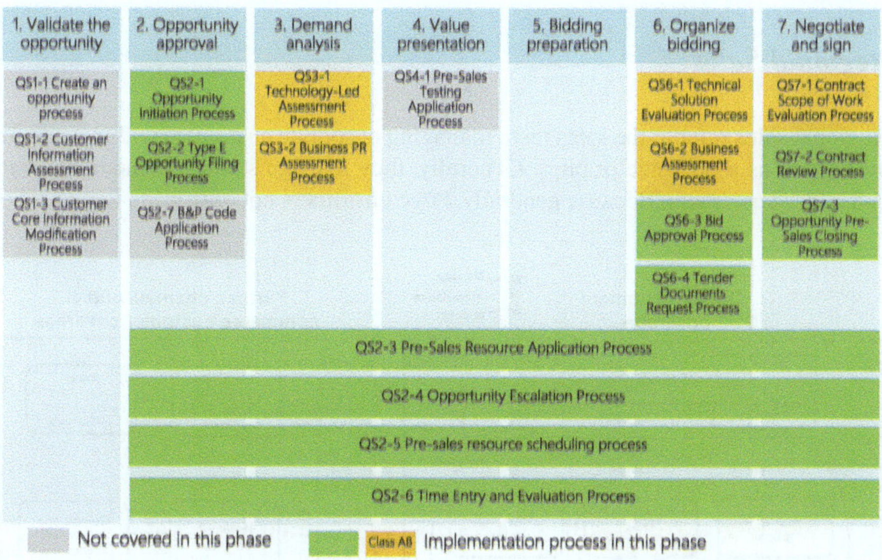

Fig. 5.16 Optimization of business processes

Customer Coverage Effectiveness Model

In the section on B2B sales and key account management in Chapter 2, I gave a simple example of managing key customer relationships. However, many large enterprises have much more complex customer relationship responsibilities. In this section, as shown in Fig. 5.17, I will detail the Customer Coverage Effectiveness Model (CCM) in CRM 3.0.

Regarding the customer coverage effectiveness model, different companies will make different adjustments according to their actual situations. Some may complicate it, some may simplify it; some may merge organizations, some may divide them more finely, or derive some new organizations. However, no matter how it changes, some basic management elements and models remain the same. For example, small and medium-sized customers are generally managed by region; large customers are generally assigned to specific customer managers, many of which are managed by industry; if the diversity and complexity of the company's products increase, solution-based sales need to be adopted, and so on. The specific introduction of the customer coverage effectiveness model is as follows:

Regional Sales

Regional sales refer to the sales team managing corporate customers within a certain area (such as a province or city). Generally, they manage small and medium-sized enterprise customers. Because generally, large customers not only bring large profits

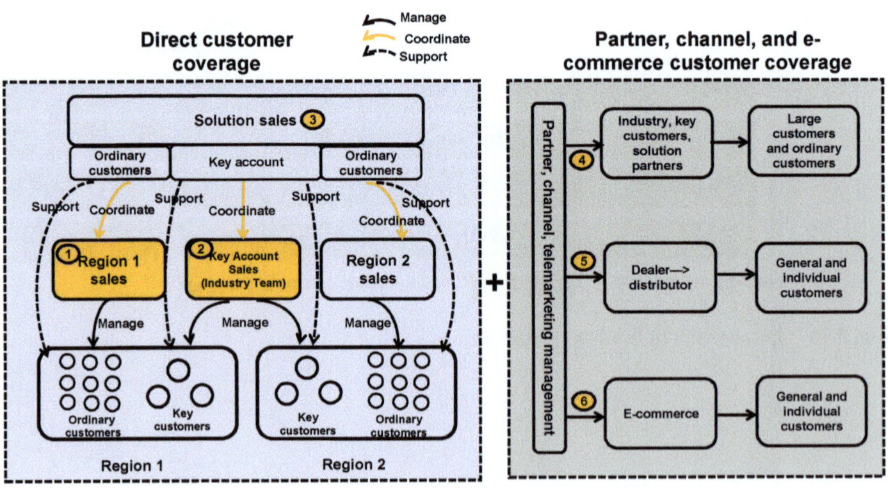

Fig. 5.17 Customer coverage effectiveness model (CCM)

to the enterprise, but also have a large scale themselves. Large customers are often cross-regional, so it is difficult to achieve comprehensive management within a region.

Key Account Sales

Large customer sales personnel are often grouped by industry, because large customers are often managed by industry. Even if they didn't divide by industry at the beginning, with the expansion of business and the increase of large customers, they will eventually be managed by industry. The main reason is that large customers often need personalized solutions. They are not willing to listen to the success stories of customers with different business formats, so sales personnel need to have a deep reserve of industry knowledge. However, the business differences between industries are very large, and sales personnel can hardly become experts in multiple industries at the same time, so the management of large customers is often conducted by industry.

Solution Sales

Solution sales refer to the sales team built for a certain type of product and solution. The solution team works together with the regional sales team and the large customer sales team to develop sales solutions, and the performance is counted with both the regional sales team and the large customer sales team. In a sense, the biggest task of solution sales personnel is to empower the regional sales team and the large customer sales team, let them know what the solution is, who to sell it to, and how to sell it, playing the role of a catalyst for the solution. Some companies have weakened the solution sales team and put the solution team into the product team, regional sales team, or large customer sales team. If the solution is complex and the solution has platform characteristics, that is, the basic functions of the solution can cross industries and regions, and the market capacity of the solution is very large, it is recommended that companies establish an independent solution sales team. Because only an independent solution team can comprehensively plan and promote sales solutions from multiple dimensions such as overall market prospects, sales strategies and methods, the completeness and advancement of solutions, and the partner system.

Partners, Dealers and E-commerce

These do not belong to direct sales customer management and will not be introduced in this article.

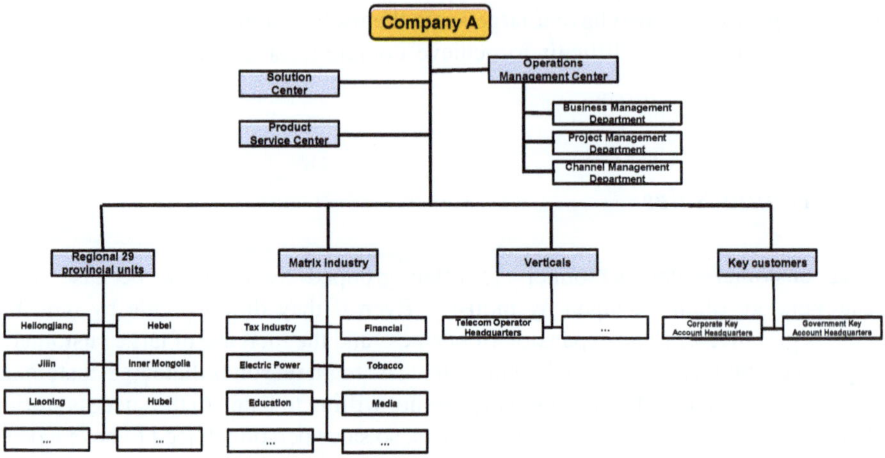

Fig. 5.18 Example of a large B2B sales organization

Next, through the analysis of a customer example, I will explain in detail how a large enterprise should adjust its organizational structure to effectively layout and fully play the roles of regional sales, large customer sales, and solution sales in B2B business.

Figure 5.18 is an example of the sales organization of a large B2B company.

(1) Regional Sales The regional unit can be considered as regional sales.
(2) Large Customer Sales Matrix industry, vertical industry, and large customers can all be considered as large customer sales.
(3) Solution Sales In this organizational structure, it is weakened, and many personnel are scattered in the solution center, industry matrix, vertical industry, and large customers, etc.
(4) Partner Management is in the Channel Management Department. However, many staff are scattered across industry matrices, vertical industries, and large customer organizations.
(5) Delivery Management has dispersed capabilities, with staff scattered across solution centers, project management, regional units, industry matrices, vertical industries, and various large customer organizations.

As can be seen, the above sales organization belongs to the structure of a large front desk and a small middle platform, that is, the front-line sales organization that frequently contacts customers is large, but the organizations that support sales, such as solution sales, delivery management, and partner management, are small in scale.

Such a sales organization is suitable for traditional product sales, that is, the products, solution functions, and processes sold are relatively simple, and the sales cycle is relatively short. However, if you want to make large orders and be responsible for large customers, such a sales organization will have some problems.

(1) Customer coverage appears blank and internal consumption. The above sales organization is divided according to industry and region to cover customers. In this way, at the intersection of industry and region, there will be situations where some customers are not managed and some customers are competing with each other. For example, in a certain region, there is a small credit cooperative. The regional sales are reluctant to follow up because the plan is complicated. The financial industry team is reluctant to travel to the local area to follow up because the scale is too small. But if it is a joint-stock bank, regional sales and industry sales are competing with each other. Even if the performance is double-counted, the control of the customer must be grabbed. Therefore, it is recommended that the customer coverage model be divided first by customer size and importance, and then by industry. Each customer is divided into different sales teams according to size and importance, and then the sales team divides customers according to industry, forming a segmented team. The direct consequence of the appearance of blank and internal consumption in customer coverage is that many "one head and one tail" customer sales opportunities will be missed.
(2) The middle platform support system is not strong enough. The product solution team, delivery solution team, and partner team are not large enough. Many functions and human resources have been put into regional sales and industry sales organizations. Because there is no strong and resource-concentrated middle platform, the development and promotion of complex solutions, the implementation of large projects, and the rapid improvement of the company's pre-sales capabilities will be greatly restricted. The direct consequence of the middle platform not being strong enough is that the company will encounter bottlenecks after reaching a certain scale and cannot enter the next level.

For complex solutions and top industry customers and large orders, I suggest: ① streamline the front-end sales organization and strengthen the middle platform support organization; ② establish sales institutions and teams in a customer-first, industry-second manner, cover all customers, divide the territory well, do not form a gray area, and avoid creating sales blank areas or internal consumption of employees.

The optimized B2B sales organization is shown in Fig. 5.19. Its key points are:

(1) The front-end sales organization is divided in the order of customer size contribution, and then industry, covering all large, medium and small customers.
   a. Small and Medium Enterprise Customer Team refers to the original regional sales organization distributed in various provinces. The customers of this organization do not need to be designated. As long as they belong to this region and are not designated to large customers and government customers, they belong to the Small and Medium Enterprise Customer Team. For example, the previously mentioned agricultural credit cooperatives, although their industry attribute is finance, as long as they are not designated customers of the large financial customer team, they belong to the Small and Medium Enterprise Customer Team. As long as the market scale of the Small and Medium Enterprise Customer Team is large enough

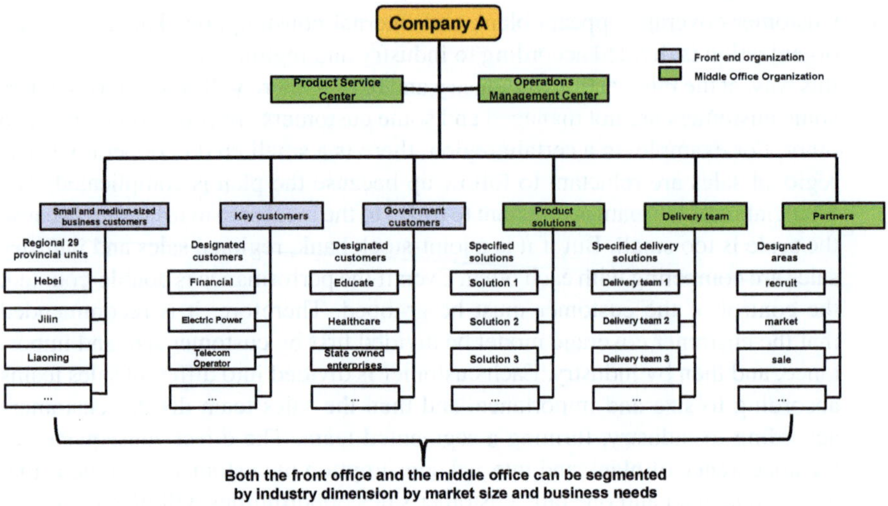

Fig. 5.19 Optimized B2B sales organization

and there is a need in business, it can also be subdivided by industry in the future. In addition, complex solutions can be The ability to pre-sell, deliver, and cultivate and manage partners is taken from the team of small and medium-sized enterprise customers and put into the product solutions, delivery solutions, and partner teams of the middle platform.

b. The large customer team is the original matrix industry and vertical industry. The large customer team will clearly specify the binding relationship between customers and sales, that is, find large customers according to certain standards and directly specify responsible sales. Each large customer salesperson is generally responsible for 2 to 10 large customers. Because large customers are often national or even global companies, the large customer sales team does not need to be subdivided into provinces, and the country can be divided into several large areas for management. Because the solution industry complexity and diversity required by large customers are very large, the large customer management team will generally be subdivided by industry. In addition, the ability to pre-sell complex solutions, deliver, and cultivate and manage partners can be taken from the large customer team and put into the product solutions, delivery solutions, and partner teams of the middle platform.

c. The government customer team is the original large customer's government large customer headquarters. Because government customers have special considerations in decision-making mechanisms and compliance, they are generally managed separately. Government customers are divided into government agencies, as well as education, medical care, central enterprises and other subdivided fields. In addition, the ability to pre-sell complex solutions, deliver, and cultivate and manage partners can be taken from the government customer team and put into the product solutions, delivery solutions, and partner teams of the middle platform.

(2) For complex solutions and large customer orders, an independent middle platform team can be established

a. Product solution team The company's main product line can establish a product solution team, equipped with product solution sales experts and solution technical experts, who will play a crucial role in the pre-sales stage. The product solution team can be subdivided into two levels, that is, according to the small and medium-sized enterprise customer team, large customer team, and government customer team; further down, it can be subdivided into three levels by industry. The sales staff of the product solution team will also meet customers and guide key projects, but the more important responsibility is to motivate and empower the corresponding front-end sales team, such as the front-line sales of the small and medium-sized enterprise customer team, large customer team, and government customer team; and coordinate product solution support resources.
b. Delivery team The project implementation team established according to the company's solution field, mainly responsible for the delivery of important and complex projects. The delivery team also has its own sales, so it is easy to control the cost of delivery and avoid the bigger the project, the more loss.
c. Partner team The importance of the partner team cannot be overstated. If you want the company's sales scale to grow geometrically, and want to establish the ecology of the company's products and solutions, partners are indispensable.

The above is an example. In the actual process of optimizing the front-end and middle-end sales organization, how to combine, refine, and focus on customers, industries, solutions, delivery, and partners, etc., must be tailored according to the company's scale, business, products, solutions, and competitive situation.

Summary > This section introduces the coverage model of customers, and through a B2B sales organization case, it introduces how to optimize the sales organization.

Coverage and Management of B2B Direct Sales Customers

The previous section introduced the customer coverage model (CCM), this section will detail how to cover and manage large and ordinary customers in B2B direct sales.

Large customers can be divided into super large customers and large customers, which are managed by industry teams. Ordinary customers can be divided into

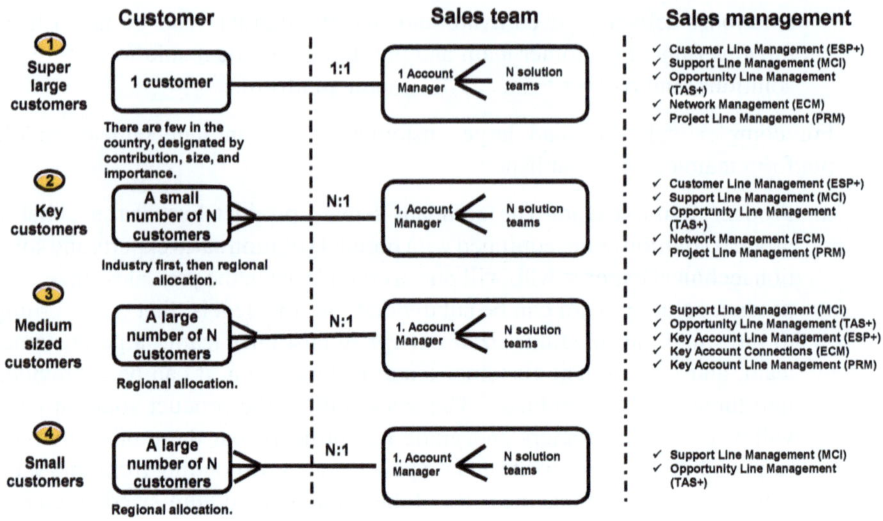

Fig. 5.20 Coverage and management of direct sales customers

medium customers and small customers, managed by regional teams. Behind the industry and regional teams, there are multiple solution teams for support.

As shown in Fig. 5.20, I divide B2B customers into four categories: super large customers, large customers, medium customers, and small customers. The left column introduces these four types of customers and their division criteria, the middle column is how the sales team covers them, and the right column is what sales management methods should be used for different customers.

Super Large Customers

(1) Customer Definition: Super large customers are often global strategic customers, with only a few hundred worldwide.

(2) Sales Team: Super large customers often have a full-time account manager assigned, who is fully responsible for the customer. This account manager does not need to distinguish industries because they are only responsible for this one customer. The performance of this account manager also depends on the output of this B2B super large customer. They are generally supported technically by corresponding product experts and account managers. At the same time, there are multiple solution teams behind the account manager for support. As for how to advance each solution and how each solution team cooperates, it is generally coordinated by the account manager.

(3) Sales Management: Because they are only responsible for one customer, they must go deep and thorough. Sales have the following 5 main lines:

customer line management (ESP+), support line management (MCI), opportunity line management (TAS+), relationship line management (ECM), project line management (PBM). Especially relationship line management and project line management are of utmost importance. This customer may bring us multiple projects and hundreds of millions of revenue each year, so the departments and key contacts involved may be hundreds of people, and the projects involved may be dozens or even more, so it is necessary to focus on managing relationship resources and project relationships to deepen and widen our "moat".

Large Customers

(1) Customer Definition: Large customers are those within a country that make significant contributions to sales and profits. They are often managed independently in each country, with hundreds to thousands of large customer enterprises within a country. Large customers are often divided by industry first, such as manufacturing, automotive, retail, finance, high-tech, health, etc., and then divided by region within each industry.
(2) Sales Team: Account managers often work in an industry team, responsible for a region, often responsible for 3 to 10 large customers. Each fiscal year, the account manager will choose a few customers to focus on and invest most resources and time. They are generally supported technically by corresponding product experts and account managers. At the same time, there are multiple solution teams behind the account manager for support. As for how to advance each solution and how each solution team cooperates, it is generally coordinated by the account manager.
(3) Sales Management: Because they are only responsible for a few customers, they must go deep and thorough. The following 5 main lines of sales: customer line management (ESP+), support line management (MCI), opportunity line management (TAS+), relationship line management (ECM), and project line management (PBM), all need to be managed intensively.

Medium Customers

(1) Definition of Medium Customers: Medium customers generally refer to those who are not industry leaders, but are relatively large-scale enterprises. Managing these customers cannot rely solely on market activities or waiting for opportunities to come. These customers often number in the thousands in each country. Medium customers do not have very obvious industry characteristics, and their internal operations are not very complex, so they are often managed by region.
(2) Sales Team: Account managers often work in an industry team, responsible for a region, and often manage hundreds of medium customers. Each assessment

year, they choose twenty to thirty medium customers to focus on and take the initiative. The remaining customers are guided to contact proactively through market activities, online promotion, and other means. Generally, product experts and account managers are paired to provide technical support. At the same time, there are multiple solution teams supporting the account manager. How to advance each solution and how each solution coordinates is generally managed by the account manager.

(3) Sales Management: Because there are many customers, it is necessary to make sacrifices and gains, focusing the main resources and time on key customers. Sales have the following five main lines: Support Line Management (MCI) and Opportunity Line Management (TAS+) must be focused on, Customer Line Management (ESP+), Relationship Line Management (ECM+), and Project Line Management (PBM) can be applied to some key customers.

Small Customers

(1) Customer Definition: Besides the above three types, the rest are small customers. These customers often rely on market activities, online promotion, brand promotion, and other means to promote, waiting for customers to have needs and come to find them. These customers often number in the hundreds of thousands or even millions in each country. These small customers do not have very obvious industry characteristics, and their internal operations are not very complex, so they are often managed by region.

(2) Sales Team: Account managers often manage a region, responsible for thousands or even tens of thousands of B-end small customers in that area. Account managers mainly create sales opportunities through market activities, online promotion, brand promotion, and other means. Customers with needs see the market promotion or hear about it through word of mouth, and then contact sales proactively, who then follow up on the opportunity. There may be corresponding product experts and account managers paired to provide technical support. At the same time, there are multiple solution teams supporting the account manager. How to advance each solution and how each solution coordinates is generally managed by the account manager.

(3) Sales Management: Account managers are responsible for thousands or even tens of thousands of customers, and the general transaction process is relatively simple and fast-paced, so the most important thing is the efficiency and success rate of making deals. Among the five main lines of sales, only Support Line Management (MCI) and Opportunity Line Management (TAS+) need to be focused on.

Summary > This section introduces how to establish sales coverage relationships and how to manage sales for direct sales customers, including super-large customers, large customers, medium customers, and small customers. How to establish sales coverage relationships and how to manage sales.

The Soul of Large Customer Sales, Solution Sales, and Project Sales

There is an anime called "Douluo Continent", which tells the story of how seven genius teenagers from Shrek Academy, through seamless cooperation, protect each other's weaknesses and maximize their strengths, creating an unbreakable team. The story of a team that ultimately walks the path to becoming gods. In the management and sales of major clients, there are three types of sales positions: major client sales, solution sales, and project sales. These three types of sales each have their own attributes and characteristics, and they must complement each other to form a combined force and achieve invincibility. Only when everyone in a team divides and cooperates well can they form a god-like team like the Seven Monsters of Shrek.

Let's discuss the job positioning of major client sales, solution sales, and project sales, and how to achieve win–win cooperation. The success of major client sales lies in trust, the success of solution sales lies in wisdom, and the success of project sales lies in intelligence.

Major Client Sales

Major client sales are generally responsible for a few, at most a dozen major clients. Generally speaking, no matter what products and solutions these clients buy from the company, they are counted as the performance of major client sales.

The success of major client sales lies in "trust", which is to gain the trust of clients. The most important thing for major client sales is to establish deep, wide, and transparent relationships with clients. Deep means that there should be many contacts with each department and business, and the relationship should be deep; wide means that the departments and businesses involved should be wide; transparent means mutual understanding and trust. All of this is based on trust with clients, and the most important thing for major client sales is "trust". Major client sales need to control the people and events in the client, and also suppress competitors.

Major client sales should focus more on Enterprise Contact Management (ECM) and Major Client Management (ESP+).

Enterprise Contact Management (ECM)

Many companies generally only pay attention to sales figures and do not pay attention to the improvement of relationship closeness, resulting in fluctuating sales performance, sales leaving, and clients being taken away and other difficult problems. In the final analysis, companies have a lot of homework to do in contact resource management, for example.

(1) Three types of relationships and four individual portrait dimensions We need to manage them to deepen, widen, and make transparent customer relationships. The three customer relationships are: customer reporting relationships, customer influence relationships, project decision-making relationships; the four individual portrait dimensions are: behavioral orientation, relationship status, interaction level, importance level (decision-making role).
(2) Customer Relationship Closeness Management We need a quantifiable method to measure the dynamic changes in our relationship with customers. Are we covering and contacting more and more departments, more and more key decision-makers trust us, and the relationship closeness is getting higher and higher? The vast majority of companies have no insight into this area, and can only evaluate based on whether the relationship is close if they win the order, and the relationship is poor if they don't win the order. We need a more scientific, quantifiable, and predictable method to manage and measure, which is Enterprise Contact Management (ECM).

Major Client Management (ESP+)

In major client management, many major client sales do very well in the two links of customer overall planning (Account Planning) and project excavation and conversion, but there is still a lot of room for improvement in influence projection. The so-called influence projection is to project the company's strength, solution and product advantages to the customer decision-makers and project decision-makers as widely and deeply as possible, so that these decision-makers form a more favorable image of us. Major client sales convey favorable information to us through various channels and methods to key customers, constructing our perfect image in the minds of customer decision-makers. in the elephant. This is to be complemented with the management of three types of customer relationships, four types of individual portrait dimensions, and the closeness of customer relationships. Only when major customer sales continue to project influence can the three types of relationships and four types of individual portrait dimensions be continuously improved, and the closeness of customer relationships deepened; only when the closeness of customer relationships is deepened, the information of the three types of customer relationships and four types of individual portrait dimensions is improved, our projection of influence can be more effective.

Solution Sales

Solution sales often manage many major customers in a region, corresponding to multiple major customer sales and multiple partners. Solution sales need to build a wise and powerful middle platform, and a global perspective is very important to them. For solution sales, it is important to have the ability to charge and fight, and to fight with bayonets; but what is more important is to inspire and empower all major customer sales and partners in their own region, help them succeed, that is, to build a win–win ecosystem for the solution in the region.

The success of solution sales lies in wisdom, that is, a global perspective, so solution sales should pay more attention to the sales support system (MCI).

Solution sales need to focus on building a sales support system, empowering major customer sales, partners, and major customers, matching the most suitable resources, making the project process smoother, and resource integration more efficient. The ultimate goal is to build a win–win ecosystem for major customer sales, partners, and major customers. To achieve these, solution sales must adhere to the following three principles:

(1) Fairness and transparency If there is too much bias and self-interest, many major customer sales, partners, and customers will not be willing to continue to cooperate with you.
(2) Abandon the small self Fully help partners and major customer sales succeed, and do not over-control. Only in this way, partners and major customer sales will think this is their own business, will be willing to take the initiative and go all out to do it, and can derive many new opportunities and solutions.
(3) Service is timely and in place Do your best to coordinate resources to help partners and major customer sales, do not make yourself a bottleneck, but make yourself an engine of acceleration and promotion.

In addition, solution sales can also play a role in filling gaps and penetrating. Filling gaps means that in some blank areas, solution sales replace major customer sales to manage customers; penetration means that for some customers who can sell a large number of products and solutions, solution sales should play a leading role, actively and continuously expand the breadth and depth of product and solution applications, thereby selling more products and solutions.

Project Sales

Project sales is the sales person in charge of the project, who needs to complete the conversion from lead to order (LTC). It can be said that if this project wins, then project sales is also successful.

Because project sales is dynamic, it is born from the project and ends with the project. The sales of a project may be led by solution sales, or by major customer sales or partners, so there will be a situation where one person holds multiple posts. For example, if solution sales leads a project, it will become project sales, and adapting to role changes will be a challenge for sales.

Summary > The success of major customer sales lies in trust, that is, establishing mutual trust with customers, and should focus on enterprise human resources management (ECM) and major customer management (ESP+). The success of solution sales lies in wisdom, that is, a global perspective, and should focus more on the sales support system (MCI). The success of project sales In wisdom, speak of cunning strategies, the interplay of reality and illusion, and defeating the enemy. We should focus more on the management of the sales process (TAS+).

Software Platform Selection for Chinese Companies Going Global

I have participated in many projects for Chinese companies going global (Go Global) in selecting software platforms. There are many countries in the world, and business models are not all the same. Culture, customs, language, taxation, laws and regulations are all vastly different, and Chinese companies lack understanding of overseas markets. Previously, selecting an overseas software platform was more difficult than selecting a domestic one. Recently, under the influence of the COVID-19 pandemic and political factors, there are more factors to consider when selecting an overseas software platform.

As shown in Fig. 5.21, the following seven points are the most critical factors in the selection of software platforms for Chinese companies going global.

Functionality and Company Strength, etc.

These are the most basic considerations, whether selecting domestically or for overseas software, companies will consider these factors.

Compliance, Language, and Taxation, etc.

(1) Compliance: Doing business overseas, the first thing is to comply. We are more familiar with the EU's GDPR, but actually overseas, each industry has its own standards, each region has its own standards, and each country has its own standards, which are very complex. To meet these standards, the cost will be very high. Regulatory oversight is becoming stricter in various countries, and a slight oversight can lead to heavy fines and have a significant negative impact on the brand.

(2) Language: There are many countries overseas, and a country may have multiple languages, so if Chinese companies want to expand globally, the selected software platform should ideally support dozens of mainstream languages.

(3) Taxation: If the software involves costs and income, because each country's tax department has its own regulations, the software platform should ideally meet the tax requirements of different countries.

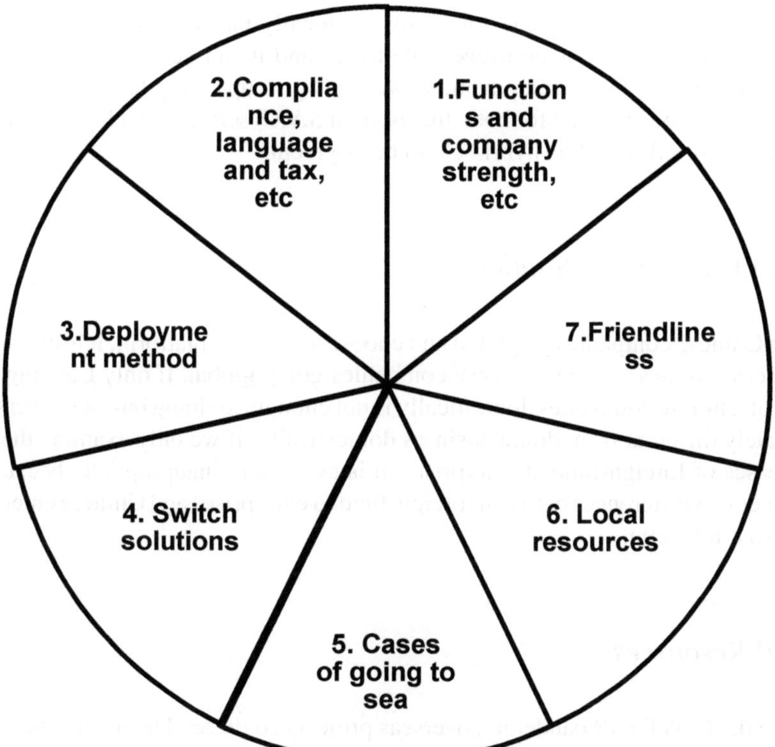

Fig. 5.21 Key elements of Software platform selection for Chinese enterprises going global

Deployment Plan

A hybrid cloud software platform is the best choice, i.e., the software platform can support both SAAS services and local installation. Many Chinese companies expand overseas very quickly after going global, promoting in multiple countries at the same time. At this time, choosing SAAS services is very suitable, with on-demand use, and the number of users can change with business needs. But some overseas countries have strict requirements for data export, such as Russia, and there are no SAAS services locally, so local installation and deployment are necessary.

Switching Plan

There are many force majeure in the business environment, and overseas data assets are the core assets owned by Chinese companies after going global. Therefore, Chinese companies should prepare in advance to switch from SAAS services to local installation. But why can't we only use locally installed software platforms? Because SAAS service is an irreversible trend, and it can help companies quickly support local business development, so we can't give up eating for fear of choking, but we need to be prepared for both, that is, both SAAS services and local installation can be supported, which is hybrid cloud deployment.

Going Global Case Studies

When Chinese companies go global and choose a software platform, it is best to look at the case studies of other Chinese companies going global. If only Looking at the cases of Chinese companies domestically is not enough, as doing business overseas is ultimately different from doing business domestically; if we only examine the overseas cases of foreign-funded enterprises, it is even more inappropriate, because the management differences between foreign-funded enterprises and Chinese enterprises are also quite large.

Local Resources

Before the COVID-19 pandemic, overseas projects could send teams for local interviews and implementation. However, due to the impact of the pandemic, going abroad has become a risky, time-consuming, and costly affair, so it is best if the software vendor also has implementation and delivery resources locally.

Friendliness

This refers to the degree of importance the software company places on Chinese enterprises and the Chinese market, and whether it is willing to make long-term investments in China. This is a point that many Chinese companies easily overlook when choosing software for overseas expansion, but it is a crucial consideration. Because when a Chinese company chooses a software platform, it is at least choosing a long-term cooperation for the next 5 to 10 years. Given the current complex international situation, at least those companies that value the Chinese market and invest heavily in China should be chosen, and the methods and strategies adopted should be beneficial to safeguard the interests of Chinese companies.

Summary > This section introduces the factors that Chinese companies should consider when choosing software for overseas expansion: ① Functionality and company strength, etc.; ② Compliance, language, and taxation, etc.; ③ Deployment plan; ④ Switching plan; ⑤ Overseas cases; ⑥ Local resources; ⑦ Friendliness.

Sharing Global CRM Promotion Experience

The problems encountered by Chinese enterprises in implementing and promoting CRM projects domestically and overseas are quite different. Domestic control is strong, and the culture and habits of different regions are similar, often following a unified model, but with great detail and unique corporate characteristics; the overseas market includes hundreds of countries, with significant cultural and habitual differences, and weaker control, so it often follows a one-country-one-policy approach. As shown in Fig. 5.22, the following introduces the six major challenges in implementing and promoting CRM overseas.

Business Value

No matter how hard the work is, it does not equate to business value. Overseas CRM projects are often very hard, but often no amount of effort gets good reviews. Many customer managers say that they have been working on global projects for many years, spending a lot of money, but have not seen any results. Those who implement CRM like to measure by how many functions they have implemented in a short time, the advanced nature of the system, and the time of going live. But customers measure

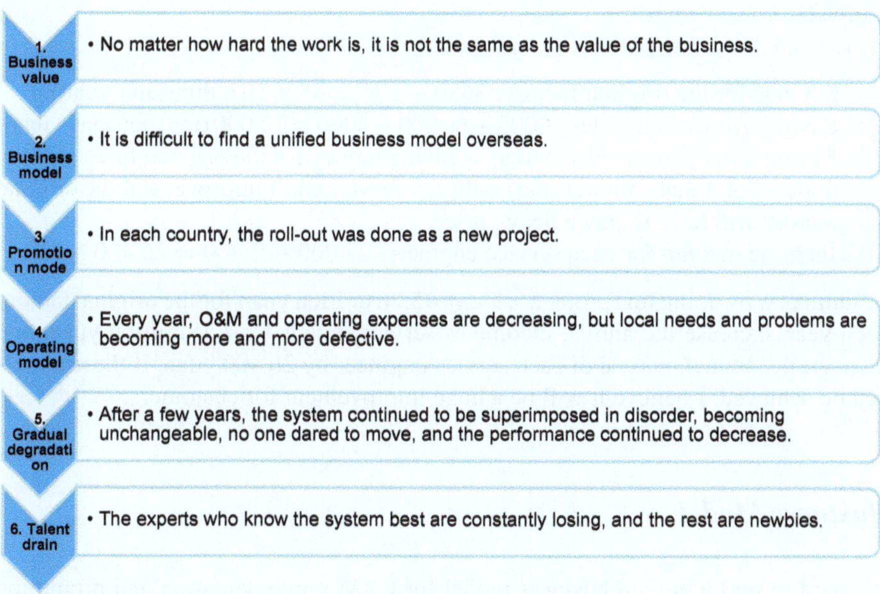

Fig. 5.22 Six major problems in the global promotion of CRM

KPI	description	target	Business value
Complaint rate	Assuming that the number of work orders per day is 100,000 and the complaint rate is 1%, the negative impact of each complaint is 1,000 yuan.	10% reduction	Annual savings: 100,000 * 0.01 * 0.1 * 1,000 * 365 = 3,650 (10,000)
Online repair resolution rate	It means that the fault is solved by phone and there is no need to come to the door. Assuming that there are 40,000 maintenance consultation calls per day, the original online maintenance rate is 20%, and the original factory pays 30 yuan each time.	10% increase	Original annual savings: 40,000 * 0.2 * 0.1 * 30 * 365 = 876 (10,000)
Dispatch accuracy	It means that the work order can be directly dispatched to the service engineer, and there is no need for the branch information staff to manually dispatch the order twice. Let's say you have 5,000 branch informants, and 50% of that time is spent on manual secondary dispatches. The fee for the information clerk is 10,000 yuan/month.	20% increase	Annual savings of service outlets: 5,000 * 0.5 * 10,000 * 0.2 * 12 = 6,000 (10,000)
Scheduling efficiency	It refers to more accurate and intelligent scheduling. On average, each service engineer can take 5 orders a day, but now they can take 6 orders. Assuming that there are 50,000 service engineers, the average cost of each engineer in the service network is 5,000 yuan per month. Suppose the average income of service engineers is 10,000 yuan/month.	20% increase	Annual savings of service outlets: 5,000 * 0.2 * 50,000 * 12 = 60,000 (10,000) Increase in average annual income per service engineer: 10,000 * 0.2 * 12 = 24,000 (RMB)
Door-to-door one-time resolution rate	The service engineer visits the site to solve the problem at one time. Let's say 10% of repairs require a second visit. Assuming that there are 50,000 service engineers, the average cost of each engineer in the service network is 5,000 yuan per month. Suppose the average income of service engineers is 10,000 yuan/month.	20% increase	Annual savings of service outlets: 5,000 * 0.1 * 0.2 * 50,000 * 12 = 6,000 (10,000) Average annual income increase per service engineer: 10,000*0.1*0.2*12 = 2,400 (yuan)

Fig. 5.23 Example of establishing a business value measurement system

by business value and business output. So the measurement and evaluation standards of the two parties are not consistent.

Overseas CRM projects should establish a customer-recognized, measurable business indicator system from the beginning, and continuously track and improve it after the system goes live. Take the after-sales service project as an example, as shown in Fig. 5.23.

Through the launch of this system, each year:

(1) Savings for the original factory: $3650 + 876 = 4526$ (ten thousand yuan).
(2) Savings for service outlets: $6000 + 60\,000 + 6000 = 72{,}000$ (ten thousand yuan). Saving money for service outlets is saving money for the original factory. If the outlets don't make money, the quality of service can't improve, and the original factory will have to pay a heavy price.
(3) Increase income for each service engineer: $24{,}000 + 2{,}400 = 26{,}400$ (yuan).

In summary, by doing this project, we save 45.26 million yuan for the original factory each year, increase the annual income of service outlets by 720 million yuan, and increase the annual income of each service engineer by 26,400 yuan. If these targets can be achieved, I believe it will be a huge improvement for customers.

Business Model

It's hard to find a unified business model for CRM implementation and promotion overseas. For example, the after-sales service model in India and Pakistan is similar to China, ASEAN countries are a bit different, and Europe is even more different. In Australia, many times it's individual businesses, running mobile service stations to take orders, with IT systems and spare parts all in the car, and the repair costs are quite expensive, sometimes up to a third of the cost of new appliances, so many locals will just buy new ones. In Japan, there is often not much innovation, and many times they are using particularly outdated service methods. So I think we don't need to focus too much on the design of a global business template, but should form regional business templates in areas with similar business and culture, and continuously optimize each regional business template.

Promotion Model

Overseas CRM projects often turn the promotion in each country into a new project. I once went overseas to promote the second phase of a CRM project and found that the way each business analyst (BA) conducts research, the level of detail in the questions they ask, is completely different, and many have not participated in the first phase of the project, and are completely asking questions and designing systems based on their own personal experience. In this way, it's not promoting the first phase of the project, but redesigning a new project.

As shown in Fig. 5.24, we need to establish a "global standardized promotion operation model" in order to ensure the continuity, consistency, and agility of the promotion. The content mainly includes four aspects: ① design of promotion-related organizations, positions, and responsibilities; ② management of the promotion lifecycle; ③ evaluation and tracking system related to promotion value; ④ global promotion template.

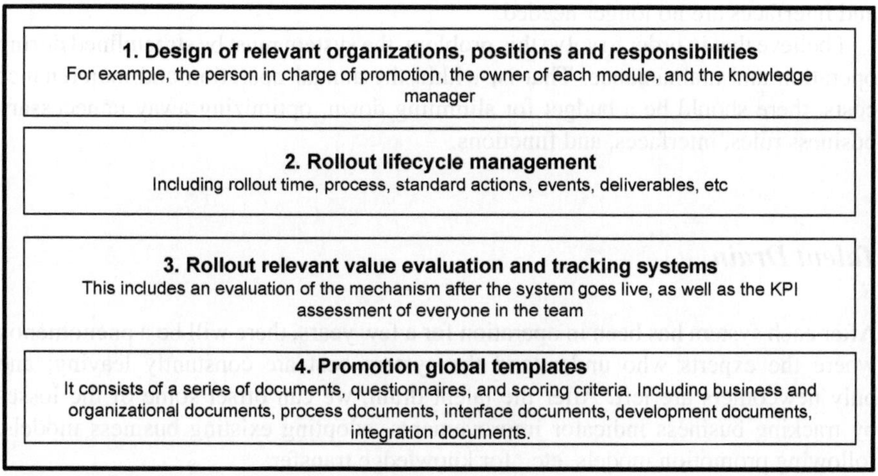

Fig. 5.24 Global rollout of standardized operating procedures

Operation Model

The annual operation and maintenance costs of overseas CRM projects are getting lower and lower, but the local demand and problem defects are increasing. Companies will think that the system will become more stable after it goes live, so the operation costs decrease year by year. But in fact, overseas business is constantly changing every year, demand is constantly increasing, but the increasingly lower operation costs can't support the system's iterative optimization needs. For sales and service projects, going live is just the first step, and it's just a prototype. Without fertilization, watering, and pruning, it's hard to grow healthily. I have detailed how to operate CRM projects in Chapter 4 "Building a CRM 3.0 Support System" in the "CRM 3.0 Full Lifecycle Delivery Method", so I won't go into detail here.

Gradual Degradation

A few years after the operation of overseas CRM projects, the system becomes increasingly disordered and stacked, becoming unchangeable and untouchable by anyone, and performance continues to decline. After going live, we add new features every year, but no one deletes useless features. Because we only assess whether new business requirements are online, no one assesses whether useless features are offline. A few years later, the system becomes increasingly disordered and stacked, becoming unchangeable and untouchable by anyone, and performance continues to decline. In some previous projects, we found that there were tens of thousands of business rules and hundreds of system interfaces, but in fact, many business rules and interfaces are no longer needed.

I believe that in order to solve this problem, the system must be streamlined during operation and maintenance. That is, within the annual operation and maintenance costs, there should be a budget for slimming down, optimizing away unnecessary business rules, interfaces, and functions.

Talent Drain

After each system has been in operation for a few years, there will be a phenomenon where the experts who understand the system best are constantly leaving, and only newcomers are left. After the talent drain, we can offset some of the losses by tracking business indicator improvements, adopting existing business models, following promotion models, etc., for knowledge transfer.

But the most important thing is to retain experienced old employees, making them treat the project as their own child, willing to continuously improve, optimize, and operate it. To achieve this, I believe it can be done in the following ways:

(1) We can't just give birth and not raise, we need continuous investment every year. The bigger the project gets, the more attention it receives, the more likely it is to retain talent.
(2) Establish a project business operation team, reward the team and project group based on business value. Only with money, can we possibly retain talent.
(3) Leading companies can turn internal project products into platforms, socialize them, and provide them to other companies within and even outside the industry.

Summary > This section introduces the six major difficulties that Chinese companies will encounter when implementing and promoting CRM overseas, and proposes corresponding solutions. The six major difficulties include: ① Business value; ② Business model; ③ Promotion model; ④ Operation model; ⑤ Gradual degradation; ⑥ Talent drain.

Analysis of the Transformation of Home Appliances, Automobiles, and Real Estate Industries Driven by User Demand

As the person in charge of Haier's service digital transformation project, I have had a prominent feeling after contacting many automobile and real estate customers: the home appliance industry's today is the automobile and real estate industry's tomorrow, and the future transformation path of 4S shops and properties will converge with the home appliance industry.

Let's review the development changes of China's "major items" over the past few decades, and we will find the following patterns:

- The three major items of the 1970s: watches, bicycles, sewing machines;
- The three major items of the 1980s: refrigerators, color TVs, washing machines;
- The three major items of the 1990s: air conditioners, sound systems, video recorders;
- The two major items after 2000: cars and houses.

Today, the three major items that were once popular in the 1970s have either exited the historical stage or become niche products. You will find that once the product market is saturated and enters the stock market, there will basically be two trends:

(1) Suppressed by cross-border products and services, only retaining a niche market. For example, bicycles and watches. Bicycles have been replaced by more means of transportation, occupying most of the market. I wonder if anyone still remembers the "Phoenix" brand bicycles and "Forever" brand bicycles; the core timing function of watches has also been taken over by various portable mobile tools.

    Over time, watches have gradually become decorative items. I wonder if anyone still remembers the "Shanghai" brand watch.

(2) Either replaced by cross-border products and services, such as sewing machines. Due to the popularization of socialized clothing production, as well as the reduction of costs and the increase in residents' income, sewing machines have basically exited the historical stage.

The three major items of the 1980s and 90s were home appliances, and after 2000 they were cars and real estate, all of which followed the same pattern:

(1) They have passed the market peak and entered the stock market. Home appliances have passed the market peak and have become commonplace.
    Household products have long been a red ocean market; cars have reached their peak and are beginning to decline, facing a brutal price war; real estate has also passed its peak, beginning to decline, with demand decreasing.
(2) Facing cross-border competition. The traditional home appliance industry has been hit by Internet companies for many years, the TV market has been subverted, and small appliances are also in danger; the traditional automobile industry has also been facing strong competition from new car-making companies in recent years; leading real estate companies are also undergoing a comprehensive transformation, diversifying development: such as urban and rural construction and life services, elderly real estate, cultural tourism real estate, etc.

In summary, although the products and services provided by home appliance, automobile, and real estate companies are different, they all provide services around clothing, food, housing, and transportation, and their essence is the same. It's just that the home appliance industry entered the market decline period earlier, and the automobile and real estate entered later. The home appliance industry entered the red ocean earlier and transformed earlier, so let's first discuss my experience in the home appliance industry.

Haier changed its name to Haier Smart Home, and Haier's direction is the "5 + 7 + N" full-scene solution. "5" refers to home spaces, including smart kitchens, smart bathrooms, smart living rooms, smart rooms, smart balconies, etc.; "7" refers to whole-house washing and protection, whole-house security, whole-house food, whole-house entertainment, etc. seven whole-house solutions; N refers to countless life scenes. Therefore, you can see that the path Haier wants to take is also a lifestyle provider. This is the same as Vanke's "urban and rural construction and life service provider".

The problem now is not that home appliance, automobile, and real estate companies don't know what to do in the future, but that they don't know how to achieve their future goals.

Before discussing how to do it, let's first look at how to achieve long-term operation, which is to definitely transform from a product-driven company to a user-demand-driven company.

But how can we transform into a user-demand-driven company? I believe the implementation path is "3 + 4 + 1", that is, "three changes, four transformations, and one construction". As shown in Fig. 5.25.

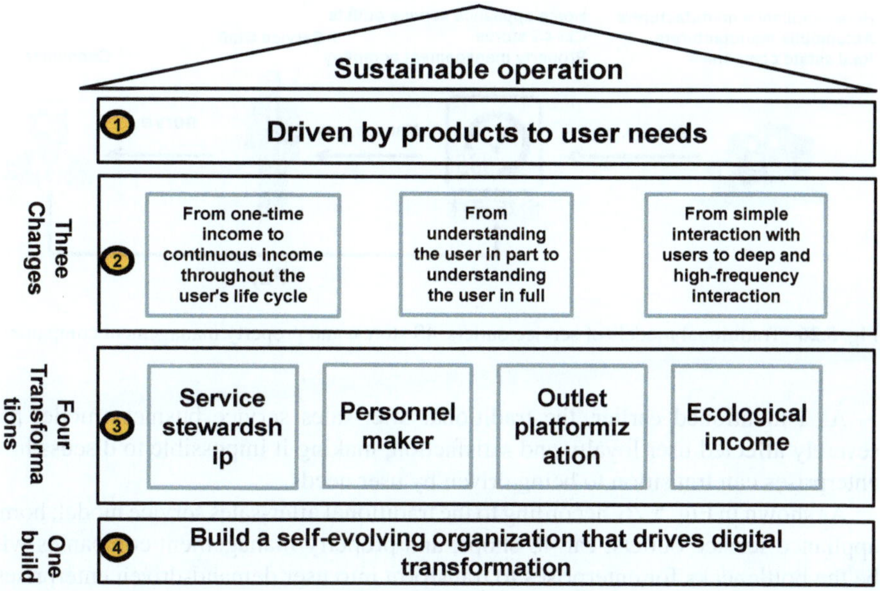

Fig. 5.25 User demand driven enterprise model transformation

Three Changes

(1) From one-time income to continuous income throughout the user's life cycle.
(2) From understanding the user in part to understanding the user in full.
(3) From simple interaction with users to deep and high-frequency interaction.

The above three changes are very easy to understand, they are changes in concepts and guiding thoughts, and will not be discussed in depth here. The difficulty lies in how to achieve these three changes, which depends on the "four transformations" introduced below.

Four Transformations

The characteristics of the home appliances, automotive, and real estate industries are low-frequency sales, with a long interval between one purchase and the next. If we want to achieve the three transformations mentioned above, the key breakthrough lies in the service link. This is because only in the aspects of home appliance maintenance, car maintenance, and property services can we continuously interact with users and provide continuous services, gradually establishing users' trust and dependence on the enterprise and service personnel.

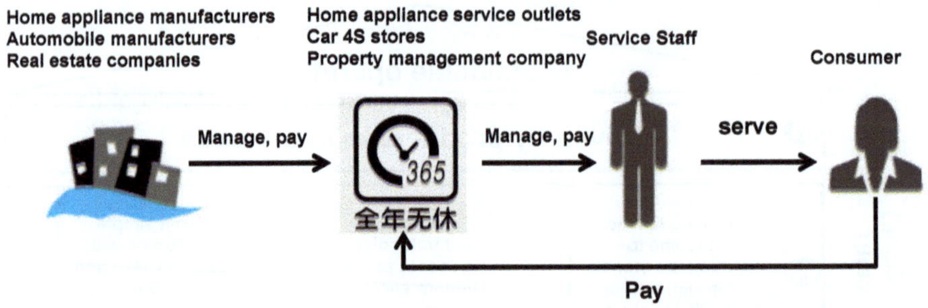

Fig. 5.26 Traditional models of service outlets, 4S stores, and property management companies

As I mentioned earlier, the traditional after-sales service business model has severely affected user loyalty and satisfaction, making it impossible to discuss how enterprises can transition to being driven by user needs.

As shown in Fig. 5.26, according to the traditional after-sales service model, home appliance service outlets, car 4S shops, and property management companies will be the bottlenecks for enterprises to transform into user demand-driven enterprises, for the following reasons:

(1) Home appliance service outlets, car 4S shops, and property management companies take too much of the revenue, putting service personnel in a relatively weak position, losing initiative and enthusiasm for service, and users lose better service.
(2) Home appliance service outlets, car 4S shops, and property management companies isolate the direct interaction between manufacturers and service personnel, preventing the effective execution of the manufacturer's real strategic intent.
(3) Home appliance service outlets, car 4S shops, and property management companies isolate the direct communication channels between manufacturers and users. Without access to users, they cannot understand users, making the transformation into a user demand-driven enterprise empty talk.

Based on the above analysis, we need to make the following changes: ① more flat and efficient management; ② higher income for service personnel; ③ better service experience for users; ④ better operation of the service system.

As shown in Fig. 5.27, I suggest achieving the above changes through the "four transformations", namely service stewardship, personnel maker, outlet platformization, and ecological income.

Service Stewardship

Service stewardship refers to establishing a one-to-one steward relationship between users and service personnel. Through various digital technologies, users can receive steward services anytime and anywhere. Service stewardship has four major benefits:

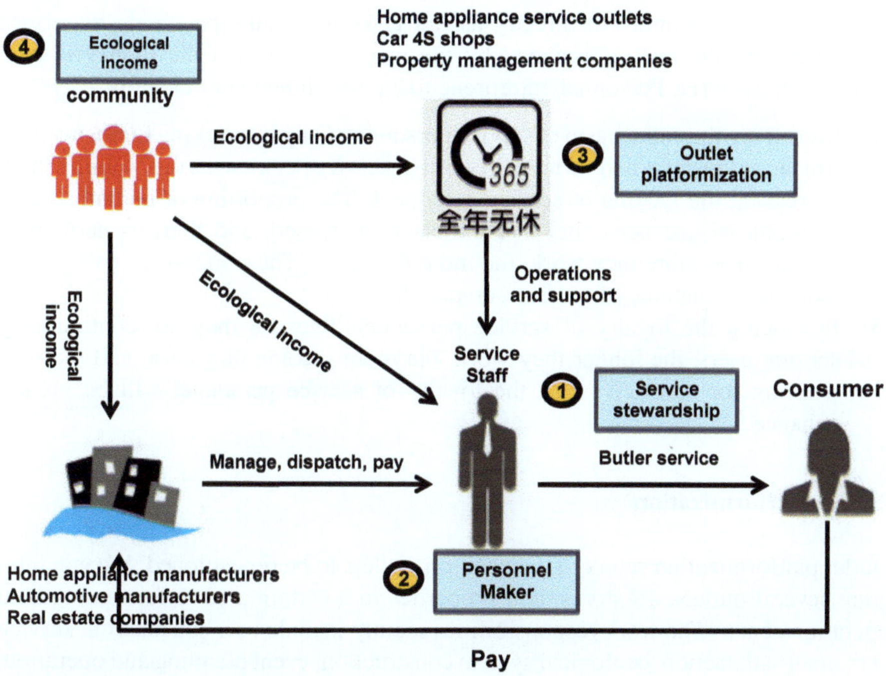

Fig. 5.27 The four transformations support the construction of a user demand-driven enterprise

(1) Enhance user experience: Through digital technology, users can receive 7 × 24 h one-to-one steward services, greatly enhancing the user experience.
(2) One-time income becomes continuous income: Once the steward relationship is established, any ecological income of the user, such as cleaning and online sales of home appliances, maintenance and cleaning of cars, and housekeeping services provided by properties, can be shared proportionally by the steward, greatly increasing the service personnel's ecological income.
(3) Achieve a comprehensive understanding and deep interaction with users: Only when users and service personnel are bound into a steward relationship, and continuous services are provided by fixed service personnel, can a comprehensive understanding and deep interaction with users be achieved.
(4) Reduce complaint rate: Users have a higher tolerance for acquaintances. When there is a problem, they will first find the steward to solve it, rather than directly complain or expose, which will greatly reduce the complaint rate.

Personnel Maker

Personnel maker refers to service personnel gradually breaking away from the dependence on service outlets, 4S shops, and properties, working for themselves, creating their own brand, and being their own CEO. The most effective way to achieve this is for manufacturers to directly assign tasks and make payments to service personnel, i.e., the task is assigned by the manufacturer, and the money is paid by the manufacturer. Personnel entrepreneurship has three major benefits:

(1) Enhancing the enthusiasm of service personnel: Only by working for themselves can the enthusiasm and ownership spirit of service personnel truly be stimulated.
(2) Increasing the income of service personnel: The proportion of income shared between service personnel and outlets is increased, and there is ecological income. The more they work, the more they earn. These measures will greatly increase the income of service personnel.
(3) Enhancing the loyalty of service personnel: Because they are continuously serving users, the longer they work, the more income they earn, and they are working for themselves, so the loyalty of service personnel will be greatly enhanced.

Outlet Platformization

Outlet platformization refers to the need for outlets to be repositioned. We can integrate several outlets, 4S stores, and properties in a certain area to form a regional operation center. The work responsibilities mainly include user satisfaction, service personnel satisfaction, ecological system construction, event planning and operation, etc. Income is no longer measured by the number of work orders, but is comprehensively evaluated based on operational effectiveness, user satisfaction, service personnel satisfaction, and ecological income. There are four major benefits to the platformization of service outlets:

(1) Enhancing user satisfaction: The income of service outlets, 4S stores, and properties is directly proportional to user service satisfaction, so service personnel will naturally put more energy into improving user satisfaction.
(2) Enhancing service personnel satisfaction: Service outlets, 4S stores, and properties will shift from managing and punishing service personnel to helping and supporting them, which will greatly enhance the satisfaction of service personnel.
(3) Enhancing operational efficiency: The income of service outlets, 4S stores, and properties is linked to the operational indicators of the responsible area, so they will naturally put more energy into improving regional operational efficiency.
(4) Increasing income: Service outlets, 4S stores, and properties can expand their responsible areas by merging, and there is also a share of ecological income, which can greatly increase their income.

Ecological Income

Ecological income refers to the manufacturer introducing and operating more products and services for users to meet their daily needs, such as our company's value-added products and services, high-frequency products and services introduced by third parties, such as housekeeping, education, tourism, consumer finance, etc. These incomes will be distributed to service personnel and outlets according to the stewardship relationship. There are three major benefits to income ecologization:

(1) Increasing the income of service personnel and outlets: Ecological income will gradually become the main income of service personnel and outlets, which can account for 40% or more.
(2) Turning one-time income into continuous income: The product sales of manufacturers are one-time, only ecological income can be high-frequency and continuous.
(3) Achieving a comprehensive understanding and deep interaction with users: Only when users continuously purchase and use ecological products and services can a more comprehensive understanding of users be achieved and deeper interaction can be realized.

Building a Self-Evolving Organization to Drive Digital Transformation

Why build a self-evolving organization to drive digital transformation? The reason is simple, "To do a good job, the tools must be sharpened first." It is now the digital age, so digital tools must be used for support. Otherwise, in the high-tech era, if you still use cold weapons, no matter how correct the strategy and tactics are, they are useless if the basic hardware does not support it. Therefore, if a company wants to transform into a user demand-driven company and wants to promote the four transformations introduced above, it must build a self-evolving organization to drive digital transformation, so that digital tools can be closely integrated with business and promote business innovation and transformation.

Chapter 3s "Building a Self-Evolving Organization to Drive Digital Transformation" has detailed how to build a self-evolving organization to drive digital transformation, so it will not be detailed here. What needs to be emphasized here is that to succeed, you must have "enough power, high enough level, and enough tempting returns". If the digital department can't even sign a contract or make a financial decision, how can it have the motivation to drive business change.

Summary > This section introduces that home appliances, automobile, and real estate companies need to complete digital transformation through.

"Three Transitions, Four Transformations, and One Construction" to achieve a complete transformation. It also emphasizes the four transformations: ① Service stewardship; ② Personnel maker; ③ Outlet platformization; ④ Ecological income.

Seven Questions to Understand Before Deciding to Purchase CRM

Under the "boost" of the COVID-19 pandemic, CRM has been pushed to the forefront again. The huge survival pressure has made the digital transformation of enterprises imminent, and as a professional customer relationship management tool, CRM is favored again.

CRM has basic functions such as customer management, market management, sales management, service management, channel management, member management, order management, etc., which can help most enterprises achieve cost reduction and efficiency improvement. In more than ten years of practical application, the effect of CRM has been well verified.

The number of CRM service providers is increasing. According to Tianyancha search results, there were 1410 CRM service providers in China in 2021, with 19 new CRM service providers registered from January to July.

How to select a suitable one from many service providers is undoubtedly a time-consuming and laborious project. For this reason, I will analyze from four aspects: selection method, required cost, procurement case, and usage principle, to help everyone better select the CRM system.

First, for Different Enterprises, Which Enterprises Are Suitable for Using CRM? Which Are not Suitable?

I believe that the deciding factor for whether a company is suitable for using a CRM system is the size of the company. The CRM system includes marketing management, service management, channel management, member management, customer management, etc., and the operation of the company will basically involve these areas, so whether the company needs CRM still depends on how many people use this system. When the number of sales staff in a company exceeds 50, Excel and Word can no longer meet the management needs of a large team, and CRM is needed for management at this time.

Whether a company chooses CRM has little to do with the characteristics of the industry and the business model, it's just that the CRM practices and features of different industries are different.

As for whether a company's CRM chooses to build its own or purchase, I believe that unless the company is large enough, willing to invest a lot of money in CRM every year for continuous research and development, and plans to sell CRM products in the future, it is recommended that companies purchase mature products on the market.

Second, There Are Many Mature Products on the Market, How Can Corporate Buyers Choose a Suitable CRM from Them?

The functions of mature products on the market are mostly similar. It depends on the company's own needs and the service experience of the manufacturer. In general, if a company wants to purchase a suitable CRM, it mainly needs to consider the following five aspects.

First, what do you want to do with CRM? Before purchasing, companies need to carefully consider what they want to achieve with CRM and what it will specifically be used for.

Second, what is the budget? Before purchasing, companies need to determine a budget range based on their own situation and make price comparisons within this range.

Different priced CRM systems have different functions and performance. Companies can choose different product manufacturers and project implementers based on different budgets.

Third, choose the required product deployment type and billing type. CRM products on the market are mainly divided into rental and buyout types. Nowadays, the products of CRM service providers are becoming more and more cloud-based, which is easier to use compared to local installations.

Fourth, past cases. The solutions of product manufacturers and project implementers may work well in some industries, but their solutions may not necessarily be applicable to industries or fields they are not familiar with.

Fifth, the implementation team is very important. Understand the understanding of the project implementer's implementation team of the industry in which the company is located, whether they have done similar cases, and their own capabilities.

Third, How Should We Examine Their Professionalism and Service Quality in Negotiations with CRM Sales Personnel?

First, you can judge by the understanding of the seller's personnel of the company's needs. CRM sellers who do not understand the industry and customers will have difficulty recommending good products and solutions. Secondly, look at the advanced nature and matching of the solutions provided by the seller, measure whether the solutions provided by the project implementer match the company, and whether they can meet the needs of medium and long-term expansion. Again, the timeliness of feedback highlights service quality. If a customer asks a question and the other party answers a week or two later, it indicates that their ability or service has a problem. Finally, it is very important for the project implementer to be able to guide the customer's future planning. CRM projects are long-term services, so this is very important.

Fourth, is It Worth It for Companies to Purchase CRM? How to Calculate the Input–output Ratio of Purchasing a CRM System?

When companies purchase a CRM system, as long as the company follows the principles mentioned above to look at the company's scale, it can basically achieve cost reduction and efficiency for the company. But as for quantifiable standards, it still depends on different areas of CRM. For example, in the service field, call centers and after-sales are relatively easy to calculate and quantify input and output. Call centers already have very complete evaluation standards. For example, you can calculate how much loss a complaint brings, or what the resolution rate is for a home visit, everything can be quantified. But some areas are very difficult, like the sales field, especially B2B sales, there should be no standard. If you really need to measure, you can do it from the customer's management ability, the control ability in the order process, the resource scheduling ability, the employee's improvement ability, the company's direction matching ability, etc., but you need experts to help customers think carefully, combine the company's actual situation to make some quantifiable indicators.

Fifth, After the First Purchase, What Additional Costs Will the CRM System Incur?

CRM systems are mainly divided into rental and buyout types. The buyout type is generally a one-time buyout for lifetime use, but subsequent addition of functions or version upgrades require secondary payment. The rental type requires annual rent payment, with basically no other costs.

Overall, the cloud is the future direction of CRM, and there are fewer and fewer local installation product manufacturers. The advantage of the cloud is that it provides many capabilities that local installations do not have, such as the Internet of Things, AI, etc. Many capabilities that require massive calculations can only be realized in the cloud. In addition, compared to locally installed CRM software, the cloud does not require To purchase hardware and databases, SAAS comes with it, saving a lot of costs compared to local installation. If you purchase in a cycle of 5 years, the cost of the cloud is much cheaper than the cost of local installation, and some products are only 50% to 60% of the cost of local installation products. CRM from cloud product manufacturers will have significant discounts and discounts.

From the implementation perspective, it will also involve the costs of problem correction, new feature development, and system operation and maintenance. But these are not much related to the product.

Sixth, from the Perspective of the Entire Life Journey, Analyze a Specific Case of a Company Purchasing a CRM Tool

The process of corporate procurement of CRM tools is also very mature, generally divided into six stages.

The first stage: Organize your own needs. Companies need to see what they want, and only after they have figured it out can they proceed to the next step.

The second stage: Contact software manufacturers and project implementers. With the needs and budget, you can roughly know which level of product and implementation team to choose.

The third stage: Preliminary communication, understanding the product. The needs of small businesses may be easily met, for larger businesses, they generally need CRM manufacturers to provide solutions. Therefore, communication on the solution and the introduction of the product are very important. Sometimes a POC is required, and larger companies may require case interviews, requiring each manufacturer to provide a case, take customers to visit the site, and discuss the landing effect of CRM.

The fourth stage: Clarify the budget, prepare bidding and bid evaluation materials. At this time, the customer has more comprehensive information, will produce a more clear budget to apply, and prepare bidding materials and bid evaluation standards.

The fifth stage: Invitation to bid or tender. Larger CRM projects generally require invitation to bid or open bidding, and the evaluation tends to favor manufacturers with deeper preliminary communication. After the bidding is completed, there are business negotiations, which may involve multiple rounds of negotiations.

The sixth stage: Choose the winning bidder, sign the SOW and contract. After the solution and price are finalized, the winning bidder will be selected, and then there are SOW and contracts. The SOW needs to describe all the details of the project, including the detailed scope of the project, so it takes a lot of time. If it is a large company and a large project, the contract will also take a lot of time for review and adjustment.

Seventh, What Are the Key Principles in the Subsequent Use of CRM by Enterprises?

The preparatory work before going online is all for better use in the future. After the system goes online, it cannot be considered as the end, it can be regarded as just the beginning. During the use process, be sure to pay attention to the following three key principles.

The first principle: This kind of product cannot only care about birth and not care about raising, it needs continuous investment. Many customers think that CRM is mainly a one-time investment, spend a lot of money online, and spend some small money for maintenance every year. In fact, CRM is just the beginning, like a newborn child. Only by continuously investing in CRM can it truly generate huge business value. CRM is a marathon, not a 50-m sprint. If it costs 1 million to go online, it is recommended to invest another 25% to 40% (250,000 to 400,000) of the operating cost to improve and upgrade CRM every year.

The second principle: There must be business value monitoring indicators. When a company goes online with CRM, it must pay attention to its continuous output of business value. At this time, business value monitoring indicators are needed. Without such indicators, it is impossible to evaluate the performance of CRM, and it is even more unclear whether it is worth investing in costs and manpower to improve CRM.

The third principle: Pay attention to digital innovation and integration with business. Digital innovation is a trend, not only It is not only reflected in its ability to enhance and optimize business, but it can also reshape and change business models. Before going live, companies may not have time to think too carefully, but after going live, they need to continuously operate and invest in CRM every year. At this time, they may need to focus on digital innovation and transformation, thinking about how CRM can better integrate with current business, optimize functions, and even change business models.

MIX
Papier aus verantwortungsvollen Quellen
Paper from responsible sources
FSC® C105338

If you have any concerns about our products,
you can contact us on
ProductSafety@springernature.com

In case Publisher is established outside the EU,
the EU authorized representative is:
Springer Nature Customer Service Center GmbH
Europaplatz 3, 69115 Heidelberg, Germany

Printed by Libri Plureos GmbH
in Hamburg, Germany